TRAVELS
OF A
Wimpy Mum

Finding courage through the Book of James

What people are saying

The idea of inserting the extracts from the children's diaries is a very good one. There are times when their comments are unconsciously - or perhaps consciously - truly funny. Vanessa writes very engagingly, and it is a great strength that means many, many readers with families will closely identify with her.

Adrian Plass
Best-selling Author of *The Sacred Diary* series

This is so much more than simply a story about a family trip around Australia. It's about family and faith, marriage and mental health, adventure and honesty. Most of all, it's about failure, success, and learning to find yourself in the love of God.

Cecily Paterson
Author of *Love, Tears & Autism*

I have always wanted to journey around Australia. Reading *Travels of a Wimpy Mum* not only gave me some "must see" places, but engaged me in the emotion of family life lived in the pressure cooker of the transient campervan family!

Vanessa's book is totally engaging and funny, and most of all very real. I felt like I was part of their family journey, living the ups and downs with them. I valued the honesty and vulnerability that oozes out of the pages and kept me turning.

The journey through the Book of James brought a stark realization to the reader – faith & the Kingdom life cannot be interchanged. It showed the power of perseverance and the beauty of seeing God in every space. Vanessa's writing has made me consider how the scripture is being lived out in my own life. It is a beautiful exploration of faith seamlessly interwoven with the tapestry of daily life – encouraging us all to consider how faith is manifested in our own lives.

Reverend Peter Neilsen, Senior Pastor,
Kilsyth South Baptist Church

Vanessa is someone I have always found engaging and willing to discuss the everyday issues in a way that is honest and thought provoking. In her book, Travels of a Wimpy Mum, these positive traits of Vanessa shine through in her writing along with her love for Jesus. As you read this book you will be taken on an adventure which will be deeply enjoyable but will also find yourself relating to different aspects within your own life's journey. I thoroughly recommend Vanessa and her book, *Travels of a Wimpy Mum*.

Reverend Tim Dyer, Minister,
Syndal Baptist Church

I'm truly delighted to share my endorsement for Vanessa's debut book, a work that stands as a testament to her unyielding determination, genuine vulnerability, and unwavering faith in Christ. Vanessa's literary journey has been nothing short of extraordinary.

With unflinching honesty, Vanessa lays bare her soul, sharing her most intimate thoughts and experiences. It takes remarkable courage to reveal one's deepest fears, struggles, and triumphs, and Vanessa does so with grace and authenticity.

Vanessa's storytelling is filled with relatable characters,

moments of triumph, and moments of heartbreak, making her book a captivating and emotionally charged journey from start to finish. She captures the reader's attention right from the first page and keeps us engaged through all her ups and turns.

Throughout the book, Vanessa's faith in Christ serves as a guiding light in her life, offering a message of hope and resilience to all who engage with her words. Her spiritual journey is artfully woven into the narrative, adding depth and meaning to the story and inviting us to view James 1:2-4 from a fresh perspective while encouraging reflection on our own life experiences.

I wholeheartedly recommend this book, firmly believing it will resonate with a wide range of readers. Vanessa's journey as an author is just beginning, and I eagerly anticipate her future works.

Vanessa Lister (MBA, MIML)

Most of us are a bit worried about sharing our parenting with the world, because, let's face it, we're often making this stuff up as we go along. So, we put on a brave face, pretending we have it all together – and that can leave us lonely and anxious.

This delightful book takes us on a family road trip though Australia, but even better, gives us a look deep inside that family. The mother's reflections (and often hilarious lack of self-reflection) ease our fears that other families are perfect and it's only ours that ever struggles.

In a culture that currently features growing anxiety in both parents and children, seeing resilient children and a mother who is trying and sometimes failing and but always growing, is a reassuring reminder that we'll all be OK.

The author writes aloud things we normally only think - and works through her faith in a far more relevant, real-life way than most church sermons. A fond reminder of the Diaries of Adrian Plass, this book helps us approach our life with more calm, trust and generosity of spirit. Read it to your kids as you plan your next family adventure – if you dare!

Susy Lee,
Prize-winning author of Raising Kids Who Care

Travels of a Wimpy Mum is a heart-warming and relatable story about facing fears and finding courage through faith. The book chronicles Jane and her family's three-month adventure travelling across Australia, complete with mishaps along the way.

It's an uplifting read, infused with gentle humour. Jane's perspective on life will resonate with many, while her husband, Hamish provides a grounding force of reason. Join Jane and her family on this engaging travelogue adventure that's sure to warm your heart and inspire you to think about life differently.

Nerissa Bentley, The Melbourne Health Writer

Travels of a Wimpy Mum is a delightful ramble. Through the challenges of a three-month camping trip, Vanessa's understanding and ability to trust God grows, and the joy and beauty of the outback shines through.

Regina Rich,
Growing into Healing and Wholeness, Bendigo

Vanessa authentically describes the many joys and challenges faced in raising children and family life, and vulnerably shares how God challenged and shaped her heart - and her broader outlook on life - as she wrestled with James' teaching from scripture.

Read this book and not only will you be stirred and encouraged by reflecting on Jane's story, but you will likely be stirred and encouraged to allow God to do a similar maturing work in your own heart and life as well.

Joel Hawting, Lead Pastor,
Liberty Family Church, Healesville

I have two events in the food truck ministry and it's probably the biggest day of the year for me and I woke up early not to prepare, but to read this book!!

The author's vulnerability throughout this amusing account of her family's adventures is endearing. The pages are riddled with a refreshing honesty as she wrestles with understanding genuine application of scripture, in the everyday, as Mum and wife. This read is light, fun, beautifully descriptive and left me wanting to know what happens next.

Carissa Rash,
Chief Executive Officer, 4Tk Australia

From the very first sentence, the Wimpy Mum draws the reader into her world of complex, quirky and totally relatable thoughts and emotions. This is an honest, raw and beautifully written book. Vanessa's awareness of her own perceived shortcomings, her devotion to her children and husband, and above all her relentless pursuit of God in the midst of the many challenges she faces on the road touch the heart and inspire at every turn. A thoroughly enjoyable read!

Penny Mentiplay, Mental Health Coach,
Breakthrough to Great Mental Health

Travels of a Wimpy Mum
Copyright © 2024, Vanessa Foran

Cover Design: Cutting-Edge-Studio.com
Formatting & Layout: Kingfisher Design
For more information email susy@raisingkidswhocare.info

ISBN E-Book: 978-0-6451410-2-3
Paperback: 978-0-6451410-3-0

Travels of a Wimpy Mum is loosely based on the author's trip around the western half of Australia in 2012. People's names and some place names have been changed to respect privacy.

All bible quotations are taken from the New International Version (2011 edition).

© 2024 Vanessa Foran. All rights reserved. No part of this publication may be reproduced, stored in a retrieval system, or transmitted, in any form or by any means, electronic, mechanical, photocopying, recording, or otherwise, without the prior permission in writing from the proprietor(s).

TRAVELS
OF A
Wimpy Mum

Finding courage through the Book of James

VANESSA FORAN

Contents

What people are saying .... *iii*

Prologue *1*
Chapter 1 .... *3*
Chapter 2 .... *19*
Chapter 3 .... *31*
Chapter 4 .... *43*
Chapter 5 .... *51*
Chapter 6 .... *63*
Chapter 7 .... *77*
Chapter 8 .... *87*
Chapter 9 .... *95*
Chapter 10 .... *107*
Chapter 11 .... *117*
Chapter 12 .... *135*
Chapter 13 .... *147*
Chapter 14 .... *163*
Chapter 15 .... *169*
Chapter 16 .... *183*
Chapter 17 .... *193*
Chapter 18 .... *201*
Chapter 19 .... *209*
Chapter 20 .... *219*
Chapter 21 .... *223*
Chapter 22 .... *231*
Chapter 23 .... *243*
Chapter 24 .... *257*
Epilogue *265*

Discussion questions *267*
Note from the Author *269*
Acknowledgements *273*
About the Author *275*

Prologue

Australia is big. In three hectic months of travel, you can only see half of it. The eastern half is full of people, sandy white beaches, and tropical resorts. The western half is mainly desert, with a few isolated attractions that were marked with a red star in our guidebook. I'd told Hamish the eastern half was better: more cities and landmarks and more likelihood of finding cafes serving proper, espresso-machine coffee. But Hamish thought we could do the east another time. We were using his long service leave and we'd never get a chance to do such a journey again, so we should see the vast and barren west of Australia.

I'd learnt that it pays off to take a chance on Hamish's ideas, like the time he suggested knocking down a wall in the kitchen and installing a breakfast bench. The mess was terrible at first, but the feeling of space it created once all the dust from the demolition was cleared away was liberating. I agreed to go west.

Hamish got busy with equipment. He'd had our old four-wheel drive upgraded, with four new tyres, and a "snorkel" that ran alongside the windscreen and then pointed forward, like a watchful antenna. He'd bought a camper trailer which hitched to the back of the car and would be our home for three months. I was in charge of communication, which meant telling the neighbours we'd be away, finding house sitters and convincing teachers it was okay to take the children out of school for a term.

My part of the packing was easy. I made sure we all had coats and walking shoes and thongs and bathers and sun hats. Then I let the kids add some of their favourite things.

Jenna chose books. Faith insisted on bringing her Tinkerbell T-shirt. Gideon added dinosaur toys and his favourite blue rug with a stegosaurus on it.

Hamish's packing took weeks. He stowed cutlery and plates, sleeping bags and beds, boxes of cereal and an oven mitt. He packed things I didn't recognise. I didn't ask questions. I needed to conserve my energy to prepare for what was coming. Would we really get to go whale spotting, see the red sand of Broome, and marvel at the magnificence of Uluru? It was thrilling, but I was still terrified. In the week leading up to our departure, my heart went into spells of beating wildly. What if we couldn't get the camper trailer to open and there was no-one around to help us? What if I hadn't packed the right clothes? Were we doing the right thing, taking the children out of school and away from their friends? Life as a full-time parent to Gideon wasn't easy, but it was predictable. On the road, with no permanent home for three months, would I cope?

Chapter 1

Monday, 4th June 2012

When the alarm went off, my heart beat even more wildly than it had all week. Had we remembered everything? I woke the children while Hamish put the last of the food into the car fridge. I locked the back door and turned off the power. I gave the house a loving look before ushering the children to the car. We'd promised them breakfast on the road.

We'd gotten away by 6.10 am, only ten minutes later than we'd agreed on thanks to Hamish's good planning. My heart rate slowed to a more regular rhythm once we reached the freeway. Maybe we *did* have everything we needed and the trip *would* go smoothly. Even though he has crazy ideas, Hamish is organised. At least the first stop would be Adelaide, which is a city, like Melbourne or Sydney. I didn't have to worry about being somewhere remote, with no one to help if we got bogged, or Hamish had accidentally left the cereal behind.

The children were well-occupied with the new DVD players Hamish had installed behind front-seat headrests. After two movies, two food stops, and eight hours on the road, we arrived at the Squiggly Creek Caravan Park, on the outskirts of Adelaide, late in the afternoon. My heart sank. The caravan park was not like a city park at all. The amenities were tiny and makeshift. The camping area was in an unmarked field. It was raining and the ground was soggy and covered in duck poo. It wasn't the comfortable start I'd hoped for.

We put our raincoats on and stood around the camper trailer. We'd practised setting up in our backyard, but it felt different doing it "for real". Hamish unzipped the trailer cover. It opened easily. *Phew!* Then we unfolded the bedrooms on either side of the trailer. *So far so good.* Next came the poles. They became slippery in the rain. Jenna and I shuffled into position under the canvas and held the poles in place while Hamish extended guy ropes and hammered in tent pegs. Eventually the tent was standing, with Hamish and my "bedroom" above the trailer and two other rooms extending out either side.

We abandoned our plan to heat tinned soup in the camp kitchen and went to the little caravan park restaurant instead. The plastic menus were sticky and there was a noisy video game in one corner called the Wild West. The girls chatted excitedly and wrote in the diaries I'd brought along to occupy them. It was hard to keep Gideon away from the Wild West game, where you had to shoot deer and other wild animals, but he was eventually persuaded to sit at the big wooden table with us. He drew a scary-looking dinosaur in his new scrapbook, while we waited for our food. The meals tasted like they'd been microwaved from frozen packs, but I was grateful I hadn't had to cook.

When the children had gone to sleep, Hamish and I sat up on our bed in between them. We'd been so busy getting ready, we hadn't had a chance to share how we were feeling about the trip.

"Do you still think it was a good idea, Hamish?" I'd forgotten it was going to be winter all across the southern part of Australia. Even though I had thermal pyjamas on and was inside our sleeping bag, I was freezing.

"Of course. We've put ordinary life behind us. We can focus on the important things. I can forget about work. We can do something different, together, as a family."

Hamish had a point. It was hard being the stay-at-home parent while he went to work. I'd enjoyed mothering the girls, apart from the hard bits, but Gideon was difficult to connect with. As a toddler he had no interest in toys or books unless they related to dinosaurs. When he reached preschool, I bribed him with lollies to get him to go to the park, to stop him from watching shows about dinosaurs all day. Ten-year-old Jenna and eight-year-old Faith were neglected while I tried to work out how to engage Gideon in wholesome, educational activities. It was awful. I was sure I was a terrible mother.

So perhaps Hamish was right about doing something as a family. He knew how to discipline the children and still have fun. I had a mental picture of three pleasant, simple, easy-breezy months, where I shared all the responsibilities of child wrangling with Hamish: fourteen weeks where every day was like a Saturday.

Hamish stretched out on the bed and stared up at the canvas ceiling. "I've told you our family moved to Cyprus when I was eight."

"Mm-hmm." I knew all about Cyprus. Sometimes at family get-togethers his parents, May and Richard, would bring out a slideshow about their time there.

"Dad was stationed there with the Air Force for two years, and it was fun experiencing something different as a family." Every Sunday after church for two years his parents took them to a different beach for a picnic. They would bring a gazebo, chairs and tables, and a badminton set, and Hamish and his brothers and sister would help set it up. It always made me feel tired watching the slide show and looking at the equipment they'd brought for a Sunday outing. But nothing was too much trouble for Hamish's family. They were smiling in all the slides.

His parents had moved a lot with the Air Force, living in Cyprus, and Ireland, and all over England, while Hamish and his brothers and sister went to boarding school. They always spent holidays together. Family was important. After retirement, Hamish's parents had moved to Melbourne to be close to their grandchildren. They were our family's biggest supporters.

Hamish folded his hands over his chest. He looked happy thinking about the trip ahead of us. "This trip is a chance for us to help the kids with their faith. Instead of them going to Sunday school, we can learn things together as a family. Maybe have family church services."

I frowned. I couldn't imagine how we could fit in running church services as well as all the hiking and four-wheel driving Hamish told me he'd planned.

"It will be good to visit an indigenous community too, don't you think? I really want the children to see a different way of life. Like I did." Hamish had arranged to visit missionaries in an indigenous community in the Northern Territory. He wanted to teach the kids about indigenous culture. I was worried about that too.

"What do you think, Jane? What are you looking forward to?" Hamish rolled over and looked at me.

"Teaching the children new things will be wonderful." I forced a smile. I didn't want to ruin Hamish's happy moment. I wouldn't tell him that I didn't want to have family church services and I was worried we'd be a burden to the indigenous community. What I was *really* looking forward to was not having to deal with the kid's arguments and a four-year-old's challenging behaviour all on my own.

I *would* keep my commitment to the girl's teachers though, to make sure they kept a diary. I didn't want them getting in any trouble.

I picked up Jenna's spiral bound journal. Her first diary entry was written as if the trip had finished and had been a wonderful success. I hoped her teachers wouldn't mind her using the past tense.

Probably when you think about journeys and adventures, the thoughts that go through your mind are of tropical resorts, or jungles and rainforests, or maybe even life at sea, but you must understand that my story is set far from any of those places. In fact, my stories are about the outback. I've never been out of this incredible land of Australia but my travels to the western part when I was ten years old were quite extraordinary.

On our first day my heart was pounding as I got into my seat, and as we slowly left Melbourne, the only home I've ever known, I knew that our adventures had only just begun. In Adelaide, we stayed in a place called Squiggly Creek. Although it took such a long time to get there, and it was raining, there were trees everywhere and a perfect spot to park. We frantically set up the trailer. When we were done, we went to the restaurant where the food was delicious. We went to sleep in awe of the sights we had already seen, and excited for all the adventures that lay ahead.

Perfect spot to park! Food was delicious! Excited for all the adventures that lay ahead! I couldn't believe how positive Jenna's diary entry was. And I felt a bit guilty, as I turned off my torch and let my eyes adjust to the dark. I'd gone along with what Hamish said about getting closer as a family. I hadn't told him that was the last thing on my mind. *I must be a bad wife and mother.* I wriggled down further into my sleeping bag. My mental image of fourteen weeks of easy Saturdays was starting to fall apart. I was worried about what lay ahead.

Tuesday 5th June

I woke up before daybreak in a panic. I could hear rain, and the wind was shaking the canvas of the camper trailer. I thought of our friends who were looking after our house while we were away. They'd be sleeping in our bedroom with four solid walls. I wished I was home. What had we done?

It was still dark, and the rain was pouring. I remembered to read the Book of James again. I'd felt anxious over the past year. Gideon's behaviour had been particularly challenging and I didn't know how to manage it. I felt overwhelmed and inadequate. I'd turned forty in May, but I still didn't feel like a competent mother. There were a few verses that always helped. Hamish had installed a Bible app on my phone—he's good at that sort of thing—and in the dark I scrolled down the screen and found my favourite verse:

> *"Consider it pure joy, my brothers and sisters, whenever you face trials of many kinds." (James 1:2).*

I'm sure the verse was written for early Christians facing serious trials, like persecution or even death; not for mothers who struggled with mothering. I also didn't know what James meant. If something was a trial, then how could it be joyful at the same time? Yet I was fascinated by the verse. I loved the possibility that a trial could bring about benefits.

The panic subsided. By the time everyone else had woken up, I was able to help them figure out where their clothes were and organise breakfast. We ate cold cereal in collapsible space-saving bowls that Hamish had bought especially for the purpose. I looked at my red bowl and thought about how much organising and planning he had done. I took a few deep breaths. I owed it to Hamish not to panic and wreck this for him. After breakfast, we walked across the soggy ground, avoiding the duck poo, to shower in the cold and draughty amenities block. We were finally ready to explore Adelaide.

We drove along a scenic route to the Central Market, on the outskirts of the CBD. I was pleasantly surprised. In spite of our dismal introduction to Adelaide, the market turned out to be as good as anything in Melbourne, full of amazing gourmet produce, and a huge food court that sold every type of Asian food you could imagine. I wanted to try the Korean food, but Hamish thought it was too expensive. I felt irritated, but wasn't confident about the financial situation, as I usually leave Hamish in charge of the budget. The stodgy doughnuts he'd bought at the supermarket weren't nearly as exciting, but they were familiar and filled us up.

We walked into the heart of Adelaide, a small version of Melbourne, with attractive old buildings and businesspeople going about their normal midweek lives, well-dressed in smart suits. We found the impressive State Library and Museum. Hamish took the girls around the exhibit about the local indigenous culture, while I stayed with Gideon who was preoccupied by a model of a T-rex in the foyer.

Back at the campsite, the girls complained about having to write in their journals. It wasn't a good sign for only the second day of their homework assignment. Eventually they opened their books and made a start. I dragged Gideon away from poking a muddy puddle with a stick and persuaded him to do a drawing, another sharp-toothed dinosaur, while Hamish heated up soup. Later that night I read Faith's diary. She'd spilt some hot chocolate on the page, but I could still read her neat round writing.

She wrote:

> On the second day Mum, Dad, Jenna, Gideon and I went to the museum. As you may already know, Gideon is obsessed with dinosaurs. Every time Mum put a dollar in the dinosaur at the front it went "Rooooaaaaarrrr". Gideon found it fascinating.

I'd been left once again managing Gideon while Hamish was able to go around the museum. I shuddered remembering how many times I'd listened to that dinosaur roar. Still, Gideon had been happy listening to the T-Rex and the day had turned out easy and uneventful.

I went to sleep looking forward to one more easy day to relax, hoping to save my energy before heading to the bush on Thursday, where there would be no museums or restaurants and it would be harder to find ways to occupy the kids.

Wednesday 6th June

I studied the guidebook this morning. Heading west, there's not much of interest until we get to the Pinnacles (limestone rock formations), north of Perth, 2000 km away. But we had another "guidebook" called *Fifty Big Things in Australia*. I discovered that Adelaide was home to its very own "big thing"—the Big Rocking Horse, and it was only a ten-minute drive away!

As well as the enormous horse made of steel, the Big Rocking Horse was home to a toy factory, wildlife park, shop and café. I accompanied Gideon to the wildlife park, where he wanted to feed the birds. "The cocky bites!" read a large sign. I dismissed it. I was sure I knew how to get around that. I showed Gideon how to put his hand flat and place the birdseed on the tips of his fingers. The cocky ignored the seed and bent his head round as far as possible to chomp down hard on the tip of Gideon's little finger. Gideon screamed. *Argh. That shouldn't have happened.* But I could be calm in a crisis.

When Hamish and the girls came to comfort Gideon, I was redeeming myself with the sound and self-sacrificial technique of firmly wrapping the sleeve of my sweater around his little finger. Hamish had insisted that First Aid training be part of my preparation for the trip. Eventually Gideon stopped screaming and bleeding, though the sleeve of my sweater was stained with blood. Hamish applied a band aid.

In spite of Gideon's cocky bite, the children still wanted to visit the next and bigger animal enclosure. A large kangaroo knocked the bag of feed out of Jenna's hand and onto the floor where he could eat it with less fuss, plonking his tail down on Faith's foot at the same time. Then the black llama started heading for us. I remembered the sign at the entrance that said, "If the black llama bites, bite him back." I'd thought it was a joke, but suddenly I wasn't so sure.

Faith's face was white. Not trusting the llama either, I took her back into the shop so she could distract herself by looking at the homemade wooden toys for sale, while the others explored the park. Eventually they returned, apparently unharmed by the llama. Hamish and the kids all climbed the big steps up to the top of the Big Rocking Horse, were photographed smiling, and received a certificate! I was relieved they all looked so happy, seeing as it had been my idea to come here.

Next, we visited the Haigh's chocolate factory, where we watched women wearing hair nets adding flourishes to chocolates. Then it was off to historic Hahndorf in the Adelaide hills, where the late afternoon sun glowed on the sandstone buildings and the windows of the designer shops. It turned out to be another successful day. Gideon even said, while eating chocolate-coated almonds, that the bird hadn't hurt him at all.

Thursday 7th June

The panic was back. We were leaving Adelaide, and going somewhere called Streaky Bay, where Hamish wanted to camp at a free site that didn't even have toilets. Why couldn't we stay in a motel? And why were two such different people taking a three-month holiday together? What were we thinking?

As I lay next to Hamish, who was still soundly sleeping, and seemed not to have a worry in the world about camping somewhere without toilets, I remembered that we'd met on holiday. I'd been lucky enough to travel Europe after university. I met Kathy and Jackie in a lecture theatre - they were majoring in History like me, and the three of us put our money together and bought an old kombi van and went around the continent in a clockwise direction. By the time we got to Italy, I didn't want to move around anymore. I said goodbye to Kathy and Jackie and took a boat to Israel, where I could volunteer on a kibbutz, maybe soak up one culture, even learn something.

For six weeks, I worked in a plastics factory in the kibbutz that made bottles for orange juice. It wasn't the exciting cultural experience I'd hoped for. Two weeks before my return flight to Melbourne was due to depart from Heathrow Airport, I met an English girl working on the other side of the conveyor belt. Her name was Lizzie, and she persuaded me to take a bus to Egypt with her, my last destination before returning home. That's where I met Hamish, at a youth hostel in a coastal Bedouin village called Dahab.

The first time we met, I noticed him staring at me. I thought it was because my curly hair had gone extra frizzy with the salt water.

Our relationship started by accident, when Lizzie organised a picnic dinner on the beach for a group of travellers we'd met from around the world. It was windy, and Hamish suggested I sit on his lap, so we'd both be warm. To this day, he says he was simply being practical. We walked along the beach together every day for the rest of the holiday, while our new friends slept or sunbaked next to the Red Sea. On one of our walks, we discussed our plans for the future. Hamish told me he was planning to go to Africa to work with an aid organisation.

"Really?" I asked him, surprised.

He'd looked at me with his blue eyes that never seemed to blink. "I've had a really good life, so I want to give back to someone else."

I looked at him in astonishment. I'd never heard anybody say anything like that. I wanted to be around that sort of kindness all the time.

Hamish postponed his aid work and moved to Australia to see if we could make a relationship work. He'd made a lot of sacrifices, particularly giving up English beer and streaky bacon, to be with a girl who wasn't even sure about marriage. My Mum had been married three times, so I was nervous about making a commitment. After the fourth time Hamish asked me to marry him, with no definite response from me, he told me I needed to propose to him. I did eventually, on Valentine's Day three years and two months after we'd met.

After a trip to England to get married, we settled into life in Australia. Hamish had been a good support. He was there for me through the bad times, especially when I lost my Dad, and then a few years later my Mum, both to cancer. I didn't have siblings to share the load. Hamish had been my rock.

Right now Hamish was snoring softly and contentedly. Remembering Hamish's goodness and faithfulness, my feelings for him warmed up again, even if he was taking me camping where there were no facilities. To overcome my anxiety about having to dig a hole for a toilet, I read again the verse from the beginning of James.

"Consider it pure joy whenever you face trials of many kinds." (James 1:2)

I felt miraculously calmer. I resolved to endure camping in the bush and digging my own hole. When Hamish woke up I was already cheerfully packing.

The first part of our journey was peaceful. The kids watched movies, which gave Hamish and I time to talk. I told him how helpful I was finding the Book of James. I asked Hamish if he understood the meaning of James 1:2.

Hamish had been acquiring a lot of interesting facts about the Bible through a podcast called *The Bible in Context*. "James is a practical book," he explained. "It tells us how to live life as followers of Jesus."

"But what does the verse mean? How can something be a trial and joyful at the same time?"

Hamish tapped his fingers on the steering wheel. "Jesus suffered," he said at last. "When we go through trials, it reminds us he suffered for us."

It reminded me of a story about my Dad. After my parents separated, I kept asking Dad if he loved me. No matter how much he told me he *did* love me, I kept asking the same question. One day instead of telling me he loved me, he said: "If we were on a deserted island, and there was nothing to eat except two potatoes, I'd let you eat both of them."

I didn't know about Jesus then. My first exposure to church was my high school chapel, where the chaplain had two sermons. The first was the sinfulness of gambling. The second was that we should tolerate others regardless of their race or religion. Therefore, I'd thought being a Christian involved giving up the worship of money and living in harmony with people different from us.

When I went to the little Anglican church Hamish had discovered near the cafe where he washed dishes, I discovered Christianity was much more than that. I learnt we all make mistakes that separate us from God. God wanted to be close to us, in spite of our flaws and weaknesses. In fact, God loves us so much he was willing to give up his only child, even though that meant horrible suffering. I remembered Dad telling me he would give up both potatoes because he loved me. God demonstrating love through a sacrifice had made sense.

"You're right, Hamish," I told him. "We can be joyful because suffering reminds us God loves us."

Later, we must have spent too much time taking photographs at the Big Galah, a concrete statue of the Australian bird on the Eyre Highway between Streaky Bay and Port

Augusta, because at some point in the afternoon, we realised we were a long way from our campsite, and it was getting dark.

We found the dirt road we were looking for, but couldn't find anywhere to camp. My stomach churned. We found a sign to an alternative site and headed down a rocky road along a cliff. The few camping spots were already taken.

I yelled at Hamish. "Hurry up and find somewhere! It's nearly dark."

"Should we continue down this road, or turn around again?" he asked.

"I have no idea!" I yelled again. "Just find *somewhere* to camp!"

He continued for a while, then not seeing a space, turned the car back around again. It was almost completely dark. My heart was pounding so hard it felt like it was going to escape from my chest. This was more than I could cope with. I knew this challenging situation was nothing compared with the suffering of Jesus, but the thought didn't help me whatsoever.

I asked God in a silent prayer to help me. I knew God would look after us. My heart rate slowed down a little. I stopped yelling, but I was still annoyed with Hamish. I calmed down enough to only give him the silent treatment. Soon after, we found the turn-off to the camping area. We set up on a flat spot and set up before the sun disappeared completely.

In the end, it was wonderful to be by ourselves, right next to the sea. I was in awe of it, but didn't say so. I still wasn't talking to Hamish. Jenna, on the other hand, was talking non-stop about how amazed and delighted she was at our situation. By the light of a torch she wrote:

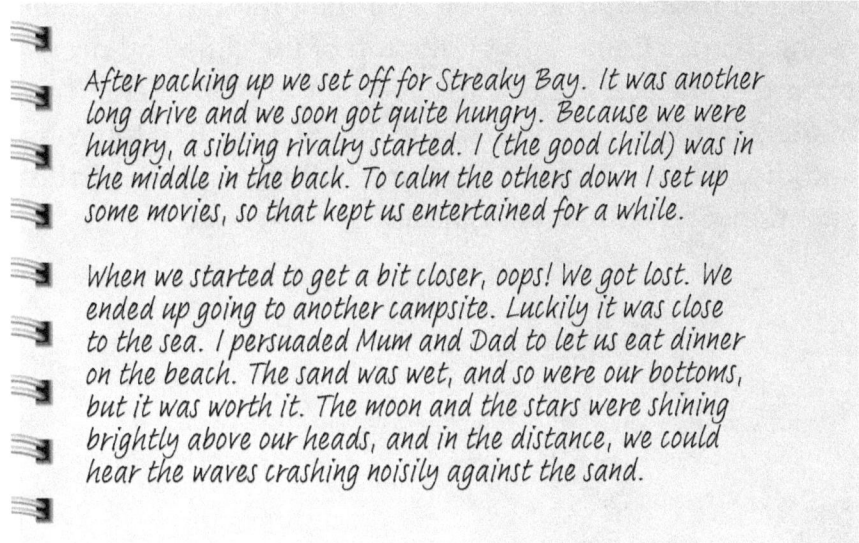

After packing up we set off for Streaky Bay. It was another long drive and we soon got quite hungry. Because we were hungry, a sibling rivalry started. I (the good child) was in the middle in the back. To calm the others down I set up some movies, so that kept us entertained for a while.

When we started to get a bit closer, oops! We got lost. We ended up going to another campsite. Luckily it was close to the sea. I persuaded Mum and Dad to let us eat dinner on the beach. The sand was wet, and so were our bottoms, but it was worth it. The moon and the stars were shining brightly above our heads, and in the distance, we could hear the waves crashing noisily against the sand.

I felt guilty again reading Jenna's diary. She was only ten years old, and so positive about everything. And she was right. I may have hated getting my bottom wet, but it was lovely listening to the sea.

Friday 8th June

I scrolled through my Bible app looking for James this morning, but accidentally opened 1 Peter. My eyes saw "rid yourself of all malice" (1 Peter 2:1). I tried to scroll back to James, but annoyingly, 1 Peter opened up again. Then I realised that I had shown Hamish "malice" by snapping at him and giving him the silent treatment yesterday. When he woke up, I apologised. As expected, he graciously forgave me.

We had an invigorating morning walking along the beach. The kids were so pleased not to be trapped in a car, they ran wild. Faith and Gideon collected shells, crabs, sponges, rocks and anything else they thought was interesting. Jenna climbed up on the top of the cliffs and drew a picture of the scene, her curly red hair blowing behind her in the wind. Later we visited the tiny Streaky Bay township and discovered another "big thing" which captured Faith's attention. She wrote in her diary:

> On the 5th day we found a humongous model of a whale shark. It's a girl shark, which I think is really cool, and it's a model of the biggest thing ever caught!!

Hamish made steak sandwiches back at the campsite. To "save time", he suggested we eat without plates, cutlery, chairs, or a table, and showed us all how to spread our legs wide and bend over to avoid getting the tomato sauce on our clothes. I tried, but it felt totally unnatural. I ate leaning over to one side instead.

    I realised that in just two days here at Streaky Bay, I had gotten used to life without a toilet. It wasn't that hard to dig a hole. Even more surprising, I was starting to trust Hamish with his decisions about the trip, although I wasn't going to tell him that. He might have us sleeping under the stars! I was proud of myself for letting things go. Perhaps my Bible reading was helping. Either way, I was doing well. The next week didn't appear to be too daunting. I might even enjoy it.

Chapter 2

Saturday 9th June

I woke up with a pain in my neck. It must have been from leaning sideways to eat the steak sandwich. It was so bad I had to search for the first aid kit and took two Panadol. As well as the burning pain in my neck, I had that churning feeling in my stomach again, despite all my positive thoughts the night before. Another long drive ahead! Having to set up camp again! It all seemed so much more real, and so much more daunting in the morning.

I pulled out the small paperback Bible given to me by Kara, an earnest Canadian woman who had been working at the Christian Youth Hostel where I stayed before joining the kibbutz 20 years ago. The front cover was a picture of stalks of wheat in a field; there was a small tear in the top left-hand corner. Kara also gave me a novel about a Jewish woman who became a Christian. I read the novel, and enjoyed it, but I didn't read the Bible at all until Hamish introduced me to the Anglican Church in North Carlton, and I started flipping through the gospels. In the last few years, I'd tried to read through the New Testament, but I'd gotten stuck on James.

I was determined to understand the entire Book of James by the end of the holiday. It's a short book, with only five chapters, and I should be able to manage it. Although Hamish was right about it being a practical book, about how to live out the Christian faith, and I am not a practical person. I prefer the book of Ephesians, which is all about God's love for us. But strangely, I always felt God drawing me back to James, the practical book. I flipped through the fine pages of my paperback Bible and found my favourite verse.

> *"Consider it pure joy, my brothers and sisters, whenever you face trials of many kinds, because you know that the testing of your faith produces perseverance."* James (1:2-3)

I felt encouraged. Not only would trials bring joy, but they would help me persevere. I remembered panicking two days ago when we got lost. I needed to stop giving up so easily when things were difficult.

The children had one last run along the beach and were allowed to bring one sandy rock or shell souvenir into the car with them. We had hours of travelling west ahead of us, as we made our way to Eucla (pronounced Yooklah) on the other side of the Western Australian border. All we could see was flat scrub, in every direction all the way to the horizon. But the Australian Bight, that section of coast down south that looks like a giant has taken a bite out of it, did have one attraction! I discovered in my guidebook that you could go whale watching at the head of the Bight, halfway along our day's journey.

"And," I read to Hamish, exultant, "between June and October there are *usually* several whales and their babies swimming near the shore."

I was delighted. It was June! We were going past the Head of the Bight! We were going to see whales—something I had always wanted to do!

We found the viewing platform down some steps at the end of a boardwalk. The wind was whipping my hair across my face, and all I could see when I moved my hair out of my eyes was miles of foamy blue water, with no sign of any life whatsoever. Hamish said he thought some foam several kilometres from shore was probably caused by a whale family squirting water from their spouts. I screwed up my eyes, but I wasn't sure which bit of water he was talking about. I went back to the car to make sandwiches, thinking if we ate lunch at the platform, we would have the longest possible time to sight any whale families. It also gave me an excuse to get out of the wind.

When I returned with lunch, Faith yelled, "We saw whales! They were playing together!" Her cheeks were flushed pink with excitement.

"Are you sure?" I thought she had probably imagined it.

"We saw two grey blobs". Jenna tugged at some hair that had blown into her mouth. "One was bigger than the other. Dad thinks they were whales."

Hamish nodded, his mouth full of sandwich.

We waited a while after finishing our sandwiches, but the grey blobs didn't come back. It got cold.

As we walked back to the car, I zipped my sweater up impatiently. Why had *I* missed the whales? It was my idea to look for them in the first place. Then I remembered I'd read we could see dolphins in Monkey Mia. Surely dolphins wouldn't be elusive? I'd heard they were very curious creatures. I cheered up thinking maybe I would see some marine animals yet.

We continued our journey, crossing the Western Australian border late afternoon, and arriving at Eucla soon after. We saw the caravan park, and drove past it, thinking we would check out the rest of the town. Hamish and I laughed when we realised that the caravan park *was* the town, drove back, booked in and set up. Thankfully it was easy today, with everybody playing their part to put up the trailer tent. And I felt comfortable being in a caravan park with other people around, even if the park *was* the entire town.

Sunday 10th June

The caravan park was well-equipped with a general store, a museum, a petrol station, a laundromat, a pub with a cafe, a gift shop, a motel and a playground. The few people working there ran between the different areas, depending where they were needed. I bought some postcards and stamps at the general store and some tokens for the washing machines. I sat writing letters in the laundromat while the machines spun and tossed our beach-stained clothes. An old man came in and asked if I had any washing detergent.

I handed him a box of powder.

"I'm Jane, from Melbourne," I said, after he'd loaded his washing and sat down next to me.

"I'm Silvio. I'm 90 years old." His eyes sparkled.

"Have you come far, Silvio?"

"All the way from Albany." He could see I had no idea where it was. "South of Perth."

I nodded.

"I want to show you something." His eyes twinkled at me. I followed him out to the car park. He stopped next to a small blue sedan with scratched paint work. The front of the car had been pushed in. The bonnet was buckled and formed a little tent over the engine. It looked awful.

"Never drive at dusk, Jane. There are kangaroos everywhere."

What are you going to do?" I stared at the crumpled bonnet.

"Oh it's fine. I tied it down." He pointed to where he'd wound some rope around it.

Perhaps it wasn't safe for him to drive anymore. But he seemed so pleased with himself, I didn't want to upset him. "Wow. That's very resourceful of you."

When my washing finished, I wished Silvio good luck. He was heading west tomorrow. "And God bless you," I added. I thought he might need it.

"God bless you, Jane from Melbourne." He smiled.

After Hamish had helped me hang out the washing, we spent the afternoon at the only tourist destination in Eucla, the ruins of the old telegraph station. Jenna wrote in her journal:

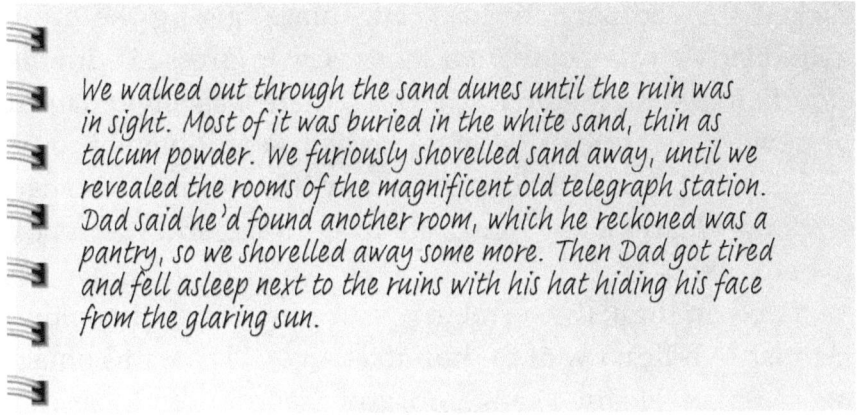

We walked out through the sand dunes until the ruin was in sight. Most of it was buried in the white sand, thin as talcum powder. We furiously shovelled sand away, until we revealed the rooms of the magnificent old telegraph station. Dad said he'd found another room, which he reckoned was a pantry, so we shovelled away some more. Then Dad got tired and fell asleep next to the ruins with his hat hiding his face from the glaring sun.

Hamish slept so soundly he didn't wake up when some quad bike riders zoomed past his feet. When he finally woke, he'd regained some energy and we walked toward a massive mound of sand we could see in the distance. From the foot of the dune, the sand rose up steeply to meet a cloudless blue sky. I took a video on my phone as Hamish and the children ran to the top of the dune, then jumped over the crest and disappeared from sight. It was wonderful to see them having that much fun. For all his over-practicality, Hamish did know how to enjoy himself. I felt a lightness inside.

Monday 11th June

As we drove away from Eucla later that morning, a grey-haired lady in a pink dressing gown stepped out of her caravan and waved at us. At first, I thought she was saying goodbye. I waved back enthusiastically. Then I realised she was pointing at the foot of the trailer, the prop that keeps the trailer stable. It was dragging along the ground. Hamish stopped the car, and I jumped down from my seat and clicked the camper foot back into place, giving the grey-haired lady a wave of thanks. I was very impressed with the elderly folk we'd met in Eucla. First, there was Silvio, who'd persevered in spite of hitting a kangaroo and having to tie his bonnet down with rope. And now this woman, who had obviously learnt a few things about camping and was ready to help others.

"Do you think the secret to perseverance is getting older, Hamish?" I didn't wait for him to answer. "I met this amazing old man. He hit a kangaroo, and the front of his car was all smashed in. But he didn't let it stop him. He's heading west."

"Wow. That is perseverance. Or maybe stupidity."

"I don't agree with you, by the way, about James meaning we should be grateful for Jesus' suffering."

Hamish glanced at me. "Really? Why?" He sounded troubled.

"I don't think that's what James meant when he said, *"Consider it pure joy whenever you face trials of many kinds." (James 1:2)* If James was talking about the sort of suffering that Jesus had to go through, then he wouldn't have said the next bit, about trials producing perseverance."

"Why?" Hamish sounded interested now.

"Jesus didn't have to learn perseverance. Jesus was perfect

from the beginning. James means something else. But I haven't figured out what yet."

"There could be a few meanings to the verse I suppose." Hamish adjusted his position in his seat. "James was writing to the early church, who were suffering persecution. Maybe he was talking about trials that come from being a Christian. Like being mocked and ridiculed."

I remembered how Mum laughed at me when I told her I'd started going to church. It was horrible. She changed eventually, and had even come to church on special occasions, like Jenna's baptism.

"So should we consider it joy when we're suffering for doing God's work? Like witnessing to others, even though they might make fun of us?"

Hamish nodded. "Yes, we should be happy even if others *hate* us for telling them the gospel."

"But how are we going to share the gospel out here, in the middle of nowhere?"

Hamish took his eyes off the road and frowned at me. "You can't plan that sort of thing. It'll happen sooner or later. There'll be opportunities."

We continued in silence. I realised I'd missed an opportunity to witness. I'd told the old man Silvio "God Bless you" after he'd shared his troubles. I hadn't told him the gospel. How was I going to learn perseverance on this trip, if I couldn't witness to a ninety-year-old in grave danger? I silently asked God to give me another chance.

Near Norseman, we found a free campsite at a place called Dundas Rocks, 20 kilometres from the town. We couldn't see anyone else camping there, which was strange after friendly Eucla. I was a bit worried about who would help us if we needed it. It was windy and wet and almost completely dark by the time we set up camp. Hamish cooked some sausages in the rain, and we ate them in bread in the tent.

Tuesday 12th June

In the morning light, I could see that we really were the only people for miles. There was just dirt, a few scattered gum trees, and some rocks off in the distance. It was eerie. What if something happened to us? Where would we get help? But then I remembered that I was trying to learn some perseverance. I decided to embrace the opportunity to show courage. We had pancakes, which warmed me up on the inside. Jenna yelled at Faith for using up the last of the chocolate spread before she had a chance to have any. This started a shouting match between them that echoed all around us and hurt my head.

To get away from the noise, and conquer my fear of the deserted landscape, I took Gideon to explore the rocks in the distance. On top of the highest rock, we could see flat dirt and small shrubs all the way to the horizon. I enjoyed the quiet. Gideon found some stones and threw them below.

I couldn't remember which way we'd come up. We climbed down the way I *thought* we should, and walked in the direction I thought we'd come from, but I couldn't find our camp site. Argh! Now what? We called out "Coooeee!" to get Hamish's attention.

He didn't reply. (He thought we were just calling out to listen to our echoes—it didn't occur to him I could get lost so close to the campsite). I felt my heart thumping in my chest. What if we never found our way back? I regretted heading off without Hamish.

Then we heard high pitched screams of, "Go away!" and

"Leave me alone!" drifting toward us on the wind, which revealed the way back. I had never been so glad to hear the girls yelling!

We drove into the tiny town of Norseman. At the tourist information centre, we read that the town had been home to a population of 27,000 when the gold mine was operating, but now less than 1000 people live here. I was right about being in the middle of nowhere. It started to rain. The weather was another chance to learn perseverance, but I decided that could wait for another time. I suggested we give up our plans to have a picnic and go to the one cafe I could see open. I persuaded Hamish that eating out would be economical if we just ordered a big bowl of hot chips. The café was surprisingly full—it seemed like half of the population of Norseman was in there, and there was a buzz of conversation and colourful pictures on the wall. I was so happy to be out of the rain and amongst people again, I couldn't stop smiling.

While we were waiting for our chips, a wiry old man wearing a blue sweater entered the cafe. He was walking fast and with purpose, even though he was clearly very old. Suddenly, I realised it was Silvio, the 90-year-old I'd met in Eucla. His face lit up when he saw me. Only two days after hitting the kangaroo, his car had flipped over when he tried to overtake someone. "The road was too narrow," he explained. He was unharmed, apparently, but his car was now a total wreck. I couldn't believe it. A second accident? I'd asked God for an opportunity to witness again, but not this. I invited him to sit with us. He ordered an espresso from the counter, then pulled up a chair next to me.

I didn't want to muck up. God had given me the second chance I'd asked for. But first I had to talk to Silvio about his driving.

"I'm worried about you," I told him.

"Why?" I noticed that twinkle in his eyes I'd seen in Eucla. I started to second-guess myself.

"You've had *two* car accidents in three days."

"Don't worry about me. I'm getting a lift to Adelaide this afternoon to buy another car."

I realised the situation was urgent. "Are you a Roman Catholic, Silvio?" It seemed likely, with a name like Silvio.

He raised his eyebrows. "No. Too much focus on the Virgin Mary." He took a sip of his coffee.

"We're Baptists," I said. It seemed like a good place to start.

"Well, we're Anglican Baptists." Hamish had never let go of his home church.

"Do the Anglican Baptists believe in Jesus?"

Hamish wriggled in his seat. I answered for him. "We believe we're saved through faith in Jesus."

I'd done it. I'd shared my faith.

"I'm glad to hear it." He downed the last of his espresso. He shook Hamish's hand. He smiled at the children, who were fighting over the last bit of tomato sauce to dip their chips in. Then he looked at me. "You've got a beautiful family, Jane from Melbourne. You're blessed."

"Thank you." I hoped Silvio would be okay.

Wednesday 13th June

I was unsure about my attempts at witnessing to Silvio yesterday. I hadn't been able to influence him to stop driving and the conversation about faith had been awkward. I was no longer sure James was referring to trials that came from sharing Jesus either. I opened up the chapter again.

"Consider it pure joy, my brothers and sisters, whenever you face trials of many kinds, because you know that the testing of your faith produces perseverance. Let perseverance finish its work so that you may be mature and complete, not lacking anything." (James 1:2-4)

The idea of being mature and complete sounded wonderful. But did James really mean it would come from persevering with sharing Jesus? Spreading the gospel was important, but I couldn't see how it would lead to being mature and complete, not lacking anything.

It rained hard when we were packing up this morning. We told the children to wait in the car while we packed up as fast as we could. It was a trial, getting drenched while we pulled pegs out of the mud. But when we had finally finished, and sat in the car with the heating on, I felt exhilarated.

"I've still got questions about that verse in James," I told Hamish once we reached the freeway.

"So you don't like either of my interpretations so far?"

"I think in this passage, when James is talking about trials, he's talking about trials in general."

Hamish was quiet for a while. "Well, if we're talking about trials in general, you *could* look at it another way." He straightened up in his seat. "Problems are necessary. If everything was easy, we'd never change. When we face a trial, we have to fix it. So we learn something."

"You're right Hamish! We learn something new and we get more mature, from going through trials. That's why we could consider it a joy." I was relieved. I felt sure I would be better at enduring trials now that I knew this.

Hamish smiled and tapped his fingers on the steering wheel.

We made a stopover at Kalgoorlie, to show the kids the open-cut mine. The wind was blowing so hard we took a quick look at the diggers and then bundled the kids back in the car.

We made the rest of the trip to Perth in silence. For the next few days, we were going to stay with my aunt and uncle at their new home. I hoped it would be easy. I was a little worried we'd be a burden. They were very quiet, and clean and tidy; we were covered in red dirt and had three children and an enormous camper trailer. But I was looking forward to a comfortable bed, and an ensuite bathroom. I needed a break from learning perseverance.

We arrived at Aunty Noni and Uncle Gordon's house just before dark. Gordon directed Hamish back and forth in the narrow street one hundred times until he finally got into the right position to back the trailer into the carport. I apologised for the red dirt all over our clothes. Gordon told us to make ourselves at home. Their new house was even more comfortable than I'd expected. It was palatial, with two levels, polished stone floors and calming grey and white furniture. Noni showed the children the study where they would be sleeping and led me to the spare room. It had white curtains, wooden bedside tables with antique lamps, and a queen-sized bed topped with fluffy grey and white cushions. It was like a beautiful haven of peacefulness. The perfect place to take a break.

Chapter 3

Thursday 14th June

The bed turned out to be extremely comfortable as well as beautiful. Underneath my bedside table was a selection of library books. I read a few chapters of *Murder on the Bay* this morning, a very exciting story. My relaxation was interrupted because we had to visit Hay Street Mall to buy a few things we needed, but I went quickly, so I could get back to my book. I was really enjoying my break from learning perseverance!

Friday 15th June

Another peaceful, relaxing day! I almost finished *Murder on the Bay*. There were a lot of twists and surprises. I had to stop reading because Noni and Gordon had planned a visit to King's Park, which is apparently the largest city park in the world. It was absolutely beautiful, but I still preferred to be at "home" in the spare room.

At dinner time I noticed the kids and their Great Aunt and Uncle were getting on well. Gideon had the cutest way of saying "Aunty No-neeee!" Gordon asked Jenna a lot of questions, which she loved answering.

Saturday 16th June

Today was not as peaceful as I'd hoped it would be. I finished *Murder on the Bay*. It had a very unsatisfying ending.

Downstairs, I could hear Jenna getting frustrated with Gordon. He kept asking questions until she forgot the point of whatever story she was telling.

Later I noticed Gideon was loving Rupert the dog a little too much. Noni told him Rupert needed to rest. Remembering we would be leaving soon, we went to Fremantle and bought Noni and Gordon a present to thank them for having us. It was a grey and white vase to match the grey and white bed cushions. I think they liked it. I tried to have a relaxing evening. I started reading *The Adventures of Max and Twitch* (a story about a young boy and his guinea pig) to Jenna. It's a bit young for her, but she still enjoyed it.

Sunday 17th June

I think it's time to leave. I finished reading *The Adventures of Max and Twitch* while Jenna was asleep. It was cute, but I didn't learn much. At breakfast, I discovered Faith had stained one of the cream-coloured placemats on the dining room table with a purple texta. Noni said it was okay, but I know they were a gift from my great grandmother. Rupert ran away and hid in a corner whenever he saw Gideon. Apparently, he doesn't like being picked up and squeezed.

Hamish and I went out to get food supplies for our trip up north. Hamish doesn't usually do grocery shopping. He looked at every product we don't have in Melbourne, and insisted on comparing the price of different brands. I usually buy the home brand; it makes life easier. I can do a week's worth of shopping in thirty minutes.

After two hours of shopping with Hamish, I couldn't stand it any longer. I told him he was being naive. Supermarkets put different brands on special each week so that customers like him will be forced to switch back and forth, trying out different products and spending more and more money. Hamish looked hurt. He said the supermarket was not forcing him to do anything. I apologised. I hope I can do better tomorrow.

Monday 18th June

I returned *The Adventures of Max and Twitch* back to its place under the bedside table. It was time to get serious again about our own adventure. I was feeling anxious about the journey north. What if we got lost again? What if we couldn't find somewhere to camp or had to set up in the dark? I read the next section from James to calm my nerves:

> *"If any of you lacks wisdom, you should ask God, who gives generously to all without finding fault, and it will be given to you. But when you ask you must believe and not doubt, because the one who doubts is like a wave of the sea, blown and tossed by the wind." (James 1:5-7)*

I loved the idea that God would give me wisdom willingly, without saying, "Oh, so you finally decided to ask me, did you?"

We said goodbye to Gordon and Noni. Noni gave me a surprisingly long hug, and said she was going to miss us all. I was relieved; I thought we'd been a nuisance. Gordon high-fived each of the kids and answered Hamish's questions about the nearest place to buy fuel.

We found the Petrol Express fuel station just before the turn-off to the highway. Hamish operated the bowser while I went inside to pay. I'd almost reached the front of the queue, and had my credit card ready to hand to the teenage boy behind the counter, when Faith rushed in.

"Wait Mum!" She had red cheeks and was panting. "Dad says there's a special deal. If you spend four dollars, you get four dollars *for free!*"

Oh no. Hamish was being naive again. "No-one gives you money for free Faith!" I told her. The deal would be that if you spent four dollars, you got a second four-dollar purchase *for free*. It was the service station's way of getting you to buy something you didn't need.

Hamish was never going to learn. "Okay. I'll get some chocolate," I sighed.

I could see some chocolate frogs in front of the counter. I could feel the young man serving and the customers behind me in the queue watching me. I scooped up eight at fifty cents each. That was four dollars' worth. Then I scooped up another eight and handed them to Faith. I felt like an idiot.

Back at the car, Hamish saw all the chocolate frogs.

"How much did you spend?" He screwed up his face in frustration. "You were supposed to spend four dollars so we could get four dollars off the price of fuel."

My irritation turned to anger. I'd just bought chocolate we didn't need, and now Hamish was treating me like a fool. He was the fool!

"Don't be stupid!" I shouted. Faith squirmed in the backseat. The other two were watching *The Parent Trap*, one of their favourites, with headphones on. "Use your brain, Hamish!" I yelled again. "Why would we get four dollars off the price of fuel, for spending four dollars in the store? That would make the purchase free! What shop is going to give us four dollars, for *free*?!!"

Hamish calmly drove out of the petrol station and turned onto the main road. My anger subsided a little. I felt bad for yelling. But if I could prove that I was right, my anger would be justified. I'd make it up to Hamish by explaining the truth nicely.

After Hamish had joined the freeway, I looked up the Petrol Express website. The home page had a purple background with bright yellow text. I read "Spend four dollars in the store, and get four dollars off the price of fuel!" I was shocked. Nothing was ever for free.

Then again, the offer might attract customers who'd go there instead of somewhere else. Maybe Hamish wasn't as silly as I thought.

I felt horrible. The most trivial misunderstanding had me yelling at Hamish, and in front of Faith too. I really was a terrible person.

Out of the blue, the words of James came into my brain, as if God was speaking to me.

"If any of you lacks wisdom, you should ask God." (James 1:5)

I knew if I was to pray for wisdom, I had to be prepared to accept the answer, like it or not.

I took a deep breath. I prayed. It was as if God put his arm around me. At that moment I knew God wasn't angry with me, and he didn't see me as terrible either. He nudged me to apologise to Hamish. It was freeing, not humiliating.

Hamish forgave me graciously. Then I apologised to Faith for getting angry and yelling at her Dad in front of her. She gave me a steely look. I obviously would need to wait a while for her forgiveness.

Our next stop was Nambung National Park, a few hours north of Perth. We took the circuit road through the Pinnacles desert marked with a red star in my guidebook. The landscape was amazing, and I was glad I was calm again, so I could enjoy it. The Pinnacles are limestone pillars, which look like little old men wearing capes. They have a round "head" at the top, and a wide curved "back", and they go straight up and down at the front. There are hundreds of these figures, in groups of four or five throughout the desert, like a large, spread-out army. We had some lunch at a lookout, then finished the circuit, before continuing our journey north.

We arrived at Coronation Beach, near Geraldton, just before dark. The only spots still left at the campsite were far away from the beach, on a grassy slope. Two friendly grey nomads, Barry and Norm, came over to offer some advice on getting our trailer into what was clearly a tricky location. The larger man, Barry, took charge, wordlessly handing me his dog lead, which was attached to a little white dog. I held the dog lead awkwardly. Barry told Hamish that he and Norm could help him push the trailer up the slope into a good position, and chock up the trailer wheels with a piece of wood, to keep it in place. Hamish thought the trailer was too heavy and would roll backwards. I also wasn't convinced Barry's idea was a good one, but Barry acted like a guy who was used to calling the shots. It seemed easiest just to give in to him.

I should have listened to Hamish.

Barry, Norm and Hamish pushed the trailer uphill, while I looked on. With a lot of effort, they managed to get it up the slope a metre or so, but when Norm and Barry let go to chock up the wheels of the trailer, Hamish couldn't hold the weight on his own. The trailer pushed Hamish backward as it rolled downhill, threatening to crush him. Somehow, he managed to straddle the draw bar, with one leg either side of the pointy end, and shuffle backwards down the hill, before being nearly impaled by the trailer as it crashed into a fence.

I lost all faith in Barry, and tied the dog's lead around a fence post. Now I listened to Hamish, who I wish I'd trusted in the first place. He thought we should camp to the side of the slope, still on a bit of an incline but on an area as flat as he could find. Norm, Barry, Hamish and I pushed the trailer into the spot, and it stayed there. Relieved, I gave Hamish a big hug.

In the middle of the night, we were woken up by Jenna, who was lying with her head facing downhill, and had gotten a headache. We had to turn her around. We'd just gotten back to sleep, when we were disturbed by Faith, who was lying at right-angles to the slope and fell out of bed.

Tuesday 19th June

I woke up with a big headache too. I told Hamish that camping was too hard, and I wanted to stay in motels from now on. He was surprisingly sympathetic. After nearly being run over by the camper trailer, he had apparently walked along the beach last night when the rest of us were asleep, praying and thanking God that he was unharmed. He was grateful to be alive, and didn't want to argue any more, although he did tell me motels would be too expensive.

Thankfully, a flat spot had become available. Norm and his wife had left in their caravan. I wondered if they had departed earlier than first planned, shocked by Hamish nearly being run over by the camper trailer. Their departure left a nice big space on level ground, so we carried out the kids' beds and all our bags without having to repack them first in the car. Then we moved the trailer, and the rest of our things, safely to the new spot, which was right next to Barry and his wife Beryl's caravan.

My head was still hurting, so I had a nap. Hamish must have told Barry about my head, because when I woke up and was sitting with Hamish under the awning, he came over with a selection of essential oils that he believed would help. Barry was obviously the sort of person who thought he had a solution for everything. I doubted his essential oils would help. He got me to smell them and choose my favourite scent—rose—then he applied it himself, dabbing oil on my forehead and temples. I don't know what exactly helped: the essential oils, the feeling of being looked after, or the after-effects of the nap I'd just woken up from, but in a few minutes my headache was gone. Perhaps Barry was not such a bad person after all.

It was the warmest day we'd had so far, a balmy 23 degrees, so the kids and I went down to the beach. Jenna and Faith jumped over the waves, laughing and splashing each other. The two girls are united in their love of water - hot, cold or lukewarm it doesn't matter. Water has to be at least 28 degrees before Gideon would consider going in. Gideon ran back and forth occasionally letting his toes touch the cold water.

It started to rain. I took Gideon back to the campsite to get my coat. The rain got heavier, and the girls came running back from the beach, breathless and excited. It continued to rain steadily, and big puddles formed around the tent. As we were stranded and couldn't go anywhere, I found it quite relaxing in the end. Although to read Jenna's journal, you'd think it had been awful.

Tuesday the 19th June: The worst beach day ever! We had to go "quick quick" and get all our stuff out of the camper, pack the trailer and push it to another spot. When we finished we got changed into our bathers and headed to the beach. The water was cold but Faith and I jumped around and splashed each other to take our mind off it.

A few minutes later, it started spitting so Mum said she would go get her coat and come back. The rain got much heavier, until every time it hit your skin it felt like rocks being thrown at you with great speed. We got out of the water, but then we started to panic as we were running barefoot on stones and it took a long time to find the path. We ran with all our might to the tent thinking all this time, "What on earth has Mum been doing?" We could see the tent and dashed under the awning to get cover from the rain.

To our surprise Mum was standing there with Gideon. We began to pour out questions. Mum said she took a while to find her coat once she arrived, then as she was about to find us to bring us home, she realised we were rushing toward her. (I think she forgot about us. I strongly doubt it took that long to find a coat, especially a bright red one like Mum's).

The awning was about to break with the weight of the rain. Dad went around every five minutes pushing the awning up with a stick so the water went off the side and made a huge river circling our tent.

Mum was stressed out so she had a nap, while Faith and I distracted Gideon with a few imaginary games, pretending we were on a desert island. Dad's friend Barry came to see the river around our tent. He threw us some Oreo-flavoured biscuits: banana, strawberry and chocolate. We shared them out eagerly and gratefully. For the rest of the day we did not do very much, but we had a good time playing in the deep puddles, too scared to go back to the beach.

Wednesday 20th June

It had cooled down again after the rain. I hoped we wouldn't have a repeat of the cold wet weather we'd had travelling the Nullarbor. It was definitely no good for more swimming; we'd need to find another activity. I had a look at the directory of Western Australia that I'd picked up in Perth. I thought the Geraldton Museum looked interesting. I was fascinated to see that an area near Geraldton was discovered by Dutch explorers, more than 100 years before Captain Cook arrived with the First Fleet. But the kids didn't want to go to a museum. We compromised and took them to the Bureau of Meteorology, which offered free tours at midday.

The Bureau was in a modern building surrounded by paddocks, on the outskirts of town. We arrived just in time for the tour. Lachlan, the earnest young meteorologist, seemed very excited to see us, as if he had not had any contact with humans for a month. I thought briefly about what awesome parents Hamish and I were, and how great it was that we were stimulating our children's minds. My thoughts were interrupted by Gideon, however, who kept asking me if he could have something to eat. It was infuriating. We were providing a great educational opportunity for him, and all he could think about was his stomach. I took Gideon out to the car and found a "fizzer" lolly to satisfy him, so he could concentrate. Back inside the bureau, the girls and Hamish were still waiting for the tour to begin. Lachlan was pointing to a display shelf of brochures and telling the girls that they were welcome to take as many brochures as they wished, even "several copies of each" if they liked. They looked shyly in the direction of the brochures, then told Lachlan, "No thank you, we don't want any." His face fell.

Nobody else arrived for the tour. Undeterred, Lachlan led us outside as if he was in charge of a whole class of school children. His phone beeped and he explained that he needed to make a report. He looked at the sky and told us there was no cyclone, or any other unusual weather activity. He made a report about this on his phone. Then he took us across a series of stepping stones to see the wind vanes and rain gauges that were fenced off so nobody could disturb them. Lachlan asked the children if they had questions. There was silence until Hamish and I came up with some. Finally, at the climax of our tour, Lachlan told the girls he needed their help with something. Faith explained it later like this:

> We went to a place where they work out the weather. We had to stand behind a yellow line. We were not allowed to put our feet over the line. Locklin put on a special suit. He filled a balloon with hydrogen. It's called a sound balloon and it's to tell you the weather. Jenna and I got to push the button. We had to push it together, because there's only one button. The balloon went really high.

Hamish and I watched the balloon for several minutes, wondering if it would burst. We watched it get smaller and smaller until we couldn't see it anymore, feeling proud that our children had played a part in predicting the weather. Being ever-practical, Hamish asked Lachlan what the weather was going to be like tomorrow at our next destination, Shark Bay. I expected him to put a special code in his phone to get an up-to-date report, or perhaps phone weather headquarters.

Instead, Lachlan looked up a website on his computer (the same website we look up ourselves) and told us there would be fine weather and sunshine. I was relieved about that. There would be no more getting caught out at the beach in the rain. We thanked Lachlan very much, and I persuaded the girls to collect some brochures on our way out, if only for the sake of Lachlan's feelings.

Back at Coronation Beach, I tried to pack up inside the trailer, preparing for our departure tomorrow. Clean clothes were tumbled with dirty clothes. There were wet towels and toys everywhere to be sorted. I was at my wit's end when Hamish poked his head in and said he needed *my* help. He explained that the alternator (whatever that was) on the camper trailer wasn't working to charge the trailer battery, so he couldn't use the battery-operated pump to push out the water stored in the trailer to cook dinner.

"You're saying we can't cook dinner," I said.

"Yes," he said. "What should we do?"

I knew the answer to the problem! After all, I had grown up in an inner-city suburb of Melbourne. The solution was of course that we should *go out to eat!* Hamish nodded. (Given how quickly he agreed with me, I suspect that he knew that's what we should do, but didn't want to be the one to say it).

We drove back into Geraldton and ate fish and hamburgers at a plastic table outside a fish and chip shop. It wasn't exactly fine dining, but I enjoyed every minute of it. The fish was fresh and delicious, no-one had to wash up, and in the distance, we could hear the roar of the sea. As I ate the salty hot chips, I was thrilled. Hamish had been able to lean on me with the broken-alternator crisis, and I had come up with the answers. Perhaps I was learning to have wisdom after all.

Chapter 4

Thursday 21st June

I was challenged by James again this morning, this time about blaming someone else for my own mistakes.

> *"When tempted no-one should say, 'God is tempting me'. For God cannot be tempted by evil, nor does he tempt anyone; but each one is tempted when, by his own evil desire, he is dragged away and enticed. Then, after desire has conceived, it gives birth to sin; and sin, when it is full-grown, gives birth to death." (James 1:13-15)*

It's my own evil desire that leads to sin. Maybe evil desires could be ordinary things, such as wanting to avoid something tedious, like taking advantage of a good deal when you bought petrol. I remembered my outburst three days ago. I'd let myself be dragged into cynicism, which had "given birth" to my angry outburst. Thankfully Hamish had forgiven me. But I didn't want to put him through it again. I needed to tolerate doing boring activities. Today there was a big task right in front of me: *packing up*, one of the most tiresome activities of any camping trip. *Stuff* was everywhere, in spite of my efforts to start putting things away last night. But I decided I would embrace the challenge!

The problem was, I didn't know where to start. I stared at the trestle table we had our meals on, which in three days at Coronation Beach had become a dumping ground for miscellaneous items. I wasn't sure what some of the things on the table were, let alone where to put them. I moved a few things around into different boxes, not sure I was doing it right. I spotted the tube of toothpaste and put it in our black toiletries bag. I knew everything had a particular place and had to be packed away in a certain order, or other stuff wouldn't fit. I was pretty sure it was too early for the toiletries bag, which went in, quite last minute, in its spot near the roof of the car. *I know*, I thought finally, *I'll sweep out the tent. I know how to do that.*

I couldn't find the broom.

"Where's the broom?" I asked Hamish sheepishly, as he placed bags carefully into the car in his particular configuration. I was embarrassed I had to ask.

Hamish walked to the back of the camper trailer, and swung open the metal lid of the trailer drawer.

"I've found a way to save space. The handle fits in here." He pointed to the handle, in a tiny recess under the lid.

I found the broom head in the main part of the trailer drawer. While I screwed the brush onto the handle, I realised I didn't know you could take a broom apart, and I definitely didn't know about the tiny recess for storing the handle. How would I ever get the hang of this?

As I swept inside the tent, my heart started to race and I felt flustered. Why had Hamish packed so much stuff he had to hide the broom handle? I bet we didn't need half of the things he'd brought with us.

Then I realised how quickly I had gone down the same path again, even after committing to embrace the hard stuff this morning. I was blaming Hamish again. If it continued, I would end up yelling and regret it, and I didn't want to do that. As I swept the last of the mud and sand out of the tent, my thoughts slowed down and became clearer. *Was it Hamish's fault that packing was hard? Anyway, what was I achieving by getting angry about it?* My breathing slowed a little.

Hamish gave Faith a lesson on how to repack the cereals into a plastic box, so that they all fit perfectly and the lid didn't bow in the middle. After I finished sweeping, Faith and I helped with the last of the bags and boxes and we packed away the tent. I was glad I had stopped myself from blaming Hamish and hadn't acted crazy again.

We said goodbye to Beryl and Barry, who had lots of last-minute advice about what we definitely shouldn't miss on the rest of our trip. On Barry's recommendation, we made a stop to visit Hamelin Pool and the stromatolites — ancient rocks which are bound together by living organisms. From a boardwalk, we looked at the ancient brown mossy rocks shaped like four-leaf clovers. Nearby were the ruins of a telegraph station built out of bricks made from shells. The bricks were dazzling against the blue sky. I felt peaceful surrounded by so much beauty. All the trouble of packing and travelling and setting up felt worth it at that moment.

We found a camping spot near a place called Shark Bay. The kids were pleased to camp on the beach again. Jenna wrote:

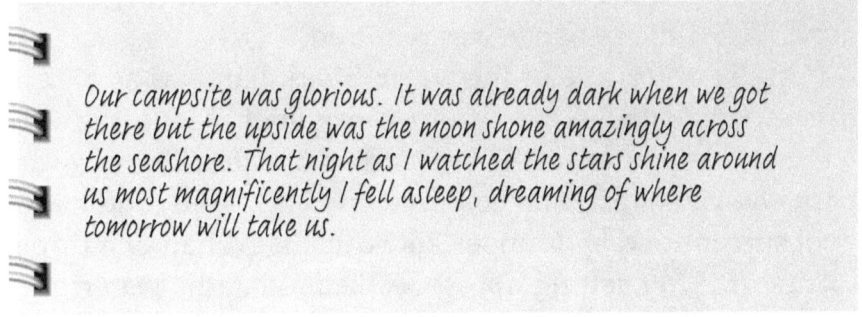

Our campsite was glorious. It was already dark when we got there but the upside was the moon shone amazingly across the seashore. That night as I watched the stars shine around us most magnificently I fell asleep, dreaming of where tomorrow will take us.

We were camping at the beach without any facilities, not so Jenna could see the magnificent stars, but because you were allowed to stop here one night for free. Tomorrow we would have to move to a caravan park in Shark Bay, to use as a base for going to see dolphins at Monkey Mia. I hated that we would have to pack up for the second day in a row, however, it was such a short stop we'd barely unpacked at all. I wouldn't be wandering around wondering what items were, and where to put them.

Hopefully, it would be easy. And if it wasn't, I would try my best to be patient.

Friday 22nd June

In the morning light, I could see the spot we had camped at *was* beautiful. Jenna was right. The fine sand was pure white and we were sheltered by some dunes behind us. The sun sparkled on the water, and on the other side of the bay we could see the palm trees and low-rise buildings of the Shark Bay township. Gideon dug holes with a stick in the sand dunes behind us, while the rest of us packed up with ease. Faith hopped on top of the trailer to stop the groundsheet blowing away then hopped off so Hamish could zip up the canvas cover. I was relieved at how quickly it was done. Very little patience was required.

On the other side of the water, Shark Bay was as attractive as it had looked from our camp spot. Along the waterfront was a boardwalk and dozens of cafes. The caravan park was full of brightly coloured tropical plants, and had a pool surrounded by lounges, like dreams I'd had of a tropical resort. After setting up, we walked along the waterfront and stopped at a cafe with wooden tables and umbrellas. As the kids ate their ice creams and Hamish and I sipped our coffee I told Hamish this was much more my idea of a holiday. I felt relaxed and peaceful, spooning the froth off the top of my caffè latte and looking out to sea.

In the late afternoon the wind blew hard off the sea and the tropical plants swayed and nearly toppled over in their ceramic pots. In spite of the wind, the girls decided to swim in the icy outdoor pool. They inched down the steps into the water, then stood shivering and urged each other to put their heads under. After a few seconds of being underwater, they shrieked with excitement while Gideon and I, safe and warmly dressed on the comfortable lounge chairs, watched and shook our heads at them.

The cold wind spoiled the illusion of a dream resort holiday. But we hadn't come to Shark Bay to lie around the pool. We were here to go to Monkey Mia tomorrow to see the dolphins. I hoped they wouldn't be shy, like the whales at the Bight.

Saturday 23rd June

Just after sunrise, we arrived at the wide white sandy beach at Monkey Mia. There was already a good crowd. The water sparkled and rippled before us, but there was no sign of dolphins. A ranger wearing a khaki shirt and shorts arrived and we followed him to the water.

Standing ankle-deep in the gently lapping ocean, the ranger told us the sea-living mammals had been coming to Monkey Mia since the 1970s, when fishermen first started feeding them. These days, the feeding was controlled, because the dolphins had become too fond of the fish handed out to them, and had forgotten how to fish for themselves.

It made me think back to James 1:2.

"Consider it pure joy whenever you face trials of many kinds."

Without trials, such as needing to find one's own fish, or work for a living, there would be no opportunities to learn new skills or perseverance.

Five fins appeared, cutting through the water toward the shore, and then five curved mouths stuck out of the water, in big smiles as if they were happy at the mention of fish. The crowd gave gasps of delight. I was thrilled.

One of the grinning dolphins had some marks on her otherwise smooth fin. Her name was Nicky, named for the "nicks" in her fin that she'd gotten from being sliced by a boat propeller in her search for food. Nicky leapt out of the water, giving us a good view of her fin, while the ranger was repeatedly nudged in the thigh by another smiling creature called Piccolo, named for her small size. In spite of the availability of human-caught fish, Piccolo preferred to catch her own food, coming to shore at feeding time for social reasons.

The ranger asked for a volunteer to feed the dolphins fish from his plastic bucket. I hoped Faith would be chosen. She looked ready for dolphin feeding in her denim shorts and T-shirt, her hair in pigtails. She stuck her left hand straight up into the air, but the ranger chose a white-haired lady wearing a flowing dress instead.

The old lady's arm shook as she held a shiny silver fish out for Piccolo, who sniffed at it, then stuck her beak up in the air in a show of indifference and swam proudly away. Piccolo was replaced by Nicky, who accepted the fish immediately.

"No more," the ranger told the lady, who was looking pleased with herself. Over-feeding in the past meant that Nicky had failed to fish for herself and to teach her children to fish. Sadly, seven out of Nicky's eight children were missing.

At the mention of children, I wondered where they were.

I saw Faith and Jenna bobbing down close to the water near Hamish. They were making swirling motions in the water with their hands, probably wishing they could swim. But where was their brother?

"Where's Gideon?" I shouted to Hamish, my heart pounding.

We ran back up the beach and spotted him near the carpark running in circles around a pelican, like one of the dolphins circling the ranger. Gideon saw us and ran in faster and more determined circles. Gideon squawked and flapped his arms, as if trying to get the pelican to fly. My heart rate slowed and my breathing returned to normal. I hugged Hamish.

Later that night after the kids had gone to sleep, Hamish and I sat up in bed.

"That was scary today." Hamish ran his hand over his forehead, as if trying to erase the memory.

I nodded. "Maybe Gideon thought the pelican was more interesting than the dolphins. It looked like a Pteranadon."

"Do you remember when he used to like round things? Like balls. And playing with peas on his plate," Hamish eased himself into the sleeping bag.

I nodded. "We thought he was going to be good at ball sports."

"Then you took him to a little soccer league and he wouldn't share the ball."

We'd taken him to see a paediatrician then. He'd diagnosed Gideon with Autism. He told us Gideon's brain works differently from other children. He's fascinated by things that interest him—at the moment it was dinosaurs—but lacks some of the skills to understand social cues or connect with other children. Hamish and I changed our attitudes and behaviour. I still felt guilty - as his mother I should have realised something was wrong and had it checked out earlier. But I loved the happy look on Gideon's face when I stopped getting angry, and gave him simple explanations that helped him make sense of the world.

"Do you think Gideon will be okay?" I asked Hamish.

"Of course he will be."

"I don't want to be like Nicky, handing him everything on a plate. He needs to fish for himself." I remembered most of Nicky's dolphin children were missing. I shuddered.

"Let's start by teaching him who he belongs to. Make him feel loved and safe."

"You're right." Hamish was right about a lot of things lately.

Hamish began the slow even breathing that meant he'd fallen asleep. I looked at the sharp-clawed long-tailed dinosaur next to Gideon's head, resting on his pillow: a fierce velociraptor, one of his favourites. I went to sleep feeling grateful for Gideon, and wondering what I'd learn next.

Chapter 5

Sunday 24th June

Hamish asked me to plan our next destination and find accommodation. I was considering Point Quobba, which had been recommended as a good stop after Shark Bay by Barry, the grey nomad who made the camper trailer roll downhill then redeemed himself by healing my headache.

First I read from James. Finding our destination was important, but I could sort that out on the road. It was more important to start the journey with a good heart.

> *"Do not merely listen to the word, and so deceive yourselves. Do what it says. Anyone who listens to the word but does not do what it says is like a man who looks at his face in the mirror and, after looking at himself, goes away and immediately forgets what he looks like." (James 1:22-24).*

It made sense. I wouldn't look in the mirror and then not do anything to fix my appearance, especially if my face was smudged with the red dirt of the outback. In the same way, why would I consult the Bible and not take any notice of it? I was determined to put what I was learning into practice.

As Hamish drove up the North West Coastal Highway, I finally consulted the camping guide. Point Quobba was 400 km away. The GPS gave an estimated arrival time of 2 p.m. It seemed like a waste to only advance 400 km in our journey, and arrive at our next destination in the middle of the afternoon. I noticed Coral Bay, one hundred kilometres further north, had free campsites. Doing a longer journey seemed like a better use of our day, and free camping would fit with Hamish's new schedule. He was determined to alternate between caravan parks, where we had to pay but got use of showers and washing machines, and bush sites, where we could camp for low or no fees. I told Hamish to head for free camping at Coral Bay, 500 km away.

I was feeling optimistic and accomplished, having made a decision about our journey. The sky was a blue dome above us, and it seemed nothing could go wrong. Even the crack of a stone hitting the windscreen leaving a star-shaped chip was nothing to worry about. At our lunch stop, I made a phone call to check our insurance policy covered windscreens (it did!), while the others sat on the camper trailer next to the bright yellow concrete "Big Banana" of Carnavon and ate sandwiches.

After lunch, the sky clouded over, and the windscreen crack got bigger, making a larger star-shaped chip. The children started to argue. Was it too ambitious to go to Coral Bay? We were supposed to arrive at 5 pm, and it would be completely dark an hour later, which didn't give us much daylight to set up. I began to doubt my decision.

I looked at the guide to see if there were any free camping sites closer. There wasn't. I noticed a yellow oval symbol next to the Coral Bay campsite in the guide I hadn't noticed before—and four words written next to it. 'Must have chemical toilet!' My heart skipped a beat.

"The map guide says we have to bring our own toilet!" I told Hamish.

Hamish frowned. "We can't just dig a hole?"

"Apparently not. And it has to be a *chemical* toilet, whatever that is."

"Why don't we stay at Exmouth National Park further on. They'll have drop toilets."

"That's 150 km further. We'll have to set up in the dark." Last time we set up late Hamish was nearly run over by the trailer, we camped on the side of a hill and Faith fell out of bed. My heart started to race.

It was 6:30 p.m. and darkness had settled over the bush like a cloak when we reached the National Park.

I jumped down from my seat and approached the gate. In the light of the car headlights I saw a sign in red letters: "No Camping!"

My heart sank. I grabbed at the only solution I could think of. "Forget the sign. We'll have to camp here anyway," I told Hamish. "We haven't got a choice."

"We'd better not." Hamish frowned. "Let's keep going to the town of Exmouth. We'll find a caravan park."

I sighed. It was annoying Hamish was such a stickler for rules, but at least he was giving up the free camping schedule. It would be good to have flushing toilets again. Maybe it would turn out okay after all.

Entering the town I noticed the "Sea and Sands resort", a large hotel with a huge concrete crustacean out front, the "Big Prawn" of Exmouth. What would it be like to stay at the resort? They probably gave out fluffy guest towels as well as fully made-up beds. It would be out of our budget, but the idea was appealing.

We continued past the giant crustacean and the Exmouth Youth Hostel. We would be too old now, and the kid's too young for a *youth* hostel. We found the caravan park. That was where we fit. I left Hamish in the car and went to book in. The lights of the office were out but I could make out a "closed" sign hanging on the other side of the glass door. My heart started racing again.

Hamish wasn't concerned. He stretched. "Let's get something to eat."

"Are you serious Hamish? It's after 7 p.m."

"I know. I'm so hungry."

My heart was still racing, but I spoke surprisingly calmly. "We can eat later. We need to find somewhere to stay before everything closes. Let's check out that resort with the Big Prawn statue. It will be expensive, but we're running out of choices now." I could already feel the softness of the guest towels.

"What about the youth hostel opposite the Big Prawn? They might have some family accommodation."

I sighed. So we wouldn't be staying in the hotel. But I could live without a fluffy towel. We just needed beds to sleep in.

Hamish drove back to the hostel. I felt the Big Prawn's beady eyes on me as we went inside. The office was open! Of course, it was still early for its twenty-something travellers. A young woman with a sleeve of tattoos on one arm said we could book two double rooms, at seventy dollars each. Hamish was shocked at the cost. He thought a youth hostel would be cheaper. I didn't care. I was so relieved to have somewhere to sleep I wanted to hug her.

The rooms were small, with corrugated tin walls. But the beds were made, and the sheets smelled clean. I was thrilled.

Hamish and the kids enthusiastically ate pizza and chips in the hostel restaurant, which was full of young people drinking and playing pool. Then Gideon and I snuggled on one of the sweet-smelling beds to the accompanying laughter and "thwack" of pool balls being hit next door.

While Gideon watched a documentary about polar bears, I put "Shark Bay to Exmouth" into my phone and found that we had travelled 691 km! An estimated travel time of seven and a half hours. It was a huge journey, all because I'd ignored the sign in the map book indicating we needed a chemical toilet at the free camping in Coral Bay. I remembered the verse from James this morning, about there being no point looking in a mirror if you didn't notice your appearance. Really, there was no point having the map book if I wasn't going to take any notice of it. I would pay more attention from now on, if I took over navigating again.

Before going to bed, Jenna and Faith proudly showed me their diary entries. Faith had included a picture of herself in front of the Big Banana. Jenna's diary featured the Big Banana too:

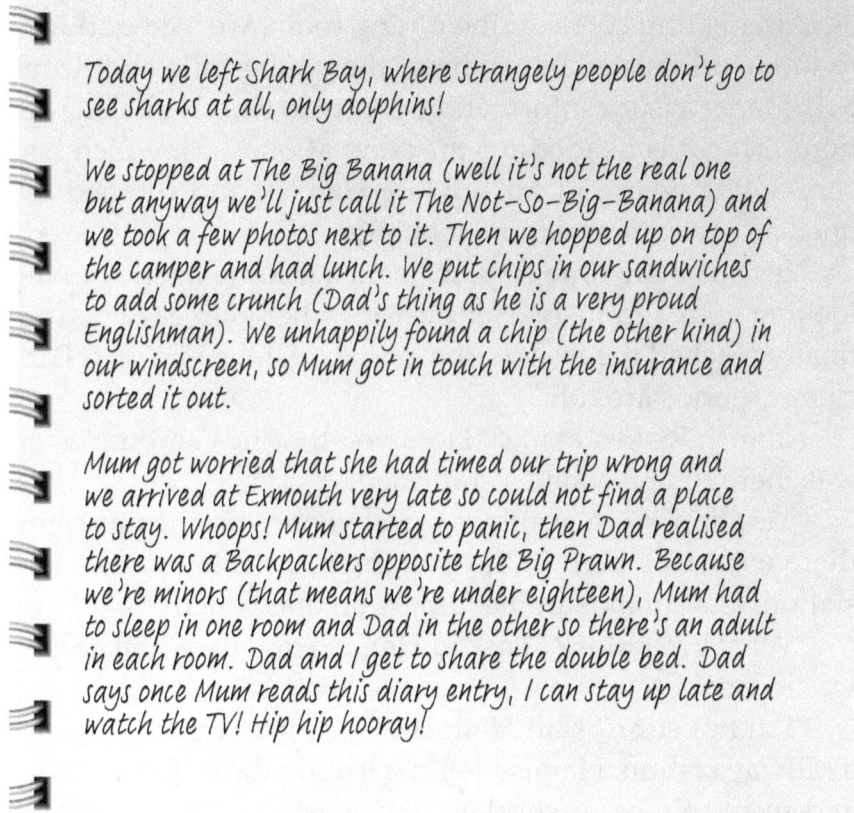

Today we left Shark Bay, where strangely people don't go to see sharks at all, only dolphins!

We stopped at The Big Banana (well it's not the real one but anyway we'll just call it The Not-So-Big-Banana) and we took a few photos next to it. Then we hopped up on top of the camper and had lunch. We put chips in our sandwiches to add some crunch (Dad's thing as he is a very proud Englishman). We unhappily found a chip (the other kind) in our windscreen, so Mum got in touch with the insurance and sorted it out.

Mum got worried that she had timed our trip wrong and we arrived at Exmouth very late so could not find a place to stay. Whoops! Mum started to panic, then Dad realised there was a Backpackers opposite the Big Prawn. Because we're minors (that means we're under eighteen), Mum had to sleep in one room and Dad in the other so there's an adult in each room. Dad and I get to share the double bed. Dad says once Mum reads this diary entry, I can stay up late and watch the TV! Hip hip hooray!

Monday 25th June

I woke up to a little head snuggled next to me, its blond hair tickling my chin. My enjoyment of the situation was short-lived when I remembered what happened yesterday. We had to find new accommodation, and fast. We couldn't stay at the youth hostel (I didn't really want to blow the budget and go home yet: I was just starting to learn something after all) and we had to find a camping spot where we wouldn't be breaking any rules. Most of all, we had to get wherever we were going and set up before it got dark or everything closed. I didn't want any more unnecessary drama.

After eating cereal in the dining room, we said goodbye to the youth hostel and some of the young folk, and drove to the large Visitor Information Centre to investigate our options. The kids headed for the shop at one end, which had snorkelling gear and gifts, while Hamish and I joined the queue for accommodation bookings.

"It's our busy time of year," said a middle-aged woman, looking at us seriously over the top of her glasses, when we finally reached the front of the queue. "All the National Park campgrounds are full."

Hamish looked at me. "I told you the "no camping" sign was there for a reason." I squirmed.

"Yes, and there are fines for anyone who tries to camp there without a permit. But you might be able to camp at a station. Have a look in the folders on that bench."

"What's a station?" I asked Hamish quietly when no-one was in earshot.

"I'm not sure," said Hamish. I was pretty sure it wasn't a railway station. Hamish left me leafing through the folder and went to look at snorkels and masks with the children while I found a listing for a "station" that allowed camping and wasn't too far away. I called the number.

"H-e-ll-o?" The woman who answered sounded surprised that someone had called.

"Is this Ningaloo Station?"

There was a pause and then a "Yes!" as if she had just remembered where she was.

"Do you have space for a camper trailer?"

"Well yes." She sounded uncertain. "But you must bring your own chemical toilet."

I called out to Hamish, who was helping Faith try on a mask, and he rushed over, keen to see if I'd had any luck.

"Somewhere called Ningaloo Station has vacancies. But we have to bring a chemical toilet."

"Oh no. Not that again." Hamish looked annoyed.

"We'll buy one," I told the woman at Ningaloo. I didn't want to lose our spot. Hamish began researching chemical toilets on his phone, while I listened to some rather confusing directions to Ningaloo before ending the call, assuring the woman we would bring a toilet.

Behind us, we heard a crash. Gideon had knocked over a glass toothpick holder filled with water, scattering toothpicks everywhere. As Hamish ushered him and the girls out of the shop, Gideon bumped into a small wooden lighthouse souvenir. It snapped in half as it hit the floor. I remembered a sign that said "Please supervise your children. All breakages must be paid for."

I picked up the bottom half of the lighthouse and turned it over to see the price. It was seventeen dollars. I considered just quietly leaving the shop, hoping no-one had noticed.

A young shop assistant arrived with a mop and a "caution, wet floor" sign. I busied myself looking at the snorkels and masks. Perhaps I could pretend I knew nothing about the broken souvenirs, and buy some snorkels for the girls, as a kind of unspoken compensation.

Then I remembered how things went wrong when I ignored the rules. I apologised to the shop assistant who had started to mop up the mess.

"Would you like me to pay for the souvenirs?" I asked her.

"Don't worry about it. Those things break all the time." She checked to see that the older woman was busy and then added quietly and conspiratorially, "I don't know why they keep buying them."

I felt good. I'd done the right thing *and* kept my seventeen dollars.

Hamish's internet search had revealed a camping shop nearby. It was easy to find, in the centre of town. We spotted a blue and white chemical toilet. The helpful sales assistant explained that a chemical toilet was small and portable with a tank at the base for water and chemicals. It wasn't good enough on a beach to dig a hole and cover it, because soft sand was easily blown away, taking campers' toilet paper with it. Enlightened, we bought a toilet with a square white tank and a green lid, and some blue chemicals. The girls persuaded us to buy them their own snorkels and masks, which were cheaper than the ones in the information centre with the expensive souvenirs.

After stocking up on groceries, which Hamish chose even more carefully than usual due to a new plan he had of spending under ten dollars per meal, we decided it would be a good idea to set off for Ningaloo. We didn't want to be late and arrive in the dark again. It was 2.30 pm when we set off, with plenty of time to travel the 130 km to Ningaloo Homestead. We headed south down the same highway we'd travelled up yesterday, enjoying the blue skies and easy driving, and confident we had a good plan, complete with a toilet. After an hour of cruising down the highway, we turned off onto "Ningaloo Road," which sounded promising. The road was rippled like the corrugated iron of the walls at the Exmouth youth hostel. Hamish had to slow to what felt like walking pace, and even then our bones felt like they were rattling as we went over the bumps. The bumps went on and on. Whatever a "station" was, it was remote.

When we finally reached Ningaloo Homestead, it was 5.45 and it was starting to get dark. We realised we had done it again. Despite all our planning and determination to arrive in plenty of time, we were late.

Hoping to make up some time I ran from the car to the front door of the homestead, arriving breathless. A man in his fifties, with thinning ginger hair opened the door. There was no sign of the nervous-sounding woman I'd spoken to earlier in the day.

"We rang about camping." I was breathing heavily, and shaking too, anxious about having to set up in the dark again.

The man looked at me thoughtfully, his head tilted to one side, as if he was deciding whether to tell me off, or reassure me.

"You want to go down to the beach? At this time of night?"

"Yes, please."

"Who are you here with?"

"My husband. And three children."

"Why didn't your husband come to the door?"

"He's in the car," I said. The ginger-haired man looked at me sternly. He wanted more of an explanation. "With the children," I said. "We have our own toilet," I added.

"Tell your husband to come and talk to me."

I ran back to the car and told Hamish he was needed.

Hamish shook hands with the ginger-haired man, who introduced himself as Jeff, the owner of Ningaloo Homestead.

"It's too late to drive down to the beach," Jeff said matter-of-factly to Hamish. "It's a long way, and a rough road. You'll arrive in the dark. You'll get bogged. Your wife will be very unhappy." He looked at Hamish disapprovingly.

Hamish nodded.

"And you know what they say: a happy wife is a happy life," added Jeff. Hamish nodded again.

Jeff seemed satisfied he had made himself clear. "We have some temporary camping in a paddock nearby. You can move to the beach tomorrow."

He gave Hamish some paperwork to sign, asking him not to trespass on private property. I gave him the required $100 bond, and fees for four nights' camping. In turn Jeff gave me a map, with directions to our temporary camping spot, and the beach camp spot we would head to tomorrow.

"Remember, no trespassing," he reminded Hamish. "And you," he looked at me kindly this time, "take it easy."

I directed Hamish through a series of paddocks. I jumped out of the car to open the gate for each new paddock, then closed each gate and ran back to the car. I was still feeling anxious, but opening and closing gates was easy and made me feel capable. I calmed down a little.

When we finally arrived, the sun had completely disappeared. We did a simple set up by the light of a few stars and the car headlights. I couldn't believe we were late, and setting up in the dark, again.

Before I went to sleep, I considered whether to blame Hamish for all the stress and anxiety. I went over my familiar complaints—Hamish had suggested a camping trip in the first place, and he'd suggested going to the west of Australia, which as I'd feared, apart from a few tourist hotspots, was largely deserted. Once again he spent too long in the supermarket making sure we bought the specials, which had delayed us this afternoon, adding to our late arrival. I had a new reason to be upset with him today: judging by Jeff's obvious disapproval, Hamish had clearly acted inappropriately. He'd allowed me to get out of the car and book in, instead of doing it himself, or at least coming with me. Jeff's wife did not have to endure that kind of trial. I imagined how cared for she must feel, having a husband who protected her and tried to make her happy. It was very romantic, thinking about Jeff and his wife, living out here all alone at Ningaloo Homestead, like an outback prince with his princess. I wished I had a caring husband like Jeff.

My eyelids flew open. What was I thinking? Did I just wish I was married to someone else? All because Hamish wanted me to get out of the car to book our accommodation? I'd started blaming Hamish for our trials, and I didn't like where it was going. I remembered James: *After desire has conceived, it gives birth to sin, and sin, when it is full grown, gives birth to death. (James 1:15)*

I needed to stop this! I wished I'd never blamed Hamish. I sat up quickly.

"What's wrong?" Hamish had rolled onto his back.

"Nothing's wrong. Go back to sleep."

Hamish rolled back on his side, facing away from me.

I would have to embrace challenges, and be grateful, instead of blaming Hamish for them. Usually when I blamed him, I ended up yelling and acting crazy. This time I'd started to wish I was married to someone else. This was serious! I had to embrace my circumstances quickly.

"Hamish!" I grabbed his shoulder.

He rolled onto his back again. "Hmmm. What?"

"Thank you for suggesting a camping trip and going west, and taking a long time at the supermarket, and trusting me with getting out and booking in."

"What are you talking about?"

"I like being here. Even the bouncing over the bumps, and setting up in the dark, and all the packing and unpacking. And I *really* liked opening and closing all the gates. That was fun."

"Hmmm." I could see Hamish rub his eyes in the dark. He stayed on his back.

I felt so much better. And then I thought of something else.

"Hamish?"

"Yeah?"

"I think a station is a farm." It would explain all the gates. They would be needed to confine the animals.

"Hmmm. I think you're right." He closed his eyes and went back to sleep.

Chapter 6

Tuesday 26th June

We only had to travel an hour to the beach. Even Hamish and I couldn't muck that up. We would arrive in plenty of time, set up camp on the fine white sand, and spend a relaxed afternoon looking out over the sea. It was going to be easy and straightforward. While Hamish and the girls went for a walk, I stuffed sleeping bags and efficiently collapsed the kids' beds while I watched Gideon play, carefree, in a nearby patch of dirt.

I still felt optimistic on the journey to the beach. The road was stony but not corrugated. Hamish smiled with contentment, like he always does when doing easy off-road driving. Two emus on a hill turned to watch us and Hamish slowed down for some fat sheep stained orange by the red dirt. They ambled slowly across the road. Some large kangaroos hopped along beside us. With all the animals, Ningaloo Station was definitely a farm.

We turned off at a sign for Winderabandi Point, as indicated by Jeff's map. Jeff had written notes in large capital letters, telling us to drive to campsite number one, at the end of the point, as far as we could go. Sunlight gleamed off the ocean ahead of us. We were about halfway along the point, when Hamish was forced to slow down as the car dragged in the soft sand. Eventually the wheels dug in and the car sagged and stopped. There was nothing in Jeff's notes about what to do if we got bogged.

Thankfully, as we stepped down from the car, four young men in board shorts and sleeveless shirts appeared. Without speaking, they each took a tyre and began scooping sand from around it, as if they had been waiting along the side of the road to do this very job.

"Thanks, fellas," said Hamish.

"What's your tyre pressure?" said one of them, a short guy with dark hair, in a Rip Curl singlet.

"I put it down to 16." Hamish started digging out sand from around the trailer wheel. So that's what Hamish had been doing this morning with the gadget that looked like a hose attached to a watch: letting down the tyre pressure.

"Ah, that's your problem mate. You need to go down to ten on this stuff." The young man picked up a handful of the fine sand and let it fall through his fingers.

Hamish found the watch attached to the hose (the tyre pressure gauge). One of the boys went to get his own gadget and reduced the pressure on the passenger side, while the Rip Curl guy supervised Hamish on the driver side, making sure he got it right. Then the children and I watched while Hamish drove and the boys pushed the car out of the sand.

"What just happened?" I said to Hamish as we waved goodbye and drove on. "Are they like the guardian angels of four-wheel driving?"

"They must have a campsite nearby," he guessed.

"Wow. We must have got bogged in exactly the right spot."

Hamish frowned. His good mood from earlier in the day was gone. "There's no good spot to get bogged. I really wish it hadn't happened at all."

He drove to the end of the point, where the turquoise water of Ningaloo Bay stretched southwards. There were no people or buildings or roads for as far as we could see. Instead of feeling scared by the remoteness, I felt excited.

"I'll just get us in the right place," said Hamish. He drove out onto the big, wide beach to get our bearings. We were excited to see the waves crashing against the shore. Hamish turned the car around to drive back to our designated spot on the point. As we returned to the softer sand, we felt the car slow down and then sink into it. Hamish leaned forward and banged his head against the steering wheel.

"Don't stress," I said. "Those boys are not far away. I'll run back and find them."

Hamish looked at me and shook his head, as if I didn't understand the seriousness of the situation, but he clearly couldn't think of any other options. "Okay, you run back to them, and I'll start digging the car out." He banged his head on the steering wheel a few more times.

I ran back down the path. I didn't understand Hamish. Yes, we had a problem with the car, but there were also four boys nearby, operating a highly coordinated rescue service. I had every faith that they would be able to help us.

I found them sitting under an awning next to their tent, with sausages and onions sizzling on a hot plate. The smell was tantalising. The short guy, clearly the group leader, stood up to greet me.

"Sorry to interrupt your lunch." It was a little early for lunch, I thought, but carrying out rescues was probably hungry work. "Thanks so much for digging us out earlier."

"No worries. You were really stuck, hey?"

"Yeah. We really appreciate your help. I'm Jane." I stuck out my hand.

"I'm Josh." We shook hands and he introduced the other boys, who nodded or said "hey".

"The thing is," I began. One of the boys turned over the sausages with a fork. The other three looked up at me, sensing another rescue mission was coming.

"We got bogged again," I continued. "On the beach."

Josh nodded his head. "Hmm. It's soft sand out there. And that trailer of yours is a heavy beast."

I nodded. I knew Hamish had crammed too much stuff into it.

"But we can definitely get you out," he said confidently. "We'll be there in five minutes." He looked at the others, who had started stuffing sausages in bread. "Boys, we're going to need a snatch strap *and* recovery boards."

They all nodded, gulping down mouthfuls of sausage.

I started jogging back up the path toward Hamish. I knew they would help us, and in less than three minutes their ute sped past me, Josh at the wheel and the others sitting in the tray balancing two large wooden boards, obviously *recovery boards*, not unlike the ones on our kitchen floor back home, but wider.

When I got back, Hamish didn't look happy. He looked worried, and something else: embarrassed maybe. I wasn't embarrassed at all about being rescued. I found it quite relaxing.

Josh attached a snatch strap between the back of his ute and the front of our car, while the other boys put the recovery boards down in front of the wheels to give the car more traction. Hamish directed everyone to stand well back, in case the snatch strap snapped instead of snatched. The ute's engine groaned with the effort of pulling our car and trailer, but the car stayed stuck fast. Josh tried a second time, revving the engine. The ute groaned loudly as if in pain, then eased the car forward, and finally yanked it free. The kids cheered.

Josh ran over to where Hamish was now turning the car around. "Where's your camping spot?" he asked Hamish, who had the window down.

"Campsite number one. Back at the end of the point." Hamish's forehead was still creased with worry lines.

The other three boys had gathered around. "It wouldn't matter where you camp. You could just camp here" suggested a tall guy, with windswept blond hair. I could see where he was coming from. It would save a lot of effort to just stop where we were.

"No way. I'd camp where Jeff told you to camp," said Josh. It was obvious why he was the group leader. Rules were rules. Hamish nodded his head in firm agreement.

The rest of us followed on foot, while Hamish drove to the spot we thought must be campsite number one. "We'll leave you to set up then," said Josh.

"Thanks again, boys. I don't know what we would have done without you," I said honestly, as they started heading back down the beach toward their ute.

Hamish had started to unfold the trailer tent. For a second I thought he wasn't going to say anything to the boys. Then he seemed to remember himself, and went to the back of the car to get something. He ran after them and handed the blond guy a six-pack of coke, his last.

"Cheers, boys," he said.

We set up the camper trailer and awning, and assembled our new toilet and its own special tent. I was delighted about the new toilet. There would be no need to take a long walk, carefully avoiding kangaroo poo, finding a tree to hide behind, and digging a hole in the dirt. I felt very proud of it, like we'd added an extension to our home.

When we'd finished setting up, Hamish and I positioned our chairs facing the sea. "This is amazing," I said, making a circle with my arm to indicate our camp, including the new toilet, and, of course, the beach.

Hamish looked down at his feet. "I hope it was worth all the trouble. I've never really liked the beach."

I felt guilty. Hamish had mentioned a few times in the past fifteen years that he didn't like the beach. Apparently the ocean smells like fish, which is a bad thing when you have a seafood allergy, like Hamish does. I decided to distract him from the smell.

"How soft is the sand?"

"I hate sand, how it gets everywhere." He swiped the sand off his legs.

"Hmm." I pretended to agree with him, but I wasn't used to being in a happier mood than Hamish. It felt uncomfortable.

After a while, I couldn't pretend to be in a bad mood. I went on and on about how wonderful the view was, how amazing it was to be out here on her own, and how good the sand felt underneath my feet. Hamish didn't say anything, but the worry lines disappeared from his face.

Wednesday 27th June

This morning I read:

> "If anyone considers himself religious and yet does not keep a tight rein on his tongue, he deceives himself and his religion is worthless." (James 1:26).

I could see a theme. James was teaching me about consistency: *Do not ask God for wisdom and then doubt him. (James 1:6-8). Do not read the word and ignore what it says. (James 1: 22-25).* And now, this. *Do not call yourself "religious" and act like someone who isn't. (James 1:26).*

I was guilty of acting on my feelings at the time, not on what I knew to be true. I would think and say one thing, and do another. I knew Hamish found it frustrating. He always followed through on what he said. I wondered what it would take for me to change. I prayed, asking God to help me be more consistent.

I found Hamish helping Jenna fit her snorkel and mask.

"Oh good! You're awake, Mum. Dad says we need you to watch us snorkelling."

"It's a good idea to keep us safe," Hamish kissed me on the top of the head and went back to adjusting the height of Jenna's snorkel. "Your Mum is a good swimmer." He had obviously recovered from his bad mood of yesterday.

"I'm good at getting help." I remembered with satisfaction how I'd talked those boys into helping us yesterday. "I'll get those people to rescue you in their boat." I pointed to a small fishing boat not far from us.

"If we wave at you, that means we need help," said Jenna. She popped the mouthpiece of her snorkel in her mouth. Then popped it out again to speak. "But hang on, Dad. What if we wave just to say hello?"

"Don't. Keep your arms by your side."

"I know!" Jenna jumped up and down. "One hand waving means "Hi Mum". And two hands waving—" she demonstrated with big arm motions "—means we're in trouble and you've got to come quick."

"No. You'll forget which is which," said Hamish.

"Or I will." I was getting worried. I was grateful there were fishermen in boats out there.

"Just keep your hands by your side, unless you're in trouble." Hamish demonstrated keeping his hands by his side and waddling like a penguin.

I watched the two of them waddle down to the water like penguins, then make the long walk out to the reef, Jenna keeping her arms rigidly by her side. Faith and Gideon woke up and began digging in the sand and I watched as Hamish and Jenna swam around in little circles. They were so far out, the tips of their snorkels were only just visible above the water.

When they got back, Jenna was so enthusiastic about the bright blue fish and green coral she'd seen, I decided to go out myself. While the kids built sandcastles, I fitted one of our snorkels and masks and headed off, leaving Hamish on the beach to act as lifeguard. The water was beautifully warm and the sand dissolved under my feet. I walked maybe 150 m across the soft sand, but it felt like 500. I couldn't believe Jenna had made it all that way. Even when the water was up to my waist, I was still nowhere near the reef. I was about to give up when I noticed the water out in front was dark blue. In one step I was in water over my head, and the deeper water was rough, rocking me back and forth. Through my mask I saw the beautiful green coral Jenna had told me about and I looked for those little blue fish she'd seen, determined to find them, but they were hiding. Soon the water got wild, swirling around me and making the seaweed sway, but there were still no fish to be seen.

"If I can just see one little bright blue fish, I'll go back," I told God. It didn't seem like a lot to ask for. I'd walked all that way.

A wave went over the top of the snorkel and I got a mouthful of water, choking me. I spat the water out of my lungs and back up the snorkel, blowing hard until it was clear. Turning back to shore, I started to swim breaststroke, scooping the water in front of me, but a current pulled me back out. It was as if I was swimming on the spot. I felt scared. I prayed "Please God, help me get back to shore."

I started a few strokes of freestyle, arm over arm out of the water. It's the most efficient swimming stroke of course, and after I had made some headway against the current, I went back to breaststroke, with my head above water. The sea was calmer now. "Thank you, God. I'll never try to make a deal with you again." I hoped it was true.

I swam until eventually I saw the sunlight on the sand again, and then, two white legs blocking my way. I stood up. There was Hamish.

"Were you waving?"

"No waving. I remembered!" I was breathing hard from the effort of swimming.

"It looked like you had your arms out of the water."

"I did! I was swimming freestyle." I pulled off my mask and snorkel.

"I couldn't tell what you were doing. We said *no arms in the air!*"

"Sorry!" I fell against him and gave him a hug.

"Get off me! You're wet!"

"So are you now!" I splashed him as hard as I could. I was so relieved to be back. The kids saw what I was doing and stopped digging in the sand and ran into the water. They pushed Hamish over and took it in turns jumping on his back. Hamish picked them up one by one and threw them up into the air so they fell, laughing, into the water.

Thursday 28th June

Jenna and I took a walk around the bay this morning. When we were halfway to the point, Jenna shouted, "Look Mum!" Her hair was blowing across her face in the wind. "The water is dark blue near the shore. That means the reef is closer here."

"Jenna, you are an absolute genius!" I hugged her. "We won't have to walk so far out to see fish!" We ran back to tell the others.

Hamish and I gathered up towels and snorkelling gear and we walked to the midpoint of the bay, where Jenna had seen the dark blue water. Gideon looked for dinosaur bones in a sand dune, while Jenna and I watched Hamish lead Faith out to the reef. Instead of having to walk 150 m to reach a good spot, they walked five metres and were in deep water. We watched the tip of one black and one pink snorkel swimming in circles like sharks.

When it was our turn, Jenna pointed out the little electric blue fish she had told me about, darting in and out of the seaweed. I gave Jenna the thumbs up so she knew I had seen them and her eyes twinkled back at me through her mask. Black and white striped fish and colourful angelfish slid in and out between the columns of coral. I kept swimming a long time after Jenna got sick of it.

I could hear Hamish calling me. I knew the kids were probably ready to go back to camp, but I wanted to see more. I swam out into deeper water. "God please let me see one more colourful fish, then I promise I'll go back to shore."

There were no more fish, only a brown shape lying in the sand. The brown thing had a tail twice as long as its body. A stingray! Steve Irwin was killed by one. The man had been full of enthusiasm for teaching people about the natural world, and had been killed doing what he loved. I could feel my heart pounding in my chest. I had to think quickly. I'd just swum over him and was facing out to sea. Maybe he hadn't seen me yet. If I swam back to Hamish over his head, he might notice me with those big black-hole-eyes and stab me with his tail. The best option was to turn around and swim over his tail end, then get away from him as fast as I could.

"Thank you, God," I prayed when I'd got away from his tail and I was sure I was safe. "I'm sorry for trying to make a deal with you, again." I couldn't believe I'd made the same mistake so quickly. "And I don't need to see more fish," I added. "Thank you for what I've seen. It was wonderful. It was more than enough." My heart swelled with gratitude.

Back at the campsite, the children built things in the sand. Jenna wrote:

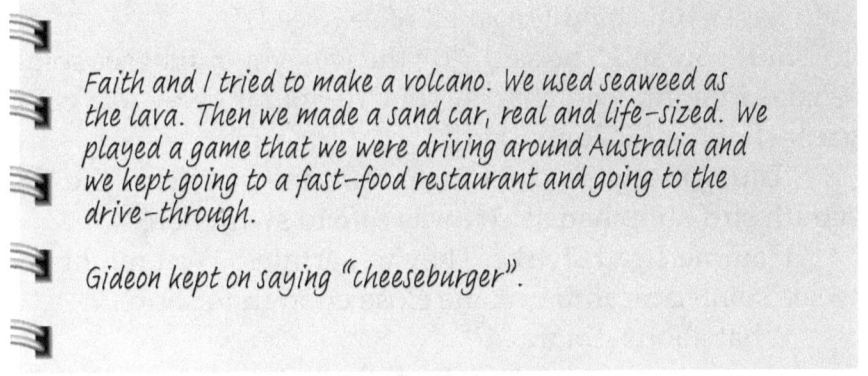

Faith and I tried to make a volcano. We used seaweed as the lava. Then we made a sand car, real and life-sized. We played a game that we were driving around Australia and we kept going to a fast-food restaurant and going to the drive-through.

Gideon kept on saying "cheeseburger".

While the kids were pretending to go to a drive-through restaurant, I tried to work out what to have for dinner. We had almost run out of water. Fortunately we had lots of apple juice. That had been on special when Hamish went shopping. We had enough water to cook the potatoes Hamish wanted for dinner, and prepare some two-minute noodles, so long as we drank apple juice until we reached a supermarket again.

I was looking through our food boxes trying to work out what else we could eat with potatoes and noodles, when a man appeared, carrying a bucket of fish. I recognised him as one of the fishermen I was going to ask for help if we got in trouble.

"Do you want some flathead?" he asked me. He put down his bucket to show me.

The silver fish were still twitching with life.

"Fresh caught today. Delicious cooked in a bit of butter on the barbeque."

I liked the idea of fresh fish. But I didn't want to upset Hamish with the smell of it. I still felt guilty about forgetting he didn't like the beach. "That's so kind of you. But my husband is allergic to seafood." I gestured to where Hamish was helping the children decorate their sand car. He was holding a piece of seaweed a long way away from his nose. "He can't even stand the smell of seaweed."

"Suit yourself," he said. "By the way you might see some whales tonight. And sharks. They're not far away. We got a great show out fishing today."

"Did you say *sharks*?" I was sure the guy from the Exmouth surf shop had said it was safe to swim here.

"Hammerhead sharks. They're harmless. You might get to see some later if they come close enough to shore."

"What about stingrays?"

"No, you won't see them from the beach. They're bottom dwellers."

"But are *they* harmless?"

"Pretty much. They only ever attack humans that get too close."

I was slicing cheese to go with the potatoes and noodles. He picked up his bucket.

"Your dinner looks interesting. Enjoy it."

"Thanks! You enjoy your fresh fish."

I watched him as he walked back to his camp, swinging the bucket beside him. Ten minutes later, we sat down to a meal of steaming hot potatoes, two-minute noodles, and cheese and biscuits, the last dregs of our food. It was a strange meal, but we were all so hungry, we ate enthusiastically.

"These potatoes are fantastic," I said. They were worth using the last of our water for.

"Yum, yum," Gideon agreed. Butter dribbled down his chin.

"Look!" Faith was the first one to see a spray of water squirting out. Then we saw the unmistakable shape of whales' tails flipping out of the water.

"Oh wow! Can you believe it? Whales, right next to where we're camping." I felt goosebumps forming.

"What are they, Dad?" We all looked to where Jenna was pointing to a pair of sharp-edged fins moving smoothly and eerily through the water.

"I think they're dolphins," said Hamish, but he didn't sound convinced.

I thought they were probably hammerhead sharks, but decided not to mention it. Even if they were harmless, the sound of the word 'shark' was frightening.

After we'd packed up and put the kids to bed, Hamish and I sat looking out to sea. I told Hamish about my conversation with the fisherman, and how we'd probably just seen sharks. I didn't mention what he'd said about stingrays being harmless. Hamish had seemed impressed by my narrow escape.

"Do you think it was worth all the trouble of coming here, getting bogged, and nearly running out of water?" I said. "I know you didn't really enjoy yourself."

"I enjoyed myself." I remembered Hamish throwing the kids up in the air. "It was just stressful, getting bogged, and dealing with the wind out here on the edge of the point, nearly blowing the tent down. I feel a lot of responsibility to look after you and the kids."

I felt grateful for Hamish. "The girls loved snorkelling," I said.

"And *you* got to see whales, finally."

"And a stingray." I wrapped my coat a bit tighter around me in the wind.

"Oh yes of course. The stingray. How long did you say it was again?"

"At least four metres."

"Well, it was definitely worth it then."

Chapter 7

Friday 29th June

Hamish was very jumpy this morning. The wind had blown extra hard last night, causing the tent to shake more than usual. He had gotten up every couple of hours to tie it down with extra guy ropes. Packing up, he accidentally put his foot through the loop of one of the guy ropes, then threw himself into a forward roll, landing on his back on the beach. Then Jenna let go of her corner of the groundsheet when we were trying to fold it. Hamish threw himself down on the ground to prevent it flying away. He lay there on his back a few moments, winded by lack of sleep and camping gymnastics.

Once we'd packed up, Hamish instructed us to run after him while he drove away from the beach. He wanted to keep the weight of the car to a minimum while he drove across the soft sand. When he'd made it to the start of the track leading away from the beach, we all jumped up in the car. We passed the tent of Josh and his team, but the boys weren't around. They were probably doing drills or undertaking a rescue somewhere. Hamish drove quickly and there was a look of relief on his face when we didn't get bogged.

When we reached the homestead, I went to collect the bond money. I wasn't afraid of talking to Jeff without Hamish. I was capable of collecting some bond money, without my husband by my side. Before knocking on the door, though, I stood up as tall as possible in case Jeff doubted me again.

Instead of Jeff, the door was opened by a tall thin woman with greying hair. I guessed this was Jeff's wife. "Yes?" she asked nervously. I was reminded of the strange conversation when I'd rung to book in from the Visitor Centre.

"I've come to collect our bond money." I gave her my warmest smile. She handed me the $100 without speaking.

"We had a wonderful time on the point." She nodded. "It was windy." She nodded again. I felt curious. She was obviously uncomfortable, but I wanted to know how she coped out here, without any neighbours.

"What do you do here all day?" I asked.

She laughed nervously. Her eyes looked left and then right. "Oh, I have different things to do around the place." She grasped the door, preparing to close it behind me.

On the journey back to the highway, the car bumped and thudded over the corrugated road. As Hamish drove carefully over the ridges, I thought about Jeff and his wife. Their marriage was nothing like ours. Hamish didn't even open doors for me, let alone talk for me. I liked it that way. Jeff's wife was obviously an introvert. Maybe she enjoyed having a husband who did the talking and a life with little human interaction. Did she spin the wool from the orange sheep, I wondered? I was deep in thought, when there was a clanging sound. It was different from the thud of going over the bumps. It sounded like something banging the underside of the car.

We jumped out to look for sticks caught under the car. My nostrils filled with dust, but there were no sticks.

Hamish leant against the car and rubbed his hands together to get rid of the dirt. "We'll need to find a mechanic," he sighed. "I'm not sure we'll make it inland".

Our plan had been to drive to the mining town of Tom Price, on our way to Karijini National Park. Instead we drove to Coral Bay, the seaside village we'd bypassed on our way to Exmouth. An on-site mechanic at the petrol station looked underneath the car and diagnosed an exhaust problem, telling us we'd have to go to Exmouth to get it repaired.

The mechanic we met at Exmouth Auto Sales and Repairs confirmed the bad news.

"You need a new exhaust," he said as he slid out from under the car. "But I can't do it this month. I'd go to Tom Price".

"That's where we were headed. But isn't it a long way to go with a broken exhaust?" Hamish asked.

"It's only four o'clock. Stop every now and then and give the car a break." He patted the dusty roof of the car. "She'll be right mate."

In spite of the Exmouth's mechanic's optimism, we decided against driving to Tom Price at four in the afternoon. We'd had enough accommodation dramas already. We drove back into the centre of Exmouth, past the Big Prawn and the Visitor Centre with the lighthouse souvenirs. We drove straight past the backpackers with the expensive double rooms, and joined the families and grey nomads in the Lighthouse Caravan Park at the end of the town.

Saturday 30th June

We didn't want to be in Exmouth, but we were too tired to move. We watched the children swim in the pool. Sitting on the banana lounges, we talked to two older couples on their annual joint trip to Exmouth. Bill and Shirley, and Betty and Jack, were typical of the grey nomads we'd met, willing to share their travel experiences. When they heard about our car troubles, and the month-long delay for a repair in Exmouth, they all wanted to help.

Bill thought we definitely shouldn't drive to Tom Price. It was risky and the mechanics in Exmouth were better. His wife Shirley agreed. She thought we could easily spend a month in Exmouth. They did every year. Betty thought we should at least stay long enough to tour the lighthouse and visit the turtle centre.

Betty's husband Jack disagreed. He had worked in the mines at Tom Price thirty years ago and they had excellent mechanics. He thought we should drive to Tom Price, stopping the car every hour to give it a break. Hamish agreed with Jack. The others all changed their mind eventually and agreed with Jack and Hamish. So it was decided.

We spent the rest of the day writing emails and washing clothes. As I hung the washing out, I noticed our clothes were becoming grey and threadbare. Time for some new clothes, I thought. Hopefully Tom Price would have the shops we needed.

Sunday 1st July

The sun was just starting to rise and our grey nomad travel committee hadn't yet emerged from their caravans, when we set off nervously for our long journey to Tom Price.

The engine was noisy, but there was no more of the alarming clanging sound we'd heard two days ago. As we headed inland, the scenery was spectacular, with red earth and rugged rocky mountains looming up everywhere. We felt as if we were seeing the real outback Australia at last. We stopped the car regularly to give it breaks, according to Jack's schedule, but still arrived at the Tom Price Caravan Park unusually early for us, in the middle of the afternoon.

Hamish had a look around the park while I went to the office to book us in. The office had a fridge in the corner with soft drinks and milk, and shelves with baked beans and two-minute noodles. In another corner was a glass case, full of clothing. I'd hoped to find clothes for sale in the town, but not in the caravan park itself. Even more surprising, I noticed there was a white dress inside the case, with a full skirt. A woman in a khaki park uniform was humming to herself while she stacked the shelves with more noodles.

"Is that a *wedding dress*?" I asked her.

"Yes it is. It came in yesterday."

"Do people actually *get married* here?"

"Not here - in Karijini National Park nearby."

I was trying to imagine why someone would buy a wedding dress from a caravan park. Did someone go to all the trouble to come out here to get married and realise they'd forgotten to bring a dress and have to rely on the caravan park shop? I couldn't imagine it.

There were a few strapless dresses in different colours, that I supposed could be worn by guests at a wedding, and another bridal dress with a long skirt and beads sewn into the bodice. The dress with the beads was beautiful. I couldn't stop looking at it.

Eventually I remembered what I had come in for and asked for a large site for our trailer tent. The woman in khaki informed me cheerfully that all the sites were large and we could pick any spot we liked.

Hamish was pleased we had free choice of sites, as he'd found a spot next to a picnic bench that would be handy for meals.

Once we were set up, we sat at the bench and researched mechanics and things to do in Tom Price and Karijini on the internet. The kids found a family with a TV in their caravan and were invited to watch a movie with them. They were excited to watch a large screen, instead of the ones in the car headrests. I was feeling quite relaxed. I couldn't wait to see Karijini. It must be beautiful if people came all this way to have a wedding. Hamish was stressed. He was worried the exhaust repair would blow out the budget.

Monday 2nd July

I couldn't stop thinking about wedding dresses. Maybe the park shop catered for brides who had a surprise proposal on holiday, and a last-minute holiday wedding. I pictured a bride and groom in front of a waterfall at Karijini. It seemed very romantic, and it also gave me an idea: what about a spontaneous renewing of our vows? Some couples recreated their nuptials at a key milestone, like their tenth anniversary. We'd never had a ten-year ceremony. And we wouldn't want to waste the opportunity when we were in Karijini. I'd have to find a good way to suggest it.

Hamish asked me to go through our receipts and work out how much we'd been spending, while he was in town looking for a mechanic. He was worried we'd already overspent on our budget and wouldn't be able to afford the car repairs. The kids played with their new friends, while I went through the receipts.

We'd spent a lot.

I took a break from the receipts and boiled some water for a cup of tea, then realising we were out of milk, made a trip to the caravan park shop. The lady I saw yesterday was there, writing figures in a notebook. While she was busy, I took another look at the glass case full of formal dresses. The dress with the beads looked like it was probably a size 12. It felt like a sign: the dress which happened to be my favourite was also my size. I would definitely have to find a good time to *propose* the idea to Hamish.

When Hamish came back he had good news and bad news: the first mechanic he'd been to could fix the exhaust today, and replace the windscreen as well. Hamish had left the car and walked to the caravan park, planning to walk back and pick up the car at five. The bad news was that the exhaust repair was going to cost $900. I told him about the spending. It was more bad news. We'd have to book into more free bush camping, Hamish thought. It wasn't a good time to ask him about a wedding.

After Hamish had collected the car, with its repaired exhaust and brand-new glass, the kids were again invited to spend the evening watching TV with their friends, so Hamish and I researched and planned a walk up the nearby mountain, "Mount Nameless." Apparently it was the highest point in the region, and the highest mountain in Western Australia accessible by car.

"Why don't we drive it?" I said.

"That's easy." Hamish sat back in his chair. "It would be fun to have a challenge."

"But you can drive up to the summit. That's what it's famous for."

"It's not famous!" Hamish laughed. "Nobody could even be bothered to name it."

"We should drive. We have a car. With a new exhaust, and new windscreen." I knew it made sense.

"Yes we do." Hamish nodded. "But a walk will be a good family activity. A challenge for the kids."

Hmm, they had watched a lot of TV the last few days. Hamish was right, a walk would do them good.

Tuesday 3rd July

Hamish likes to do things properly, of course, so we took ages getting ready. We filled drink bottles, applied sunscreen, found hats and packed a picnic lunch and scroggin (a mixture of dried fruit and nuts, and chocolate) to give us energy along the way. It was irritating how everything took so long with Hamish. He never leaves anything to chance. Finally, with Hamish and I both carrying a backpack full of supplies, we walked from the caravan park to the track that led to the base of the mountain. From the base, we climbed up some stone steps, which led to a rocky path which extended all the way to the summit, past spinifex, and wildflowers and the occasional shade-providing gum tree. At first I thought Hamish was right with the walking idea, it was invigorating and satisfying to have a challenge.

A quarter of the way up the mountain, I could feel the sun burning my shoulders and I started to sweat. It became harder and harder to put one foot in front of the other. My calves were aching and my throat was burning. I wished I had persuaded Hamish to drive. The kids kept asking if we could go home. Jenna said the mountain should have been called "Mount Awful". Faith suggested "Mount My Legs Hurt". When we were all about to give up, Hamish remembered the scroggin and suggested we have a break. Thank goodness for Hamish's planning. I was not irritated with him at all now. Gideon couldn't believe it when he received his first pile of fruit and nuts and chocolate. He stared at it, then picked up a few bits carefully and examined them, before putting them delightedly in his mouth.

By the time we reached the top, after lots more walking and several more scroggin breaks, my whole body was aching and my heart was thudding. Sweat trickled into my eyes. Most of the scroggin was gone and the little bit left was a congealed mess of melted chocolate and sultanas. The kids suddenly found a burst of energy now they didn't *have* to walk, and they started running around, picking up rocks and tossing them down the side of the mountain.

Hamish and I found a nice flat red rock to sit on. It was a relief to stop. The view below was spectacular. We could see all of Tom Price, and the cut-out mine below us. I remembered the topic I'd been waiting to discuss with Hamish.

"What do you think about couples renewing their marriage vows?" I asked him.

"What's that?"

"You know, when a couple says their vows again, when they're already married."

I blew away a bit of frizzy hair that was sticking to the side of my sweaty face.

"Oh that. I'm against it. Totally against it." Hamish drew a line in the red dirt next to him with the stick he was holding.

"What do you mean, you're totally against it? It's wonderful to say your original vows again, to recommit."

"No it's not. I meant it when I said them the first time." Hamish threw the stick away, put his arm around me and gave me a hug.

So we wouldn't be having a wedding re-enactment. My dreams of saying our vows next to a waterfall in Karijini National Park disappeared. I felt a little sad. Then I felt relieved. Wanting to wear a dress wasn't a good motivation for renewing our vows. Plus, I wasn't sure I was actually a size 12 anymore. And it would be a real pain to have to put a dress like that on in a tent. I was very glad Hamish meant it the first time. His habit of planning ahead is always tedious in the initial stage, but it usually pays off in the end, like going to the trouble of packing scroggin to keep us going on the journey.

We joined the kids, and Jenna said we needed to choose a proper name for the mountain. It wasn't Mount Awful, now that she'd seen the view from the top of it. In her diary she wrote:

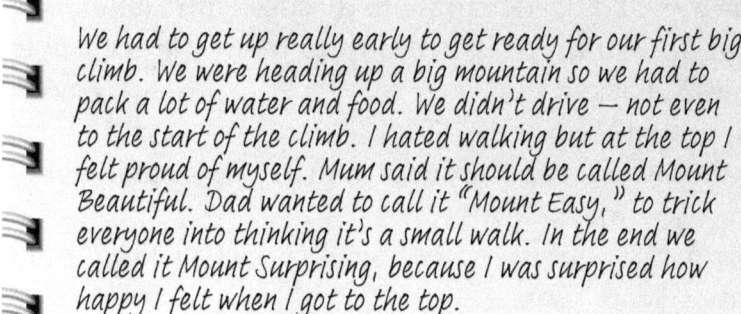

We had to get up really early to get ready for our first big climb. We were heading up a big mountain so we had to pack a lot of water and food. We didn't drive — not even to the start of the climb. I hated walking but at the top I felt proud of myself. Mum said it should be called Mount Beautiful. Dad wanted to call it "Mount Easy," to trick everyone into thinking it's a small walk. In the end we called it Mount Surprising, because I was surprised how happy I felt when I got to the top.

Chapter 8

Wednesday 4th July

The children said a tearful goodbye to their friends with the television. I'm not sure whether they were more upset to leave their new friends, or the chance to watch movies on a full-sized screen. I was happy to be going to Karijini. A mum from Gideon's playgroup, Yvonne, had done a trip around the West and told me it was their highlight. It was the most beautiful part of Australia in her opinion, and the gorges were spectacular. As we got closer, the ground around us became redder, and flatter, and dustier. No sign yet of spectacular beauty, but I was sure we would eventually find it. Gideon was fascinated to see a dingo running alongside the car.

At the busy park office, a ranger allocated us a big flat campsite. We thought it was great at first, but the earth was so hard, Hamish broke a couple of tent pegs as he tried to hammer them into the ground. In the end, he used an electric drill he had brought with him in case we needed it.

While Hamish drilled holes for the tent pegs, I took Gideon for a walk. He dragged me over to the "Beware of dingoes" sign we'd seen as we came in. The dingo pictured had a good likeness to the one we'd seen running alongside the car, with a strong-looking yet skinny body and a large head full of sharp teeth. Gideon was fascinated. I pulled him away. I wanted to find a walking trail and get a sneaky first peak at the beauty I'd heard about. But each time I persuaded Gideon to leave the dingo sign, we didn't get very far before he dragged me back. I was bewildered. Did he love the picture of a dingo? Or did he think an actual dingo might appear at this exact spot? We found a rock to sit on next to the sign and made handprints in the dirt and talked about dingoes. I'd have to wait until tomorrow to find the beautiful gorges hidden in the park.

Thursday 5th July

I tried to stay patient this morning through the long process of getting ready. Hamish's arms were aching from the effort of trying to hammer the tent pegs into the ground yesterday. Still, he insisted we pack our backpacks with a picnic, water bottles, and scroggin to keep us going along the way, as well as our bathers and towels, and a first aid kit, just in case. I felt impatient at how much time it took.

Once we were ready with the hats, sunscreen, and the good walking shoes Hamish had insisted we wear, we found the start of the Dales Gorge track. It wasn't far from the dingo sign. If I'd coaxed Gideon a little further yesterday, we would have found it. The ground opened up into a deep wide canyon. To our right, the gorge ended in a series of steps, like a large Roman amphitheatre. The curved steps were a million shades of pink stone and a cascade of water cut a trail from the top of the canyon down into a circular pool above us. No wonder people got married here.

My moment of awe looking at the gorge was interrupted when someone stood in front of me. It was a young woman wearing a pair of ugg boots, with a string bag over one shoulder. I looked around and realised that most of the sightseers were inadequately prepared with inappropriate footwear. I felt a surge of pride at Hamish's excellent packing and insisting we all wear sensible walking shoes. I was sure one of the tourists would slip.

Walking the path to the top of the falls. Jenna's pink hat came off and fell backwards into a shallow pool. Being at the back of the pack, I was the closest to the hat. I didn't want it to be swept down the waterfall. I quickly threw off my shoes and socks, then stepped onto a wet rock near the hat. I fell forward and my knees crashed into rock. I yelled out. I grabbed the soggy hat; it was floating in the shallow water, and hadn't moved an inch since she'd dropped it. I returned the hat to Jenna's head. Hamish was ready with the first aid kit. Surprisingly, given the amount of throbbing in my knees, there were no cuts or grazes on them.

We continued along a path, following some signs to Fern Pool, passing some enormous fig trees: the ones with trunks that divide into lots of different strands that looked to me like hands with fingers digging into the ground. Fern Pool was surrounded by red cliffs, with ferns growing out from between the rocks. It was empty, apart from two Aboriginal men leaning against a railing.

The kids stripped down to their bathers, ready to swim, while Hamish and I asked the men about a sign on the railing about the significance of Fern Pool.

"This is a special place," the younger of the two men said. "When our people come here to swim, they do this." He knelt down and scooped some water in his hands and held them out in front of him. "It says, I mean good. I'm here to swim and not harm the pool."

"Our people have been here a long time," said the older man. He looked over to the girls who were dipping their toes in the water to test the temperature. "When the white man came, they thought they could name everything. They call a mountain Mount Nameless, but it already had a name."

"Oh really? What's the name?" I couldn't wait to tell Jenna.

"Mount *Jarn* dun *mun* ha." He emphasised the *Jarn* and the *mun*. It sounded beautiful.

"Is that just a name, or does it mean something?"

"It means 'place of rock wallabies.'"

Oh, so not Mount Beautiful or Mount Surprising then. I remembered Aboriginal people have a strong connection with the land. It made sense they would name a mountain after its natural features or animals.

"The white man took a lot away from our people," the older man continued. "Before white man, our people had ceremonies. Young men like my grandson here," he gestured to the other man, "they would have an initiation ceremony at twelve years old. Then he would be recognised as a man."

The young man nodded in agreement. "The girls had ceremonies too." He nodded toward the girls who were sitting on a rock, kicking the water and wondering whether to dive in.

"Without the rituals, boys don't feel like real men. They start drinking. I was lost as a young man." The old man looked at us sadly. "I went to England and fought in the British army to see if that would make me feel like a man, but it didn't help."

Hamish and I looked at him encouragingly. We felt privileged that he was telling us his history. The girls had decided Fern Pool was too cold for swimming, even for them. They stood next to us shivering, listening to him.

"Then I started drinking to take away the pain. That didn't work." He shook his head. "Alcohol made things worse. I gave up twelve years ago. Now I help young people stop drinking and find their traditional culture."

"That's wonderful," said Hamish. "Thank you for sharing that with us." The men nodded.

I wasn't sure whether to say anything or not. I didn't want to add to their experience of the loss of their culture.

But the old man had shared what was important to him. I wanted to do the same.

"We're Christians," I said. "That gives us a sense of identity."

"I've looked into that." The old man looked away and then back again. I wondered what he would say next. Had he taken offence?

His eyes were alight. "I *loved* Jesus. I've read all about it. I thought he was going to be meek but he wasn't. He knew how to make the ultimate sacrifice."

I felt relieved, and also humbled. I'd wrongly assumed he wouldn't know much about our faith. We thanked the men for a wonderful conversation.

On the walk back down to Dales Gorge, I wondered about the Aboriginal names for the sights around us. High cliffs on either side of the gorge were made up of big flat square stones of grey, pink, white, red and orange, all stacked against each other in perfect layers. They made me think of liquorice all sorts. According to our guidebook, they are banded iron formations, made up of layers of iron oxide and silica. How would they have appeared to the traditional people? At the other end of the gorge was a perfectly round swimming hole, identified in our book as Circular Pool. The water was icy. Only a tiny sliver of sun got through the narrow opening of the canyon. It was definitely too cold to go in it. To the girls' disgust they spent an entire day beside water without swimming.

Friday 6th July

I reread some of James, the verse about worthless religion I'd read in Ningaloo.

> *"Those who consider themselves religious and yet do not keep a tight rein on their tongues deceive themselves and their religion is worthless." (James 1:26).*

A note in the concordance, the part that explains the verses in detail, directed me to a related section in James Chapter 3.

> *"If anyone is never at fault in what he says, he is a perfect man, able to keep his whole body in check." (James 3:2).*

Further on I read that the tongue is powerful, like the rudder of a ship.

> *"Although (ships) are so large and are driven by strong winds, they are steered by a very small rudder wherever the pilot wants to go." (James 3:4).*

I liked the idea of the tongue being powerful. I remembered how my speech hadn't influenced Gideon two days ago. I'd tried to steer him toward the start of the walk to Dales Gorge, but no amount of asking or begging had influenced him one bit. He had insisted we stay at the dingo sign. Perhaps my motivation hadn't been good. It was sneaky to try to get a peak of the gorge before the rest of the family, while poor Hamish had been drilling holes for tent pegs. Or, maybe it was wrong to plead with a four-year-old. Maybe if I had spoken with calm authority, I would have been able to lead him, like a tame horse, or an obedient ship, where I wanted him to go.

I tried out my theory on Jenna and Faith, who'd been wasting time instead of doing the breakfast dishes.

"Girls, please stop splashing each other with the washing up water. Do your job, and do it *now*." I was calm but firm. It was a success! After having flicked water and annoyed each other for the previous hour, the girls did the dishes in five minutes.

I continued to think of myself as the rudder of a ship, as Hamish drove to the other end of the national park, where our guidebook said there was a gorge with a hidden pool that was good for swimming.

As we walked the trail to the bottom of the gorge, I wondered if I had remembered to put the guidebook back in my backpack. When we reached the end of the trail, I turned the pack upside down and gave it a good shake while the family waited. Some sunscreen, and half a packet of fruit chews fell out. There was no guidebook, with its handy maps. Then I had a memory of it sitting where I'd left it on the camping table.

I told myself it wasn't a problem. I could still steer the family. "I think it's this way." I pointed along the right-hand bank. It *felt* like the right way.

The family followed trustingly. We had to clamber over big rocks to reach the end. When we got to the end of the gorge, we found an enormous ledge of dry rock. I felt deflated.

The girls groaned at the sight of a puddle of water in a tiny dip in the ledge, useless for swimming.

Okay so I hadn't gone the right way then. It was silly to think because I'd led the girls to do their chores this morning, that I could lead the family without a map. I followed sheepishly as Faith led us back to the other end of the gorge. This time the river got wider and wider. At the end of the trail, we saw a sign for the hidden Handrail Pool.

The pool could only be reached by first walking through water and then climbing onto a ledge which led to the entrance to the pool.

Hamish and the girls made their way carefully along the

narrow ledge, while I sat with Gideon on the sandy riverbank. I was happy to stop with him and catch my breath. I managed to occupy Gideon and stop him from following his sisters by pretending to look for dingoes with him. Gideon was convinced he'd found some tracks.

Apparently, the handrail pool was very exciting. Faith wrote in her diary:

> Today was the best day of the holiday! We had to walk along the cliff, holding on to the rock. There was a big hole in the ground. We went down a ladder. The water was rushing. Dad slipped and fell but didn't hurt himself. I didn't slip once.

It was our last night In Karijini. Tomorrow we were heading to Port Hedland, on our way to Broome. Even though I'd gone the wrong way and gotten the family lost, I'd learnt a lot in Karijini. I'd had success applying that verse about the tongue being powerful, getting the girls to wash up instead of yelling at them. I needed to tell Hamish. Perhaps we *should* have one of those family church services Hamish was talking about.

Chapter 9

Saturday 7th July

I read the final verse in Chapter 1 of James this morning. It continues the theme of true religion.

> *"Religion that God our Father accepts as pure and faultless is this: to look after orphans and widows in their distress and to keep oneself from being polluted by the world."* (James 1:27)

I remembered a sermon I'd heard at St Michael's, the church Hamish introduced me to twenty years ago. Orphans and widows stood for people who had no-one to care for them, and no one to stand up for them. I thought of the indigenous people of Australia. They had been oppressed by the colonial settlers, and had no-one in power to advocate for them, like the widows and orphans of Jesus' time. Was it true religion to be helping the indigenous, like the grandfather we'd met at Fern Pool, or the Smiths we were going to visit in Kalkaringi? I couldn't wait to get to Kalkaringi and find out what they were doing.

First, I needed to be sure I'd learnt the first lesson from James, to embrace trials. As Hamish's wife, the biggest trial I faced was packing. I was learning not to resent him for it, but the truth was Hamish had brought so much stuff that packing up was like Tetris, that computer game, where you scored points for fitting awkward shapes into other awkward shapes. Through trial and error, I was getting better at it. I'd learnt to put soft things, like sleeping bags, into the big metal drawer of the camper trailer first. That way when

I added the hard things, like the plastic boxes of equipment, they would push against the sleeping bags, which would give a little, and I would be able to cram it all in. It was a relief when I'd crammed it in tight enough that I was able to shut the drawer.

Hamish hummed happily to himself as we packed up this morning. He was still smiling when we left the caravan park and entered the highway. He likes driving. I once asked him what he enjoys about being behind the wheel. In the city, he likes to observe what speed the other drivers are doing to make sure he's in the most efficient lane. On long road trips, he works to maintain the best fuel economy. He pays attention to his speed, but also how many revs he's doing. Too many revs is bad. The gauge that measures revs is called a tachometer.

I have no interest in fuel economy or being in the most efficient lane. I let my mind wander on other things. I think about what happened yesterday, and what might happen tomorrow. I did a personality test once and got "reflector," someone who likes thinking about events more than they enjoy the events themselves. Hamish got "achiever," which is fitting.

With all the thinking I was doing, I had an idea. "What if I write a book about our trip?" I asked Hamish. "I could write about what worked, and what didn't." I was feeling impressed with myself: I'd finally learnt how to pack the camper trailer, and I was sure I could write a book about camping.

Hamish took his eyes off the road to look at me. "Why would you do that? Who would be your audience?"

"Other families planning a trip. I could prepare them for it."

"Do you think you're the right person to write about camping?"

"Why not?" I felt a bit defensive.

Hamish didn't say anything. He looked at the road straight ahead.

Undeterred by Hamish's lack of support, I spent hours thinking about a book. I had it planned out by the time we arrived at Port Hedland.

The caravan park was fully occupied, as the town was full of tourists and seasonal mining workers. Thankfully, the owner managed to squeeze us into a space that was right alongside the pool. It would make it tricky for others wanting to access the pool tomorrow, but the girls were pleased how easy it would be for them to swim in the morning.

Sunday 8th July

I considered suggesting a family church service. It *was* Sunday. But I was still thinking about my book. I hoped God would be pleased that I wanted to make a difference in the world, and would excuse that we hadn't worshipped him as a family yet. I started the chapter on packing:

You may be surprised to learn just how much you will need to pack for an extended camping trip. Of course you'll need a strong tent, a guidebook, good walking shoes and a first aid kit. Those items are obvious. Other equipment is essential but you may not have thought of it (I know I didn't). Believe it or not, you'll need a chemical toilet (letting your toilet paper blow across the sand is not allowed in Western Australia), an electric drill (for drilling holes for tent pegs in stubborn ground), recovery boards (in case you get stuck in the sand) and a gadget for measuring tyre air pressure (Note to self: get name of gadget from Hamish).

I spent the day thinking about other sections for the book. I was too distracted to pay much attention to the events of the day. However, I did make a discovery. I couldn't sleep, because of the "beep beep" of the trucks of the mining workers returning from shifts at all hours. I got up to make tea and found Hamish sitting at the table typing on the laptop. Hamish is writing a diary. He'd written:

> Rest day. Well we are on holiday after all. Faith was keen to go swimming, Gideon just wanted to meet friends and Jane needed to catch up on washing. Jane seemed very distracted. I think she must be exhausted. For me it was off to the shops to fill the car fridge and find Gideon socks. Yes, socks. Not sure where they had gone, but seemed to be very few around. Took Jenna with me as she wanted some Dad-time. One thing that I love about spending time with Jenna is that she loves to really talk, and discuss all manner of things in her life.
>
> Got back before midday to lunch that Jane had set up under a tree next to the pool. The days are so much hotter now with temperatures over thirty most days. Then the afternoon was taken up with the girls playing in the pool, and getting everyone through the showers as we would be bush camping, without many options for a wash, at our next destination. Although the days are hot, nights are still chilly. Made a warming chicken stir fry that everyone agreed must go on the dinner rotation. Excited for our trip to Broome tomorrow.

I couldn't believe it! I'm *the writer*. Still, it could be useful. Hamish's diary was full of detail. If I forget what the weather was like, or what we ate for dinner, I will consult Hamish's diary.

Monday 9th July

Inspired by Hamish's weather observations, I wrote:

Everywhere you go, the conditions will vary. In Western Australia, warm days can be followed by cold nights, and you'll need to be prepared.

I wondered what the weather would be like in Broome. Our guidebook described it as a tropical oasis. There would be crocodiles and mosquitoes. I'd probably need to add a chapter on tropical hazards.

We made a detour to Eighty Mile Beach, apparently the best beach in Australia for shell-collecting. We had a competition. Hamish was the winner, of course. After a long and determined search, he found a perfect pink shell that looked like it was glowing. On the onward journey, Faith told us she was planning to put a tiny hole in her symmetrical white shell to thread it onto some string. Suddenly, there was a loud crack and a tiny hole appeared in the top left side of the windscreen.

"What was that? Faith was straining forward in her seatbelt to see the damage. The other two had their headphones on and were glued to a DVD.

Hamish tapped his hands against the steering wheel. "I think a stone flew up behind the wheels of that truck in front of us."

I was shaking my head. "I can't believe it! The windscreen was only one week old!"

"Was the truck going too fast?" Faith asked.

"Probably not. It's just bad luck." Hamish tapped the steering wheel again. Faith settled back into her seat and looked out the side window.

I stared at the windscreen. "All that glass will have to be replaced, *again*."

"We'll need to ring the insurance company," said Hamish calmly.

"Well obviously we'll need to ring the insurance company!" I snapped at him. I felt so irritated, first about the windscreen, and now about Hamish being so *logical*. My heart was racing a little. "I'm not doing it *now*."

"Well, I can't ring them while I'm driving."

"Can't you just let me complain about it? You always have to solve the problem straight away." It felt good to say it.

Hamish didn't reply. He kept his eyes steadily on the road ahead.

I stared at the chip. The hole had lots of cracks coming out of it, making a complicated star-shape. Would the hole get much bigger? I wondered what the probability was of getting a windscreen replaced, and then it getting broken again after a week. The opportunity to ponder seemed to calm me down a little.

Arriving in the Broome, we got a quick look at the town's wide streets lined with palm trees, before continuing north to Quandong Point, where camping was free. The road was red sand—the colour of the outback —yet deep and soft in places, like a red beach. Not tropical after all, more like the outback by the coast.

We found a campsite on a ridge overlooking the sea. It was getting dark and the kids were tired. They moaned loudly at the thought of having to get out of the car and help put up the tent. I whispered to Hamish that we should set up quickly while the kids stayed in the car. It would be easier for everyone.

Hamish ignored my suggestion and told them to get out

and help. Faith wailed, saying that it was the worst holiday she'd ever been on and she hated camping. Gideon lay on the ground kicking and screaming. Hamish kept repeating his request for help. They continued to cry and wail. I couldn't bear it. I found some muesli bars in the car which quietened them down a little. Then I wrapped them up in Gideon's blanket and rocked them until they stopped whimpering.

Hamish set up the tent with Jenna. They didn't rush, even though Faith and Gideon were exhausted and I was sitting on an uncomfortable rock, trying to calm them down. Hamish insisted they did a proper job, with everything brought out of the car and stowed carefully in the tent.

Tuesday 10th July

My head hurt. It was Hamish's fault. Why couldn't he be more sympathetic? The kids had been beside themselves, and now I had a tension headache. Hamish needed to learn to be more flexible. If he'd taken my advice, and let the kids stay in the car while I helped him set up, we would have avoided all the tears and temper tantrums. I made some notes for the book:

Setting up camp is a lot of work. Get children to help. But use common sense.

This was where Hamish was sometimes lacking.

Be flexible and respond to the circumstances. If children are tired or distressed, lower your expectations. Maybe give them a night off.

The *good* side of Hamish's stubbornness was his brilliant organisation. I noticed how neatly he and Jenna had set up the inside of the tent. I remembered rocking the children while he and Jenna set up. Perhaps my expectations were too low? Hamish had trained Gideon to set the table for dinner this holiday. At first he'd whined and complained, but Hamish had stubbornly insisted Gideon learn to set the table. Now he did it easily and without whining. Was Hamish right after all? Was it right to expect kids to help even though they were tired and upset? I felt confused. Perhaps I wasn't a good person to be giving advice. I put my notes for the book aside.

I owed it to Hamish to be more organised. I needed to phone the insurance company about the second broken windscreen. I still couldn't believe it had been broken *one week* after it had been replaced.

There was something else I had to do as well. While Hamish took the kids to check out the town, I went to the visitor centre to find out about accommodation at our next destination, Fitzroy Crossing. We were meeting some friends there: Leon and Marion Morris, a recently retired couple who were escaping Melbourne Winter. We were arriving first, so they'd asked me to book a caravan park and email the details to them. It would also be Gideon's birthday while we were there. I persuaded the visitor centre to book the caravan park and a crocodile boat cruise, a surprise for Gideon's birthday, even though they usually only make bookings for Broome.

I was so pleased with myself, I decided not to ring the insurance company after all. That could wait. Hamish would be grateful I'd organised the birthday boat trip.

We spent the afternoon at Cable Beach, the main surf beach in Broome. I went in the surf with the girls, while

Hamish watched Gideon playing in a small pool of water in a hole on the beach. The girls were beside themselves with excitement. They jumped over the little waves and dived under the big ones, and got tossed into somersaults by a few.

At the end of the swim, Faith wanted ice cream, but the beach kiosk only sold one type.

"Vanilla!" Faith groaned. "What about chocolate and liquorice?"

"What a wasted business opportunity," said Hamish. With all these tourists, you'd think there'd be a decent ice cream business."

We still bought the vanilla ones. It was lovely sitting on the rock wall of the beach, licking our ice creams and looking out to the tumbling sea.

Wednesday 11th July

I remembered how much the girls had enjoyed themselves yesterday. We'd had so many days travelling, hiking, or visiting important landmarks. It was nice to see them relaxing and having fun. I added to my book:

Children need to relax. Find a balance between structured activities, and allowing time for children to be silly, play games, and have fun.

That was something Hamish and I could agree on.

We had a busy morning checking out Broome's landmarks. Hamish drove to the port where there was a museum in an old pearling boat near the wharf. I read all the displays about pearls while the girls took photos of Gideon and a model crocodile. The children were not that interested in pearls.

After the museum, we walked through some expensive shops alongside the wharf. We were very out of place, in old clothes that had started to take on the red colour of Broome's sand. I thought it would be nice if Hamish bought me a pearl necklace, but he never thinks about that sort of thing. Gideon ran around the glass display cases. He was convinced the pearls for sale were in fact crocodile teeth.

We decided to celebrate our last day in Broome with another ice cream. Hamish was determined to find an ice cream shop with a wide selection this time. He spotted a fancy looking one in the main tourist strip. We all had two scoops. The children sat at their own plastic table happily licking ice cream, while Hamish and I found a wooden bench next to a palm tree.

"Try this. It's fantastic." Hamish handed me his lemon and chocolate on a pink plastic spoon. He was convinced that the secret to a good ice cream was choosing two contrasting flavours: one had to be sharp and the other one sweet.

"Oh that is good," I agreed.

"I need to talk to you about *my* book."

"Ah yes, your book." Hamish threw his empty cup into the bin behind us.

"Are you enjoying it?"

"Not really." I was starting to realise what a hard task it was. "But I hope it's going to be useful, for other travellers. I just need your help on a list of equipment." I could hear the kids getting louder and more rowdy next to us, but I ignored it. I wanted to hear what Hamish had to say.

"Don't write a practical book. Write about your own experience. Do it for yourself."

"You don't believe I could write a serious book then?"

Hamish didn't answer. He'd left to gather up the kids, who were playing a chasey game around their table. I had expected him to be more supportive. Writing would be hard work, but I could do it. I would do my own research on what items to bring, like that gadget he attaches to the tyres. I was determined to prove Hamish wrong.

Chapter 10

Thursday 12th July

I spent a sleepless night thinking about my conversation with Hamish. In the end I decided he was right. Who was I to think I could be a writer? Millions of people thought they could write books, and most of them were wrong. Surprisingly, I didn't feel that bad. It was a relief not to have to worry about the names for tyre gadgets.

I clicked on my Bible app and quickly read through Chapter 2 of James. It didn't have the fascination for me of Chapter 1. The first section is about not showing favouritism. The rest is about faith in action.

> *"Suppose a brother or a sister is without daily food. If one of you says to them, "Go in peace; keep warm and well fed, but does nothing about their physical needs, what good is it? In the same way, faith by itself, if it is not accompanied by action, is dead." (James 2: 16-17)*

I remembered Silvio, the old man we'd met in Eucla and bumped into again in Norseman. I'd wished him well, but hadn't done anything to ensure his safety. Was my faith dead? I needed to do something quickly. Thankfully we'd be visiting the missionaries in the Northern Territory next month. Perhaps they'd be struggling terribly with the hardships of their role, and we could help them. The thought cheered me up.

At the petrol station just outside of Broome, Hamish filled the tank with diesel while I went inside to pay. There were no annoying signs offering money off the price of fuel if you spent money in-store. In fact, there was very little on sale in the store at all. Most of the shelves were empty. A man in a mechanic's overalls was moving boxes behind the counter.

He stopped what he was doing. "Where are you headed?" he asked.

"Fitzroy Crossing."

"Great!" Do you mind dropping a package at the roadhouse for me? I'll give you $50 for it."

I couldn't believe our luck. An opportunity to do a good deed, so soon after I'd read about helping others. I interrupted Hamish washing around the hole in the windscreen to ask what he thought.

"Of course!" Hamish seemed excited at the thought of a special mission. "Tell him we don't need the money."

For a man who had started saving money by switching brands of fruit juice every week, Hamish could be very generous. I felt proud of him.

"We'd be happy to take the package," I informed the grinning mechanic. "And don't worry about the $50. We're going that way anyway."

"No, no, I insist! That's how it's done around here," he told me. He slapped a cardboard box on the counter.

I carried the package out to Hamish and he found a spot for it in the car. In spite of being willing to forego the payment, he was happy to get the $50. I wasn't so sure. Was it still a good deed if we got *paid* for it? Maybe it was. The mechanic seemed pleased about the arrangement. Maybe he was a bit *too* pleased. What if the package contained something illegal, like drugs. It would be awful if, instead of doing a good deed, we were unknowingly acting as drug couriers.

I put the thought out of my mind. It was Gideon's birthday tomorrow. He was turning five. It was also the day our friends Leon and Marion Morris would arrive. I was looking forward to seeing them, but also anxious. I hoped the caravan park I'd booked was okay. I'd chosen it because they had vacancies and it was cheap. Perhaps I should have asked more questions. Like was there any shade? Even though it was technically winter here, it was still hot. The Morrises might burn in the tropical sun. I should have thought about that.

I was so busy thinking about the caravan park, I almost forgot the package. Fortunately Hamish remembered. The roadhouse at Fitzroy Crossing was a smaller version of the one at Port Hedland. Hamish went inside with the box while I studied my guidebook to see if the picture of the caravan park showed any trees. It was hard to tell.

"How did you go?" I asked Hamish when he returned.

"Mission accomplished." He rubbed his hands together importantly. "I've phoned the guy at Port Hedland to tell him we've delivered it."

"What do you think was in that box?"

"A car battery."

"A *car battery*?" I felt relieved. "Are you sure?"

"Yes. They've been waiting all day for someone heading this way apparently. We came along at just the right time."

I was pleased to find the Fitzroy Crossing Caravan Park was green and peaceful and full of beautiful fig trees. There was plenty of shade for the Morrises to park their camping chairs and protect their newly-arrived-from-Melbourne skin from the tropical sun.

A couple of grey nomads were sitting in the shade quietly sipping cups of tea. An elderly indigenous man was busy carving nuts from the bottle-shaped boab tree next to them. It seemed a shame to disturb the tea drinking and boab nut carving by setting up the trailer tent. But thankfully, we worked together harmoniously for once. Hamish had recently numbered the tent poles with a permanent marker so we knew the order in which to assemble them. Using the number system, the children and I confidently and cheerfully gathered poles, calling out to each other as we worked to help Hamish assemble the tent.

After we'd set up, the children ran off to explore the caravan park, while Hamish and I introduced ourselves to the elderly couple. They were Billy and Dawn, from Sydney, both in their eighties, making what they thought would probably be their last ever camping trip.

"We loved watching your children set up the tent just now," said Dawn.

"Really?" I said. I was worried they'd been noisy with all the calling out.

"They reminded us of our own children," said Billy.

Dawn was having another cup of tea. She put her cup down and looked at me.

"You really miss the children when they grow up."

It was a pleasant surprise to realise that our children had been a blessing to them.

We all had an early night. The children had worn themselves out playing with some new playmates: three energetic sisters from Holland. They fell asleep instantly. Hamish was tired too after the special mission. He fell asleep reading emails from home. His phone slipped out of his hand onto the sleeping bag. I placed it next to him where he could find it in the morning. I thought about Gideon's birthday. Hamish had promised Gideon a birthday cake. Hamish was great at birthday cakes, but he'd never made one in a camp kitchen. And what if something went wrong with the crocodile boat trip? What if they hadn't received our booking and weren't expecting us? Or worse, what if it wasn't the season for crocodiles, and we didn't see any?

I must have finally drifted off after deciding there was probably no such thing as a crocodile "season". It was so warm in Fitzroy Crossing all year round they wouldn't need to go anywhere else in winter.

Friday 13th July

We woke up to the girls singing "Happy Birthday" to Gideon in bed. We all watched Gideon open his presents: a pair of dinosaur-print shorts, and a handmade wiggly wooden crocodile we'd found in the souvenir shops in Broome. Gideon quickly tossed the shorts aside, but seemed to like the toy. He studied how all the pieces fitted together and how the crocodile could slither like a snake across his sleeping bag.

When Hamish and I went outside to make breakfast, I brought up the cake.

"I really appreciate you making the cake Hamish, but do you think your idea is a bit too ... difficult?"

"I've bought a pre-made sponge cake, and I'll decorate it with some dinosaur toys I'll put on top."

"But how are you going to make it look like a *forest*?"

Hamish didn't answer. Gideon had gotten tired of playing with the wooden crocodile and come out for breakfast. After breakfast, I took the children for a walk to a playground in the town while Hamish worked on the cake. When we returned, I noticed a new caravan next to our trailer tent. The Morrises had arrived! I'd forgotten Marion had beautiful tanned olive skin. I shouldn't have been worried about her skin burning. Her blonde hair neatly touched her shoulders and she was wearing a clean white shirt and beige three-quarter length pants. Leon had a fair, slightly florid complexion though. He would definitely need to stay out of the sun.

When Marion hugged me, I noticed her floral perfume. I was wearing an oversized T-shirt that used to be blue but was now red-brown. I couldn't remember the last time I'd had a shower. It might have been in Port Hedland, but I wasn't sure. Leon shook my hand warmly. I led them over to where Hamish had just finished the birthday cake and hidden it under a tea towel.

While Hamish followed Marion into their caravan so he could put the cake in their upright fridge, I was left with Leon. He used to be a school principal, and was the well-regarded secretary of our church. Marion was the leader of our church women's group.

"What do you think of the caravan park?" I said, after a pause.

"It's delightful," said Leon. He looked around himself, smiling. I let out the breath I'd been holding on to.

"There's a nice big tree next to your caravan. You could set up your camping chairs there. Out of the sun."

"Ooh don't worry about us. We'll be fine," said Leon. He took his hands out of his pockets and rubbed them together, like Hamish did after delivering the car battery yesterday.

There was an awkward lull in the conversation. At home, Leon raises his voice to announce that a business meeting is going to start. Now he spoke softly and said only a few words. He even looked physically smaller somehow. I wondered if he was ill.

Thankfully, Hamish returned with Marion. We told them about the boat trip, and Marion and I arranged to put our food together for a kind of potluck dinner when we got back.

We found the river easily—it was only a few minutes'

drive away—and walked down to a little jetty with a sign for the "Geike Gorge nature and indigenous history tour".

We joined a small line-up of tourists and boarded a motor boat with built-in benches covered with a plastic awning. Our captain and guide, who introduced himself as an Aboriginal elder, steered us slowly down the river and through the narrow canyon of the Geikie Gorge. The cliffs on either side were high and cast a shadow across the water. Then the river widened and the water sparkled with sunlight. I saw some dark eyes and a long snout sticking out of the water. My heart skipped a beat with excitement. Then I saw another reptilian creature with a long snout, completely motionless, its mouth slightly open, on the right-hand bank of the river. It looked like it was dead. I wondered if I should cover Gideon's eyes. I couldn't believe this was Gideon's first ever experience of seeing crocodiles, and it had turned out like this. I felt sick in the stomach.

It was too late. Gideon had seen the motionless crocodile on the bank and started shouting "crocodile!". Then I noticed more crocodiles, lots of them on either side of the riverbank.

"Why are they so *still*?" I asked our guide. He was steering the boat and had barely spoken a word so far.

"They stay still like that to save energy when it's cold. It's called brumation. "

Hmm so there was a kind of crocodile season. Gideon didn't seem to mind how inactive they were. He pointed out every crocodile he saw.

When we reached the widest part of the river, the guide stopped the motor for the cultural part of the tour. He spoke softly and slowly, like the Aboriginal men we had met in Karijini. He told us his people traditionally had several marriages, and took a spouse who was a different age to them, so they could mentor or learn from them, depending on their stage of life. I liked the way the indigenous culture revered the elderly, and their marriage structure ensured wisdom passed on to the younger generations. Gideon was not interested. He made his wooden crocodile toy crawl along the bottom of the boat, then growl and snap at his own hand. The girls told him to "shush". He made quieter growling noises.

As the boat made its way back to Fitzroy Crossing, I felt satisfied. We'd learnt something about the indigenous culture, and Gideon had seen crocodiles, even if they were lethargic.

Back at the caravan park, Marion and I placed the Morrises' small camping table next to our trestle table, and combined all the dips and cheese and biscuits we had to make a special meal. The children invited the three Dutch girls over to have cake. I was a little worried. Would Hamish be embarrassed about not having been able to create a forest for the dinosaurs? Would Gideon be disappointed? Hamish carried the cake down the steps of the Morrises caravan. He'd lit some sparklers, which fizzed and shone against the night sky. We sang happy birthday, while Gideon smiled and held hands with Sophie, the youngest of the Dutch girls.

When the sparklers sizzled out, Hamish put the cake on the trestle table. I could see a forest full of dinosaurs peeping out from a nest of leaves. Everyone said "Ooooh" with delight. Gideon's mouth dropped open. He let go of Sophie's hand and ran toward the cake, bending over it to pick up the figure of a velociraptor.

"Wow Hamish. How did you do *that*?" asked Marion.

"I used fondant icing. I dyed it with food colouring and rolled it out with a coke bottle. I made the leaf shapes with my pocket knife."

"That is amazing," said Marion. She shook her head

in wonder. Do you mind if I take a photo? Our grandson would love it."

"Go ahead." Hamish smiled proudly.

I was thrilled to see how much Gideon loved his cake. I couldn't believe Hamish had pulled it off.

I listened while Hamish told Marion about his plans to travel down the Gibb River road, a four-wheel drive trip he'd wanted to do ever since he came to Australia, while Leon and the children washed the dishes.

Saturday 14th July

I went back to my Bible reading this morning. I skipped ahead to Chapter Three.

> *"Who is wise and understanding among you? Let them show it by their good life, by deeds done in the humility that comes from wisdom." (James 3:13)*

Doing good deeds wasn't just about being helpful, it was also about the spirit in which it was done. I read on further.

> *"The wisdom that comes from heaven is first of all pure; then peace-loving, considerate, submissive, full of mercy and good fruit, impartial and sincere." (James 3:17)*

Later as I washed our clothes, and hung them on the line to dry, I was aware of a peaceful feeling. I wondered if it was due to all the old people camping with us. Old people had had time to learn the kind of peace-loving wisdom James 3:17 talked about. Billy and Dawn were still sitting calmly on their camping chairs under a tree. I watched them scrape the green icing away from the cake Hamish had given them, and enjoy the cake underneath with another cup of tea. I took some tea and cake over to Marley, the elderly indigenous boab nut carver. He spoke quietly as he showed me his carvings. He had created detailed scenes of trees and animals, white against the fuzzy brown shell of the egg-shaped boab nuts. He was obviously a sweet tooth. He ate every bit of the cake and the icing and asked me to put three sugars in his tea.

We invited Marion and Leon over to our campsite for dinner again after they got back from their own cruise to see crocodiles on the Geikie Gorge. We all shared travel stories. The Morrises were going anti-clockwise around the West, in the opposite direction to us, so they were about to head toward the places we'd already been. We told them they should definitely go to Dales Gorge in Karijini. Hamish told them about our plans to drive down the Gibb River road, the legendary 600-kilometre journey he'd been wanting to do ever since he came to Australia twenty years ago.

Then Marion leaned forward in her chair and looked at Hamish. "I've been meaning to ask you a favour."

"Sure," Hamish said. I wondered if she was going to ask us to deliver a package to a friend up north. After our last successful delivery, I was sure Hamish would say it was no trouble.

"I'm starting the women's group up again in September. We're doing a cooking series. Could you give a cake decorating demonstration?"

"Of course. That would be my pleasure." Hamish beamed.

I couldn't believe it. Hamish is already good at camping, four-wheel driving, packing *and* fixing things. Now he's going to demonstrate cake decoration at *my* women's group? How could I ever keep up with him?

Chapter 11

Sunday 15th July

I made a decision this morning. I'll stop stressing out about other people, like Leon and Marion. They were able to sort themselves out without my help. And I'll stop comparing myself to Hamish. I'll go with the flow, relax and blend in, like Leon did when he was on holiday. It will be a relief to stop striving all the time.

It was time to say goodbye to the Morrises. They were heading south, en route to Karijini. We were travelling east toward Derby to begin the four-wheel drive journey Hamish had dreamed of for twenty years. I hugged Marion, and Leon and Hamish shook hands and then patted each other's shoulders.

"It was great to spend time with you both," said Leon.

"Take care of yourselves," said Marion. She looked impeccable again, in a pink T-shirt and khaki shorts.

"Enjoy Karijini National Park," I said. "Don't forget to go to Dales Gorge. And don't step on slippery rocks. You could fall, like I did." I remembered the pain in my knees from banging them on the rocks there.

"Don't worry about us," said Leon. He smiled. I realised I'd been stressing out again.

We watched Marion and Leon drive off, towing their little white caravan. They waved to us as they turned onto the road out of Fitzroy Crossing. After saying goodbye to Billy and Dawn, who told us they would miss the sound of the children, and exchanging details with the Dutch girls so the children could email each other, we set off ten minutes after

Leon and Marion. Before long we saw their little caravan in front of us on the road to the highway. Hamish increased his speed. Leon smiled and raised his hand to wave again as we overtook them.

I looked toward Hamish. He was concentrating on the road ahead, looking for the turnoff. "Did you notice Leon was different here from how he is in church?"

"You mean more casually dressed?"

"Not that! He was quieter. In church he's loud and calls everyone to order. Out here, he didn't raise his voice once. I thought he might be ill."

"Well just because he's the church secretary doesn't mean he's an organiser when he's out here. He knows his limitations."

"You're right, Hamish!" I recalled that Leon had been content and happy, chatting with the children and helping them wash the dishes. There was nothing wrong with him at all. Then I had another idea. "Do you think *that's* what the verse means, "*Consider it pure joy, my brothers and sisters, whenever you face trials of many kinds?*"

Hamish glanced at me. "How so?"

"As we go through life, we experience more trials, we learn what we're capable of, and what we're not capable of. We learn what our role is, and what our limitations are." That was why older people had more wisdom. That's why perseverance in trials made us "*mature and complete.*" (*James 1:4*)

"Hmm, maybe you're right." Hamish tapped his fingers on the steering wheel. I was glad I'd been the one with the ideas for once. I wondered when I would be as wise and humble as Leon.

As we drove toward Derby, I wondered what *real* four-wheel driving would be like. We'd done a little bit, unexpectedly, on the long road out to the Ningaloo Homestead. But we were about to drive 600 kilometres along the most famous four-wheel driving journey in the country. I imagined it was like a roller-coaster. Much more exciting than the flat corrugated road into Ningaloo.

We stopped in Derby to buy enough food and cold drinks for a six-day journey, and arrived at the Windjana campsite, the start of the Gibb River Road, in the middle of the afternoon. It looked like a four-wheel drive muster. There were two dozen vehicles dotted around the campsite. All of them had enormous aerials, just like ours, for communication with each other via CB radio. They were all massive vehicles, with roof racks, and wide-treaded tyres. This was obviously a trip for people who took their driving seriously.

The car temperature gauge showed thirty-five degrees. When I jumped down from the car, the heat slapped me in the face. It felt hotter than thirty-five, with no wind, and no shade, except for a tiny bit of half shade from some straggly gum trees. I felt like I was gasping for air.

"Let's go down to the river and put up the tent later, when it's cooler," I said.

"No, let's get it over and done with," said Hamish. He was already unzipping the cover on the camper trailer tent, in a series of quick movements because the cover was so hot he couldn't leave his hands on it for long.

When we'd finally set up the tent and awning, Hamish was red-faced and dripping with sweat. I fetched five cans from the car fridge, and we sat under the awning. The kids drank their lemonade, a rare treat, in big gulps. I put the cold can on the back of my neck. It felt so good.

Hamish and I studied the guidebook, and watched a few more families arrive. One of the new arrivals played Dire Straits from their car sound system, loud enough for everyone to hear. The shared music made me feel part of a club. All the kids played together.

Later Jenna wrote:

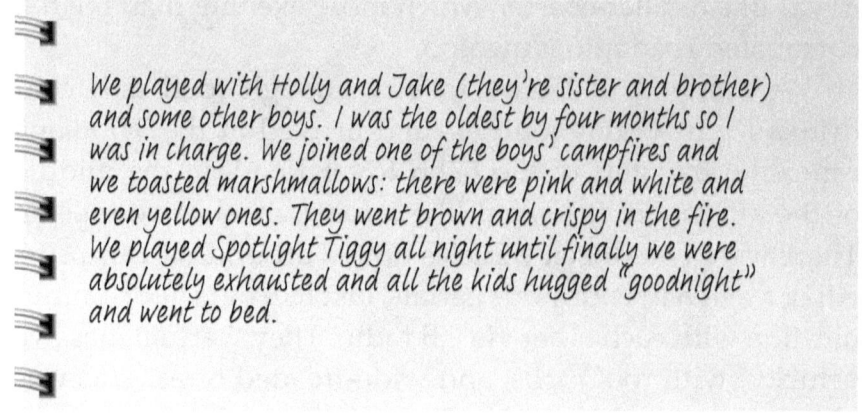

> We played with Holly and Jake (they're sister and brother) and some other boys. I was the oldest by four months so I was in charge. We joined one of the boys' campfires and we toasted marshmallows: there were pink and white and even yellow ones. They went brown and crispy in the fire. We played Spotlight Tiggy all night until finally we were absolutely exhausted and all the kids hugged "goodnight" and went to bed.

There we were, all hanging out, with our huge cars, and our cold drinks, listening to chilled-out music, all ready to take on the Gibb River Road journey together.

I wondered if four-wheel drivers in a group like this race each other. Would it be a competition to see who could be the fastest and the most powerful getting out of the campsite tomorrow? It seemed a little scary, but perhaps it could be fun.

Monday 16th July

The families left in a slow steady trickle this morning. Perhaps four-wheel drivers don't have races. I would have to wait until tomorrow to find out. We'd decided to delay the journey, and look for crocodiles at Windjana Gorge from the safety of the walking track. It seemed wrong to be so near to crocodiles and not give Gideon the chance to see some up close.

We walked down the sandy track toward the gorge. The

sun already had a sting in it. Gideon ran toward the yellow warning sign and pointed to the picture of a crocodile with its mouth open. Then the path took us away from the river along a ledge under overhanging rock. Hamish had to bend over so that he didn't bang his head. Gideon's feet slid along the rock below, but he didn't fall.

We found a series of steps leading back down to a sandy path and emerged into bright sunlight again. There, on the bank of the river, was not just one, but dozens of crocodiles basking in the sun.

Gideon took a few steps toward a crocodile who was facing us, with his tail in the water. The crocodiles' chest expanded and contracted as Gideon got closer. I didn't know what to do. Should I chase after Gideon? Or would that frighten the crocodile, and make him attack one of us? I stayed still and watched Gideon stop two metres in front of him and crouch down to get a better look. The crocodile's breathing slowed. It stiffened slightly.

"Gideon, smile!" Hamish held up his phone to take a photo.

Gideon was in danger, and Hamish was taking a *photograph*.

Gideon gave his biggest smile for the camera. I walked slowly toward him.

Hamish took a few more photos.

"Come back now, Gideon!" I called in a loud whisper. I tried to move calmly and steadily. Gideon ran toward me. I grabbed his hand and walked him firmly away from the river. I turned around in case the crocodile was following us. He was in the same spot and still appeared to be watching us. His mouth was slightly open as if he was grinning.

"What were you thinking?" I snapped at Hamish. "That was no time to take *photos*. Did you see the way the crocodile was breathing hard, ready to pounce?"

I kept Gideon close to me, away from the river, while we walked the rest of the gorge. Jenna took photos of Hamish next to a group of crocodiles. I held firmly onto Gideon's hand until we got back to the campground.

It was much quieter than the night before. Most of the families had left already. Hamish introduced himself to a guy from Adelaide who was doing the trip solo in an enormous black ute, and they chatted about the best way to drive the Gibb River. From what I overheard, the key to putting the least stress on the car was a mixture of correct speed and tyre pressure. I switched off after a while.

I obviously couldn't relax and go with the flow completely, after Hamish's behaviour around the crocodiles. I would need to be on the lookout. But there was safety in numbers. I hoped we would meet up with the rest of the four-wheel drive "club" somewhere along the journey tomorrow, and drive over the hills and dips together.

Tuesday 17th July

We headed for Bell Gorge campground, 180 km along the Gibb River Road. I was surprised to discover it was flat, apart from the ridges like the corrugated tin walls at the Exmouth Backpackers. There were no real dips or hills at all, and it was empty of other cars. I felt deflated.

"I thought it would be more challenging," I told Hamish.

"The road's been graded recently, and I'm doing the right speed. If you're fast, you skip over the top of the bumps." Hamish was looking carefully at the road ahead of him. He didn't look deflated. He had that contented look he had driving to the beach before we got bogged at Ningaloo.

Perhaps it was more interesting for the driver. I looked at the dusty road in front of me. "Can I drive for a bit?"

Hamish's shoulders sagged. I was obviously spoiling his fun. "Sure," he said. He pulled over and we changed sides.

My heart was racing. I'd done plenty of highway driving on the holiday, but this was the first time I'd driven off-road.

"You want to drive about 70 km per hour," Hamish said. "And if you see someone ahead, pull back."

It was a little bumpy at first, but when I reached the right speed, the car glided over the ridges, just like that guy from Adelaide said it would. I didn't have to worry about traffic. There was no-one in sight.

Hamish kept staring firmly at the road. "Watch out for rocks. Make sure you go around them."

I swerved around a pile of rocks in the middle of the road. Then I saw a small rock on Hamish's side. I was sure the car could handle it, as Hamish had gotten extra big tyres, and a suspension lift, especially for this trip. I drove over it. The car bounced.

Hamish raised his voice. "What are you doing? I said to avoid the rocks!" He shook his head.

"Are you serious? We've got these enormous tyres, and that snorkel and everything, and I can't go over a rock the size of my fist?

Hamish was squirming in his seat, his face red. "The rocks are small but they're sharp. You'll put a hole in the tyres if you keep doing that!" He shook his head again.

I looked out for rocks on the rest of the drive and watched the speedometer so that we didn't bump over the corrugations. I couldn't see what the big deal was about four-wheel driving. I let Hamish take over. To relieve the boredom, I took some fruit chews out of the glovebox and handed some to the children. Then I unwrapped one and passed it to Hamish. He placed it in his mouth without speaking. He was looking out for rocks. He looked happy again.

We arrived at Bell Gorge campsite after two and a half

hours' monotonous journey. Outside it was hot, but not stifling like it had been at Windjana. I saw a few families we'd seen on our first night of the Gibb River journey. The kids were ecstatic to meet up with Jake and Holly.

After setting up the tent, we walked to Bell Gorge in search of water to cool off in. It was a long walk, along a dusty path, with the occasional climb over smooth rocks. A wide ledge ended in a series of rock steps that led us down to a perfectly circular pool, half shaded by the steep cliffs, and surrounded by tall palm trees. The sun-exposed half of the water twinkled brightly, like the sparklers that shone against the night sky on Gideon's birthday cake.

I sat on a ledge with my feet in the water admiring the beauty. Perhaps *this* was the point of four-wheel driving—being able to go to remote places that could only be reached on unsealed roads. Maybe that's why Hamish had looked so happy today. He was looking forward to *this*.

Back at the campsite, Dire Straits was playing again. Jenna gathered all the children together and organised another game of Spotlight Tiggy. Hamish talked about tyre pressure with Holly and Jake's dad Matt, a big guy with a prominent Adam's apple. Matt explained that out here, the tyre pressure had to be lower than regular four-wheel driving, because the tyres heat up on such a long trip. I tuned out again.

The kids toasted marshmallows in the campfire, and when they ran out, they wrapped up the rest of the fruit chews and toasted them. I enjoyed staring at the crackling fire and watching the children lick the melted lollies off tin foil. If Hamish could stop being so technical about the driving, the rest of the trip might still be fun.

Wednesday 18th July

I read the end of Chapter 3 this morning:

"But the wisdom that comes from heaven is first of all pure; then peace-loving, considerate, submissive, full of mercy and good fruit, impartial and sincere. Peacemakers who sow in peace reap a harvest of righteousness." (James 3:17).

I remembered Leon's submissiveness and considerateness by being humble in Fitzroy Crossing. It was inspiring. But I was worried about Hamish. He wasn't being considerate at all. He'd gone red in the face and raised his voice at me when I drove over a rock yesterday. I would need to look for an opportunity to talk to him about his behaviour.

Matt had recommended a day trip to Manning Gorge, a long drive, followed by a difficult hike, but apparently worth the effort to see the stunning gorge and swim in the waterholes. I was pleased it would be a long trip. It would give Hamish and I a chance to talk. But on the way to the Manning Gorge roadhouse, the starting point of the walk, Jenna talked non-stop about her new friends and had no interest in watching DVDs. I would have to wait for another opportunity for the discussion.

At the roadhouse, I propped the back door of the car open and made sandwiches on a shelf Hamish had made that slides out from under the fridge. Hamish smothered himself and the children in sunscreen and filled water bottles from the roadhouse water tap. I couldn't wait to get the preparations over with so we could start walking and I could ask Hamish to be more considerate.

Our guidebook instructions explained that we needed

to cross a river to get to the start of the hike. We found the river and a little tin boat operated by a pulley system. The children loved pulling the rope and watching the ripples the boat made as it crossed the water. On the sandy bank a sign read "Manning Gorge: two hours return". A one-hour walk to the gorge? That sounded daunting, but then again it meant plenty of time to talk.

Hamish set out in front. I wanted to keep up with him, but Hamish walks fast. I watched him getting further and further ahead of me. Then I noticed how beautiful the surroundings were. It was a much better view of the world walking rather than driving. I slowed down for a while to take it in. I saw spinifex grasses and strappy-leaved pandanus. The children ran on ahead of me. I spotted a grevillea plant with red flowers that looked like bottle brushes. Perched on a branch at eye level, a brightly-coloured bird with a blue tail was moving its yellow head from side to side. The bird tilted his head back and tweeted out a quick little song. I was entranced.

I called out, but Hamish and the children were too far ahead to hear me. I wanted to tell them about the beautiful bird. And I still had to talk to Hamish about his temper. I tried to speed up to catch them, but their backs were getting further and further away. Then I couldn't see them at all. After a while, the sandy path was blocked by big rocks. White painted arrows showed which ones to clamber over. It was hard work. I wondered how Gideon had managed it. On the other side of the rocks, there was still no sign of them. I walked faster.

My legs hurt from trying to go quickly. The sun was stinging and my throat was parched. I remembered I had the food, but Hamish had the rest of the water. Now I had to find him so I could have a drink. I noticed my tongue was swelling up in my mouth. I saw a couple of twenty-year-olds in swimming costumes with towels slung over their shoulders, coming back from the gorge.

"Is it much further?" I was panting.

"You're nearly there!" the woman said.

"It's all downhill soon," the man said. He stopped and leant on the bushwalking stick he was holding. "And it's worth it! You'll love it."

"Thank you!" I could feel the sweat running down my face. I was happy to hear the gorge wasn't far.

A few minutes later, I saw a fork in the path. The right-hand path went slightly downhill. I couldn't see any white arrows, but the other walkers had said the gorge was close, so this *must* have been the path to the gorge.

I reached a large rock and pulled myself over it. On the other side was an enormous boulder with a smooth face. There were no foot holes to step into, and no white arrows. It wouldn't be possible to get over it. This was obviously *not* the way to the gorge.

I retraced my steps, furious that I had wasted so much time in the heat. *Couldn't those people have been a bit clearer with their directions? And why had Hamish and the kids left me behind anyway? Hadn't it occurred to Hamish to wait for me to catch up?* I grumbled to myself. I reached the original path and this time was careful to follow the white arrows, which led me to another path leading downhill. I came to a sandy beach next to a small swimming hole, where a bikini-clad woman was lying peacefully with a sun hat over her face.

She propped herself up on one elbow and let the hat fall off her face. "Are you looking for a family?"

I nodded. I was too out of breath to speak.

"They went that way." She flung her right arm up in the air, then lay back down again.

I walked uphill again in the direction she'd pointed. I got

more and more frustrated, as it occurred to me that I wasn't going to find the gorge walking uphill. *Why were people so bad at giving directions?*

I came to a ledge and looked down below to see if I could work out where I was. I could see Hamish standing on some rocks below me. Thank goodness, I'd found him. I yelled to get his attention. He waved back enthusiastically. He gestured that I had to go back down to the small watering hole, and come down a path to the right. His directions actually made sense, but I was furious as I trudged past the sunbaking woman and down the hill.

By the time I reached Hamish, I was shaking with anger.

"How dare you leave me behind. It was okay for you to come down and have a swim. What about me?" Hamish was trying to say something, but I ignored it. "Weren't you worried about me? Anything could have happened! What were you thinking?" I shouted. Hamish opened his mouth to speak and closed it again. He turned around and went back to the water. He seemed to be having trouble walking, probably because he felt so bad about leaving me behind.

Manning Gorge was a line of swimming holes that flowed into each other, via a series of waterfalls, that were surrounded by sandy beaches, sand-coloured rocks, and pandanus palms. It was hard to stay enraged with Hamish surrounded by so much beauty. I cooled off after drinking a litre of water, eating a sandwich and sitting in the shade of the cliffs watching Hamish and the girls jump off a rock into one of the swimming holes.

Gideon stayed near me watching a water monitor. It looked like a snake with legs, but was nowhere near as big as a crocodile. I was pretty sure it was harmless.

I was still angry on the walk back to the boat ramp, although my fury had subsided. I decided to make Hamish feel guilty. I explained that as I was clearly the slowest person, I needed to go in front, and we all had to stay together. I stopped self-righteously every now and then and turned around to make sure I could see everyone. Of course I *knew* they weren't far behind me, but it was important to show Hamish how bushwalking *should* be done.

Back at the river, the girls and I swam across this time, while Hamish and Gideon carried our belongings over on the boat with the pulley. By the time we drove home, it was almost dark. The children fell asleep.

It would have been a perfect time to discuss Hamish's temper, but there were other things on my mind. Not only did Hamish have a bad temper when it came to avoiding rocks on the road, but after today, I realised he could be rude, thoughtless, and inconsiderate. I didn't know where to start. I would have to sleep on it and we would talk tomorrow. Hamish didn't speak either. I guess he was still embarrassed about his behaviour and didn't know what to say.

Thursday 19th July

Strangely enough, I wasn't focused on Hamish at all this morning. I was still angry with him. It *was* rude and inconsiderate to walk ahead of me. But I realised that *I* was actually the one with the problem. If Hamish could leave me behind like that, it meant he didn't care about me. I thought back to him not wanting to have another wedding. At the time, I thought Hamish was being practical. But now I could see what was really going on. Hamish was obviously questioning his feelings for me.

I felt so awful, I needed God. And I wasn't going to read the Book of James anymore. I needed something less *practical*.

The year before, I'd been reading Ephesians. It deals with *real* Christianity. It describes God's plan for us, and has a lot of encouraging things to say about how God loves us. I found Ephesians in the Bible with the wheat on the cover I'd been given in Israel. It had a sticky note to mark where I'd finished reading last time.

Frustratingly, the next session was not typical of Ephesians at all. It was about speech.

> *"Do not let any unwholesome talk come out of your mouths, but only what is helpful for building others up." (Ephesians 4:29)*

My eyes scanned the page looking for the words about God's plan for us. But this section of Ephesians was surprisingly direct.

> *"Get rid of all bitterness, rage and anger, brawling and slander, along with every form of malice. Be kind and compassionate to one another, forgiving each other, just as in Christ God forgave you." (Ephesians: 4:31-32)*

I felt a warmth spread through me. The passage pointed to a quite obvious solution. I could forgive Hamish for being rude and inconsiderate. If I was capable of forgiveness, then I was capable of speaking to him calmly, instead of being in a rage, or putting him on a guilt trip. It was a good place to start.

Hamish was filling the kettle with water from the cask on the trestle table.

"I didn't like how you left me behind yesterday. I got lost and I couldn't see you. I was scared and hot and angry." I felt like a child. I'd enjoyed yelling and then acting self-righteous the day before. It made me feel powerful, and important. Now I felt like a five-year-old in need of help.

"I'm sorry." Hamish put the kettle down on the table and put his arms around me. "You're right, I shouldn't have done that." I snuggled into him and rested my head on his chest. It was a relief he agreed with me. His fleecy jumper felt soft.

"You didn't even turn around and look over your shoulder." My voice broke and a few tears slid onto the fleece and rested on the top.

"I'm sorry," he said again. "I was trying to go fast so Gideon didn't get bored. I didn't want to carry him."

"Oh, I didn't think about that." It made sense. Once Gideon got bored, he wanted to be picked up.

"And I thought you were enjoying yourself. You like to look at the plants." It was true. I thought of the grevillea and the bird with the blue tail.

I remembered I'd shouted at Hamish at the gorge, while he was trying to tell me something. "I'm sorry I yelled at you and wouldn't let you talk." My voice was croaky.

"That's okay, your feelings were hurt. I understand." Hamish gave me a squeeze.

The world felt normal and safe again. It had been worth telling Hamish how I felt, even though it made me feel small and vulnerable.

I looked at the computer open on the trestle table. "Have you been writing your diary?"

"I was writing about yesterday. You can read it if you want."

In Port Hedland Hamish had written about the weather, and what we ate for dinner. It hadn't made great reading. But I was curious to see what he'd written about leaving me behind.

(Wednesday 18 th July)

Up early with the sun as is our habit, and we decided to visit Manning Gorge for the day. It was a 2 km walk to the falls and pool, but first we needed to cross a river in a leaky tin boat (tinny) with polystyrene boxes inside for things we did not want to get wet, then pull ourselves to the other side using a rope on a pulley system. Kids loved it and thought it a bit of an adventure.

Successfully on the other side of the river we then walked across the rocks on a path that was well-marked, but arduous. It was really hot and we seemed to be going through our water at a fast rate, so was hoping the water at the gorge would be clean enough to drink. Jane unfortunately did not keep up well with us and with my goal-focussed approach I failed to notice as I put all my energy into keeping the children going so they didn't notice how far it was.

Kids and I found our way down to a popular waterfall / swimming hole. The kids spotted some of their new-found friends and ran ahead to see them. I heard Gideon scream for me in that way you know is not just attention seeking but something serious. I leapt across the rocks, forgetting that I was not in fact a mountain goat and so banged the ball of my foot really hard on a rock, before stumbling to his aid which was no longer needed.

Became a little worried that Jane was not behind us and after a while started making plans to find her. Then I saw her up on the cliff, so gestured for her to come down. After quite a long time, I saw her appear again on the cliff so this time gestured enthusiastically to get her attention. It was needless to say an emotional reunion when she finally reached the waterhole as she was upset with us for leaving her behind.

The girls were still swimming and jumping off rocks into the water. So glad they were having such a great time. Had to hurry them in the end as it was now 3 pm and we had a long walk and a long drive ahead of us. Jane was insistent that we all stay together and that we leave no-one behind. I think this is a marine motto.

Hurried back to the creek where Jane and the girls swam across. I took Gideon in the boat but there were no boxes this time so had to bundle our stuff on my lap while pulling us across. We were starting to lose the light and driving in the dim light on rough roads with dust quite thick that it often obscured my vision was not pleasant at all, and was in fact dangerous. Drove in silence as I had to concentrate on the road. Jane also quiet as she must have been exhausted. Took a while to sleep that night as I think I did something to my hip when I banged my foot chasing Gideon.

"I like that Hamish. I liked how you compare yourself to a mountain goat." His diary entry wasn't dull at all.

"No, I said I'm *not* a mountain goat. That was my mistake. Forgetting I'm in fact a 45-year-old man."

"How's your hip? I noticed you were limping."

"It'll be fine. No problem at all." Hamish had started packing things into the back of the car. He winced with pain every now and then. In spite of protesting otherwise, he seemed to be in trouble.

We spent the day packing up and driving to Ellenbrae, a privately-owned camp halfway between Manning Gorge and the township of El Questro, at the northern end of the Gibb River. As we approached the camp, I heard a rattle from the camper trailer. We got out to investigate. The trailer and car were completely covered in dirt, and the dust caught in my throat. Hamish lifted the lid of the trailer. It was a black mess. The electrics that powered the water pump for the trailer had caught fire and burned out. We agreed that it would have to be looked at when we reached a town with a mechanic. Hamish found the cause of the rattle: the petrol can, which was about to come loose. I was amazed when Hamish found some little screws he had brought with him.

Perhaps all those extra items Hamish had packed were necessary after all. I held the petrol can in place while Hamish screwed it on tight.

When we reached Ellenbrae, I found that the running board along the passenger side had almost separated itself from the car. It was hanging on by a small join at the back. Apparently, all the bouncing over corrugations had shaken it loose. But it was no problem as it turned out. Hamish had packed "liquid nails" and glued the board back on. Once again I was impressed.

Ellenbrae was a peaceful oasis with green lawns and tropical landscaped gardens, and surprisingly, a cafe that served scones, jam and cream, and ginger beer. After a delightful afternoon tea, we set up camp next to a couple of young police officers who told us they were on remote patrol. It was comforting to be camped next to the officers. Hopefully with them around I wouldn't get lost, and there would be no drama on the second half of the Gibb River Road.

That night, I listened to Hamish snoring. He only ever snored when he was very tired. He was obviously still exhausted after yesterday's adventures.

It was odd the way Hamish loved driving so much, and he walked too fast, and nothing was *ever* too much effort. He was incapable of taking a short cut - everything had to be done correctly and according to the book, even avoiding small rocks. It was infuriating.

Then again, he knew where everything was in the car, and how to fix things, and his eyes shone brightly whenever he was having fun. He forgave me when I yelled at him and refused to listen to him. Hamish wasn't such a bad person after all. I hoped his hip would be okay. I didn't want him to have any more trouble.

Chapter 12

Friday 20th July

I read James this morning. I can't believe I'm up to Chapter 4. It talks about judgement. The words that caught my attention were:

> "Do not slander one another. Anyone who speaks against a brother or sister or judges them speaks against the law and judges it .... But you - who are you to judge your neighbour?" (James 4:11-12).

I could have substituted "husband" for neighbour. Two days ago, I'd judged Hamish for walking ahead of me before I knew the facts. Who was I to judge him? I decided to assume the best of Hamish from now on. I would *not* jump to awful conclusions.

I heard the police officers camped next to us packing up their tent. When I got up to make tea, they drove past in their white landcruiser. The blond one in the passenger seat wound down his window and gave me a wave.

"See you in El Questro." He was bright-eyed and upbeat. How could he be so energetic? Maybe it was part of his training.

I put down the kettle and waved back at him. "See you there. Have a good trip," I croaked back.

After enjoying a quiet cup of tea, I saw the owner carrying a bucket of water. He'd introduced himself yesterday as Mick. He was a short, stocky man, with a long full grey beard.

"Good morning," he said cheerfully. "If you want a

shower, the water will be hot soon. I'm about to fill up the donkey".

I followed Mick to the other side of the shed with the amenities. I'd never seen a donkey up close, but I knew they were related to horses, and they're beautiful.

He poured the water into a large drum and threw some wood into a smaller drum underneath. "Should take about thirty minutes," he said.

He whistled as he walked back in the direction of the office and cafe. He wasn't going to give water to an actual donkey then. There was a lot I didn't know about outback life.

Back at our site, Hamish was already rolling up sleeping bags. He didn't think it was a good idea to wait for the hot water. I was disappointed to miss out on a wash. I was sticky and dusty from our drive yesterday. Then again Hamish had a point. We had a long drive ahead of us. We couldn't delay setting off too long.

While I helped the girls pack up their beds, I noticed Gideon playing where the police officers had camped. He poked the remains of their fire with a stick. I knew I should stop him. He'd get filthy, or burn himself on hot coals. Then again, the policemen would have put their fire out properly. They were policemen after all. And it made my life easier that Gideon was occupied while we were packing up.

I folded up the camping chairs and stuffed them into their nylon bags. Hamish liked them to go in padded ends first, so that the legs didn't put a hole in the bottom of the bag. It was hard work trying to squash the padded arms into a shape that could be pushed into the bag. While I was struggling with a chair, I noticed flames in the distance. I dropped the chair and ran toward the fire. Gideon was proudly holding up the stick, which had caught alight.

"Look Mum!" he yelled.

"What are you doing?" I yelled back.

I grabbed the stick out of his hand and stabbed it out in the dirt.

Hamish told the girls to fill buckets with water. Then he made Gideon pour them over the remains of the fire. Each time Gideon upended the bucket, ash and steam rose into the air. Gideon smiled and his eyes shone. He seemed pleased that he'd started a fire, and now even better, had been given the important job of putting it out.

I left the children with Hamish and went to find the bushy-bearded camp owner. He was stacking wood against the wall of the office building.

"Excuse me." I could hear my voice shaking.

He looked surprised to see me. Maybe it was past the checkout time and we'd outstayed our welcome. There were no other campers left.

"The police officers that were camping next to us didn't put their fire out. My son was poking it with a stick and got it going again."

Mick lent his head over to one side and looked at me. I raised my voice, in case he was hard of hearing. "He could have hurt himself. Or started a bushfire."

"I see." He stroked his beard, then stood up straight. "I'll have a word with the officers for you." He threw a final bit of wood on the pile, and started walking back to the office.

Hamish had finished packing, and the children were in their seats in the car. Hamish was giving Gideon a lecture about the danger of playing with fire.

When he finished his speech, I fastened Gideon's seat belt. Gideon whispered in my ear, "I'm going to be a dad one day."

I stifled a laugh. He could have set himself on fire, and all could think about was how powerful he'd felt.

"Don't you *ever* do that again. You could have hurt yourself." I tried to sound stern.

The journey to El Questro was bumpy, but there was no rattle from the petrol can or the running board. Hamish's screws and liquid nails glue seemed to have worked. The children were glued to DVDs. I watched the bush going past. It was quiet and peaceful. My pulse slowed down and my breathing returned to normal.

The calmer I felt, the less angry I was about the policeman not putting out the ashes from their fire. Maybe people didn't normally throw buckets of water over a fire out here; maybe it was a waste of water. I looked at the bush going past my window. The trees were tiny and far apart. Probably the worst thing that could happen was a grass fire that could be put out with a shovel.

If the policemen had done what was *normal* in this part of the world, then maybe it was *my* fault Gideon had set fire to a stick. Parents were supposed to supervise their children and protect them. My stomach churned. Then something else occurred to me. Because of me, Mick was going to talk to the policemen. Mick was short, but scary-looking. I would hate getting a lecture from him. I remembered the officers' happy faces and how the blond one had smiled and waved at me this morning. He'd had no idea I was about to dob on him.

I put it out of my mind when we arrived at our destination. The place was called El Questro township, even though it was just a campsite. There was a big car park, and a lawn with picnic benches. I could see an amenities block, an information centre, and a lively open-air restaurant. The guests sat at tables or around a wooden bar in the middle of the restaurant. It was a fully self-contained tourist complex; like a tropical resort, but without the luxury accommodation. In the distance were campsites full of tents, swags and camper trailers.

While Hamish and the kids walked around the campground, I joined a small queue of people at the information centre to book us in. A young man wearing a shirt that said "Lead Camp Ranger" addressed us.

"Welcome to El Questro. I'm only going to say this once, so listen up." We all stood up straight, and looked at him.

"If you're going to stay here you'll need a wilderness permit. The permit entitles you to use our facilities." *Thank goodness, a shower, finally!* I smiled at the woman standing next to me. She smiled back.

"You'll need to know the password for the amenities block, and where to buy tokens to use the washing machines." I started to get restless. Lionel Ritchie was playing from the speaker system at the restaurant. I looked over at the guests already relaxing.

I noticed the blond policeman from Ellenbrae, sitting comfortably at the wooden bar, wearing his navy-blue officer's uniform. One of the women said something and he threw his head back and laughed. He was very good-looking, and was obviously enjoying the female attention.

I looked away guiltily. It was awful, seeing him so happy, knowing that I'd betrayed him to Mick from Ellenbrae.

The ranger finished his talk. I waited my turn, then paid for our permit, and three nights of camping. It would be nice to stay in one place for a while.

Hamish had already chosen a spot to camp. It was a long way from the showers, but it was a large site, and the ground was level. Ever since Hamish had nearly been injured by the camper trailer rolling downhill at Coronation Beach, his main criterion for any campsite was that it was flat.

I was happy with the spot, but I was uncertain about our neighbours. They were two middle-aged men. They had long beards like Mick, and an impressive-looking old car. I wondered if it had a hotted-up engine. Maybe they would rev the engine and play music loudly and keep us awake. I wished Hamish had chosen a family to camp next to.

After we set up, I took the girls with me for the long walk to the shower. I remembered I didn't know the password. Thankfully I saw the nice woman I'd smiled at in the queue. She punched the password into the keypad to let us in. It was bliss letting hot water run over me. When my two minutes ran out, I waited a while and then started the shower over again.

Walking back to the campsite, I noticed Hamish sitting with our new neighbours. They introduced themselves as Ron and Alan, from Broken Hill. They invited us to join them for dinner at the camp restaurant. They were planning to have hamburgers. They seemed friendly, but I was still concerned they might play loud music. Hamish thanked them for the invitation to join them for dinner, but told them the kids needed an early night.

After Gideon and Hamish had showered in the men's facilities (apparently the password wasn't needed; someone had propped the door open, making life easier), we barbecued some sausages.

Sitting up in bed later, I could hear the distant sounds of music and laughter. I wished I was at the restaurant after all. It sounded fun. Hamish sat next to me and looked content as usual. He wasn't even thinking about anyone else. He was in his own world, writing his diary again. He writes it so people at home can know what we're doing, and what the weather's like. He posts photos to Facebook too, like the photo of Gideon next to the crocodile. I watched him tap on the keyboard. I wished I could be so simple and uncomplicated.

Saturday 21st July

Hamish decided he and Gideon needed to spend the day together. He was taking him to Wyndham to see the Big Crocodile. He wanted to talk to him in the car ride about things he would need to know if he was going to be a dad - things like being careful around fires, respect, and putting others before himself. Gideon was excited about the Big Crocodile, and some one-on-one time with Hamish.

That would give me a chance to wash our clothes. I bought some mangoes and three washing machine tokens from the town shop, then filled three washing machines.

While waiting for our laundry, the girls and I sat on one of the picnic benches, ate the mangoes and watched other campers come and go. I saw the policemen, standing in a little circle with the camp ranger. The handsome blond policeman noticed us. I had juice dripping down my chin and was pretty sure I had a piece of mango stuck to my left cheek. He waved. I wiped my cheek and smiled. The dark-haired policeman gave me a nod.

It seemed unlikely Mick would give them a hard time because of my complaint against them. He probably had a laugh to himself and forgot about the fire, or was planning to tell them, in a concerned but friendly manner next time he saw them. I shouldn't have given it a second thought.

The camp ranger came over and invited the girls to join in the day's activities, as part of a fundraiser. They were excited, especially about being led around on horseback by some junior camp rangers wearing purple polo shirts. Jenna wrote later:

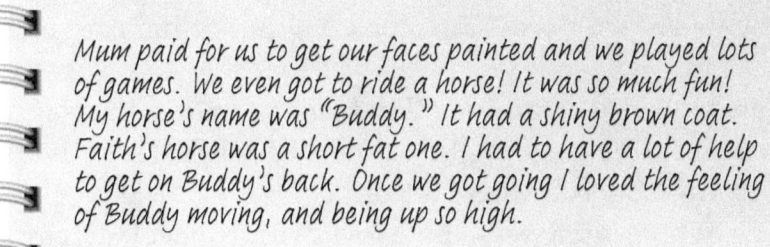

Mum paid for us to get our faces painted and we played lots of games. We even got to ride a horse! It was so much fun! My horse's name was "Buddy." It had a shiny brown coat. Faith's horse was a short fat one. I had to have a lot of help to get on Buddy's back. Once we got going I loved the feeling of Buddy moving, and being up so high.

The girls were thrilled to ride horses and raise money for the Flying Doctors at the same time. They chattered happily as we walked back to the tent. Hamish was sitting with our neighbours again. He was telling them about his trip with Gideon.

"He talked about dinosaurs and crocodiles for three hours." Hamish sat back in his chair and ran his hand over the top of his head. "I couldn't get a word in. I'm exhausted."

"Have a Pepsi." Alan handed Hamish a cold can, then turned to me. "Would you like one?"

"Thank you." I took the Pepsi and dragged a chair under their awning. Yesterday, I was wary of Alan and Ron. Today I felt relaxed, and competent, after being recognised by the local policemen, and operating the camp washing machines. I was sure I could handle the neighbours. "How was the Big Crocodile?" I asked Hamish.

"Big," he replied.

"Was that the one at Wyndham?" Alan asked.

Honestly. How many Big Crocodiles were there? Of course it was the Big Crocodile in Wyndham. What was Alan thinking? I opened the Pepsi and took a long drink.

Hamish nodded. "Big drive." Hamish definitely looked tired.

Alan leaned forward in his chair. "Did you get to Five Rivers lookout?"

Hamish shook his head.

"We're going tomorrow, aren't we Ron?"

"If you say so, boss." Ron took a drink of his rum and coke.

Alan looked at Hamish. "He lost his wife a year ago. Breast cancer. We're going to scatter her ashes. Five Rivers Lookout was special, wasn't it Ron?"

"The whole area was. She loved four-wheel driving, Angie did. Loved the bush too. So did the kids. Alan came sometimes. It's been a year since we lost her, but it's not getting any easier." Ron shook his head sadly.

I fidgeted nervously in my chair. "I'm so sorry," I said.

Hamish had become very still, his eyes focused on Ron. "Thanks for telling us your story. It sounds like you had some special times here."

"Thanks for listening," Ron said. Hamish nodded. I felt ashamed of having wanted to avoid them earlier.

Alan was looking across the grass. "Is that your son?" Alan asked. "The one threatening the other boy with a stick?"

I ran after Gideon and wrestled the stick off him. A group of girls giggled as I walked him back to the tent with me.

When I came back, Ron and Alan were getting ready to go out again. "You should come to the town with us tonight. There's a band. They do eighties covers. It's old stuff, but we like it."

"I think we'll be getting the kids to bed early again tonight," Hamish said.

We had another barbecue dinner. I appreciated every bit of it: cooking the food, eating it, watching the night fall, putting the kids to bed. Listening to the music later, I remembered Ron and Alan and hoped they were enjoying themselves.

Sunday 22nd July

This morning I read:

> "When you judge the law, you are not keeping it, but sitting in judgement on it. There is only one Lawgiver and Judge, the one who is able to save and destroy." (James 4:11-12).

I was glad God was the judge. Who was I to judge others? I'd assumed that the policemen were responsible, because of their uniforms, then got upset when they didn't do what I thought they should. Then I'd worried Ron and Alan would disturb us, because they had long beards and an old car. They'd been no trouble at all.

I even got it wrong with Hamish, the person I knew better than anyone. Who was I to think I could judge people I knew nothing about?

There was a freedom in not judging. The world felt bigger and less constricting. A burden was lifted.

We planned an exciting last day for our Gibb River Road adventure. We would drive to Zebedee Springs, which involved crossing the Pentecost River. I'd never driven through a river before. Driving the dusty tracks had seemed uneventful and hadn't lived up to the hype. But driving through a river? That sounded like *real* four-wheel driving.

As we approached the river crossing, Hamish explained the purpose of the car's snorkel, the long tube that runs alongside the front windscreen and sticks up above the car, like a human snorkel for swimming. Apparently, the engine needs air, just like we do. The suspension lift turned out to be important too. If we hadn't gotten the car lifted up, we would have water pouring in the cracks under the doors, he said. I didn't need convincing. I knew ordinary cars weren't meant to drive through water.

The engine groaned as Hamish drove down the steep embankment. We were all quiet, as if the car needed to concentrate. Then the car drove gracefully through the water, like a dog that could swim without being taught. It was wonderful, looking at the high water rippling just below my door.

On the other side, we found the car park for the Springs.

The children were amazed that it was possible to drive to a swimming hole, without then having to hike for several hours before they could swim. Faith wrote in her journal:

> We went to a warm water spring. It was a very small walk, only ten metres. We found a private pool: it was warm and deep. It was like a bath.

Gideon was excited to discover how warm the water was. He was thrilled to finally have the freedom in water that he'd seen the girls have.

He lay on his back in the water with his arms stretched out either side. "Look Mum," he yelled, to make sure I could see him floating.

He rolled over and reached down to touch the pebbles on the bottom. Then he swam, arms thrashing through the water, then lay on his stomach to demonstrate forward floating.

When Gideon got tired, he wrapped his arms around my neck. We looked up at the circle of blue sky framed by the tops of the palm trees surrounding us.

Back at El Questro township, Hamish and I celebrated our last day on the Gibb River Road with coffee and cake. We bought the kids Icy Poles. They complained bitterly that we had coffee and cake and they only had Icy Poles. Hamish and I looked at each other knowingly. The kids had no idea about how much money we had, and the cost of car repairs. They only know a part of the big picture. We generously let them have a few mouthfuls of cake, and a spoonful each of cappuccino froth.

We'd made it through one of the toughest legs on our journey. The car and trailer had taken a beating on the corrugated roads: the car running board was attached with a bit of glue, we'd nearly lost our petrol can, and the electrics in the camper trailer had burned up and died. Thank goodness we'd be back on sealed roads tomorrow. The car would be grateful. As for me, I'd gotten lost, realised my temper was *still* a problem, and learnt about not judging others. I was excited to see what adventures lay ahead.

Chapter 13

Monday 23rd July

I was determined not to judge anyone today. It was better to leave other people to God, who knew everything from the big picture to the tiniest detail. After leaving the Gibb River Road, we no longer bumped along the gravel, but travelled smoothly on the asphalt. It seemed like anything was possible, now that I'd turned away from unnecessary worries and judgement.

Hamish remembered to increase the tyre pressure. He pulled into a rest stop before the turn-off onto the freeway and found his portable tire-inflator in the back of the car. Once the pressure was right, he turned the key in the ignition. The engine made a soft whirring sound. He tried a few more times. The sound got softer. Eventually the sound turned whiny and then the engine gave up trying to start altogether.

Hamish never copes well with car trouble. He panics, like that time we got bogged at the beach and he didn't know what to do. This time he groaned and struck his fist on the steering wheel. I tried not to judge him for his irrational behaviour. I needed to be the strong one.

Anyway the solution was obvious. "We'll just ring the roadside assistance service," I said.

But it wasn't as straightforward as I thought. I couldn't find my phone, and Hamish's phone had zero reception. We were still in the outback, after all.

Then I remembered something. "Didn't you buy a satellite phone in case we got stuck without mobile coverage?"

Hamish leaned over and took a black box out of the glove compartment. The phone inside the box was a brick, like a mobile phone from twenty years ago.

"Ring Mum," Hamish said. "She'll be able to help."

Hamish's mum May was always calm in a crisis, but she was 4000 km away. "What can she do Hamish? I'll ring the breakdown service myself."

Except I didn't know the number for the breakdown service. Never mind, I'd figure out what to do about that in a minute. I switched on the power button, then I held the brick to my ear. There was no dial tone.

"Maybe you have to put in a code. Read the instruction manual." Hamish banged his head against the headrest.

I felt around the inside of the box. There were no instructions. Hamish sighed. He'd apparently forgotten to ask how to use the satellite phone when he bought it. I would have to come up with a solution, but I was out of ideas.

"Let's pray," Hamish suggested.

"That's good." I nodded. I should have thought of it myself. I'd been so caught up in showing Hamish I could solve the problem, that I'd forgotten about God.

Hamish bowed his head and closed his eyes. "Please help us Lord," he said quietly. "We're stuck and we don't know what to do."

I nodded encouragingly. "And please start the engine," I added, "or send someone to help. Amen."

"Amen," said the kids sweetly from the back seat. Hamish sat up straight. He looked better. The colour had returned to his cheeks.

He tried to start the car again. There was no sound at all this time, just the clicking of the key in the ignition. Hamish sighed.

"Don't worry, Dad, God will send someone to help us,"

said Faith. I hoped she was right. Then I saw a white minibus pull into the rest stop behind us. It was empty except for the driver.

"Look!" Faith yelled. "I told you so, Dad!"

A large man got out of the bus. He wore a black polo shirt and shorts and dusty boots. He had big bags under his eyes. He wore a badge under his collar that said "Great Outback Adventure Tours."

I got out of the car and walked toward him.

"G'day," he said. He pulled out a pack of cigarettes and lit one.

"Hi there. Our car won't start. I don't suppose you could take a look." I glanced over to where Hamish had propped open the bonnet and was staring at the engine.

"Sorry, I'm no good with engines. I just drive."

That wasn't the response I was expecting, but he was the helper we'd been given. We just needed to have faith.

Hamish had joined us. "Could you try to jump start our engine?"

"Are your lights working?"

"Yes, I just tested them," Hamish said. He sounded hopeful.

"Well, it's not the battery, if the lights are working. No point trying to jump start."

Hamish and I stood around, wondering what to do, while he finished his cigarette. The kids jumped down from the car. The girls swung upside down on a railing. Gideon squatted in the dirt and looked for stones. Once the man had finished his cigarette and ground out the butt with his boot, he got some jumper leads out of the bus and said he'd try to start our car after all. Our engine rumbled to life.

The man smiled. "Looks like that's done the trick," he said. "Gee, you would have been in real trouble without me."

Hamish smiled back at him. "You're a real blessing," he said. "We prayed for someone to help us." He shook the man's hand.

"Really? I've never been an answer to prayer." He patted Gideon on the top of his head. "I don't usually stop here, but one of the tourists complained the bus smelled like cigarettes. So here I am, smoking at a rest stop instead of in the bus. You're *very* lucky."

We drove toward the freeway. Hamish was still smiling with relief. I was proud of him. He'd panicked, as usual, but in the end he was the one who remembered to pray.

Hamish was nervous about stopping and starting the car again. We decided to drive straight through to Katherine, stopping only once so the kids could go to the loo, while Hamish kept the engine running. It meant arriving very late, so I booked the Katherine Gardens Motel, the cheapest I could find.

In spite of the long drive, I was delighted to have a night off camping.

The kids were excited too. After we'd eventually arrived and paid for our spot, Faith ran ahead to find our room. She came running back to us, eyes shining.

"There's two double beds!" she told Jenna. "*And* we've got our very own bathroom!"

Jenna ran after her. She too was amazed at the thought of having a bathroom we didn't have to share with anyone.

We ordered pizza and sat up in bed to watch the children's channel. I remembered my phone was still missing. While the others watched cartoons, I took Hamish's phone to the car so I could call myself. I heard a faint ring coming from the camper trailer. To get my phone, I would have to unzip the cover, unfold and open the trailer tent and crawl inside. There was no way I was opening up the tent when I didn't have to sleep in it.

After the cartoons finished, the children argued over where to sleep. Gideon tried out the top bunk, but it was high up, and too far from the rest of us. He came back down the ladder and hopped into one of the double beds with me. Faith stayed on the bottom bunk bed. It was cosy having the five of us in one long line, in the same room, without any canvas walls between us.

Once the children had fallen asleep, Hamish whispered to me from the double bed next to me that he thought we should drive to Darwin tomorrow.

"No way!" I told him. "We can't risk the car breaking down on such a long drive. Let's find a mechanic in Katherine. Isn't that what we're here for?"

Hamish said a few more things. The mattress was soft and my pillowcase smelt of eucalyptus. I didn't want to spoil the enjoyment of finding myself unexpectedly in a motel. I ignored Hamish and fell asleep.

Tuesday 24th July

I woke up thinking about Hamish's idea of going to Darwin. At first it had sounded ridiculous: Darwin was another 300 km away. But this morning it made sense. Darwin was a large city, the capital of the Northern Territory, so there would be plenty of mechanics to look at the car and trailer. And if the car was out of action for a while, there'd be public transport to get us around. We might even be able to go to Kakadu National Park, which was apparently beautiful.

When Hamish woke up, I whispered to him I thought we should go to Darwin after all.

"There'll be a choice of mechanics to look at the car and trailer, and we can get buses while the car's being fixed."

Hamish was glad I'd seen the sense of his idea. Apparently, he'd already mentioned all of that, but I'd fallen asleep.

If we were going to Darwin, that meant getting organised. I grabbed Hamish's phone and looked up caravan parks. I found one that was close to the centre and public transport. The receptionist said they didn't take bookings, but if we arrived by 1 pm, they would be able to fit us in.

Then I searched for a mechanic who could fix four-wheel drives and knew something about electrics. I found one not far from the centre of Darwin who told me he would try to repair the car before the long weekend. He knew an auto-electrician who could fix the trailer, but we would have to wait for that.

"Long weekend? What long weekend?"

"Friday's the Darwin Show. It's a public holiday in the Northern Territory. I'll do my best to fit your car in before that. The trailer will have to wait."

I said Hamish would bring the car over this afternoon. I was pleased. If Darwin had a show, just like Melbourne, it really *was* a major centre.

We made the most of the motel room. The kids had a bubble bath and splashed each other, while Hamish and I ate toast and watched the news. The main item was the Darwin Show. People were coming from all over the Territory to take part. I wasn't sure I wanted to take the children. We'd been to the Melbourne Show once and the show bags cost a fortune. It was probably best if we didn't mention it.

It was a strange feeling not having to pack up everything. I put our pyjamas and toothbrushes in the one bag we'd carried in with us. It was so *easy*.

The car started the first time Hamish tried. He was visibly relieved. I was hoping for a quiet pleasant journey, to continue the relaxed feeling of leaving the motel without packing up a tent. But Hamish wanted the kids to make up for the night watching TV and write in their diaries. They complained. I got a headache. Eventually some diary writing was completed. Then the books were put aside and we got excited as signs of Darwin came into view. It was a *real* city, with multi-storey buildings, and big wide streets cut in half by traffic islands with palm trees.

The caravan park was on the main road. I told the young receptionist we wanted to stay until next Tuesday.

"I can't do that long" she said. "We're completely full. I can fit you in near the barbecues until Saturday. Then we've got a booking."

"I thought you didn't take bookings? You said just turn up."

She shifted from one foot to another. "We don't take bookings *anymore*. We *used to* take bookings. Someone booked the spot near the barbecues, and they're arriving on Saturday. Come down on Saturday morning and we'll find you another spot."

"Why don't you find a new spot for the people arriving on Saturday?"

"I can't do that." She sighed. I noticed her forehead was shining in the heat. "Look, why don't you go and have a look. See what you think?"

It was a good site, nice and flat, with the barbecues on one side and an enormous fig tree providing shade on the other. About twenty metres beyond the tree, I could see a blue and purple playground. That was a bonus. The children would love it. Then there was a loud noise, like an enormous clap of thunder.

"Does that happen all the time?" Hamish called out to one of our neighbours, who was reading a magazine under a tree.

"Yes, it's always noisy here." A plane flew overhead, casting a shadow. "We're right next to the airport!" he shouted. "And the showgrounds!"

Ah, of course, the Darwin Show. The blue and purple playground was actually a jumping castle inside the showgrounds. When I looked closely, I could see it was behind a wire fence. The kids had already discovered the showgrounds. Jenna wrote in her diary:

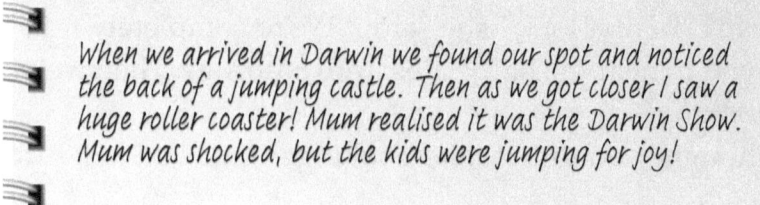

When we arrived in Darwin we found our spot and noticed the back of a jumping castle. Then as we got closer I saw a huge roller coaster! Mum realised it was the Darwin Show. Mum was shocked, but the kids were jumping for joy!

We booked in. There was no point arguing with the woman at reception about having to move on Saturday, and now the kids had discovered the Show, we might as well be near it. We'd be able to walk there.

We set up the trailer tent, then Hamish dropped the car off at the mechanic. When he returned, we grilled sausages on the park barbecue. It was almost peaceful. The Show didn't start until Thursday, so the bouncy castle and the roller coaster were deserted. Then some young Germans camped next to us and started playing dance music. It had no words, and the same beat over and over. It was annoying.

I couldn't sleep. I'd retrieved my phone from the pocket next to the bed. While Hamish slept, I searched the internet for "Motels in Darwin." Because our tent was attached to the trailer, we'd need somewhere to sleep while the trailer electrics were repaired. The cheapest motel I could find was $300 per night. Perhaps we would need to buy another tent.

I looked up camping shops. There were lots close by,

probably because people camped at nearby Kakadu National Park. Kakadu was known for its spectacular gorges and waterfalls, and ancient cave paintings. I hoped we would be able to go. The challenge was that we were visiting missionaries Jim and Debbie Smith next week. They were squeezing us in between other commitments. We would be cutting it fine to get the trailer repaired *and* go to Kakadu.

But what if we went to Kakadu *while* the trailer was being repaired? If we bought a tent, we'd have somewhere to sleep. And since we had to pack up and move within the caravan park on Saturday anyway, we might as well go to Kakadu.

It was a brilliant idea. I tore a page out of Gideon's scrapbook and scribbled down an itinerary:

Thursday: Buy a tent.
Friday: Take the kids to the Darwin show. (Packed lunches may reduce the cost? Hamish will approve).
Saturday: Drive to Kakadu.
Sunday: Return to Darwin Caravan Park.
Monday: Drop off trailer at auto-electrician. (Could also get the front windscreen repaired for the second time?)
Tuesday: Morning: Drop off car for the general service. Hamish is insisting.
Afternoon: Take bus to collect car, drive to auto-mechanic to collect trailer.

I was delighted how many things we could achieve in six days. I put the piece of paper in the canvas pocket next to the bed to share with Hamish tomorrow.

Wednesday 25th July

I read from my Bible app this morning.

> *"What causes fights and quarrels among you? Don't they come from the desires that battle within you? You want something but you don't get it. You kill and covet, but you cannot have what you want." (James 4:1-2).*

I was pretty sure my six-day plan would avoid fights and quarrels. I'd considered everyone's needs: the kids would go to the Show, I'd go to Kakadu, and Hamish would get the car serviced. Reading James was working.

When Hamish woke up, he was in a hurry to go into the centre of town to look around. I would have to wait to share my plan with him.

We caught a bus on the main street all the way to the Smith Street Mall. After looking at the souvenir shops and letting Gideon explore the playground, we found a food court for lunch and shared a butter chicken with naan bread. It was so good after having been on a diet of barbecues for so many weeks. It was another bus ride to collect the car. We walked the last few blocks, past warehouses and factories, eventually finding our car behind a wire fence like a forgotten zoo animal. The mechanic explained that he'd had to replace the car's starter motor, which had gotten wet. I remembered crossing the Pentecost River near El Questro. Even with big snorkels and special lifts, it was like I'd suspected - cars were not *really* meant to go in water.

Hamish looked ill as he used the EFTPOS machine to pay the $600 bill. I was glad I'd come up with a way to spare us the cost of a motel while the trailer was being repaired. I was looking forward to cheering Hamish up with my money-saving ideas.

Back at camp, we cooked another barbecue, and after putting the kids to bed, I was finally able to present Hamish with the itinerary. I unfolded the crumpled piece of paper from the trailer tent and read to Hamish aloud. I omitted the part about Hamish insisting on getting the care serviced.

Hamish tapped his fingers against the table. "That's a lot to do in six days. Do we have to go to Kakadu?"

"Of course. There's ancient Aboriginal rock art. And gorges and waterfalls."

Hamish rubbed his forehead. "The thing is I'm tired. I just want to stay in Darwin and chill out for a while."

I was a little worried. Hamish was never tired. That wasn't good. But I ignored the thought and persisted with my agenda to see the waterfalls and rock art. "Everyone goes to Kakadu. Even my mum has been there."

Hamish wasn't persuaded. He usually didn't care what other people did. He shook his head. "I'm not sure about buying a tent either," he added. "It seems like a waste of money. I'm going to see if we can hire one."

Hire a tent? Whoever heard of hiring a tent? I was sure that was not possible. I left him sitting outside and lay down on the bed.

I stewed over our conversation. Hamish should have been glad I'd come up with such a great plan. Why didn't he want to go to Kakadu? We'd done the Gibb River Road journey, which was arduous and rocky. The poor car had nearly drowned crossing a river. Kakadu was on sealed roads, with no river crossings. It would be *much* easier, and it was just as spectacular. That's why *everybody* went there.

I could feel myself getting more angry. My heart raced and I felt hot. I didn't want to continue down that path and end up yelling again. I prayed, asking God to help me. A verse from James came to mind.

"You cannot get what you want so you quarrel and fight. Submit yourselves then to God." (James 4:1-7).

It was obvious. I was holding on too tightly to what *I* wanted to do. I needed to give up going to Kakadu. I found Hamish researching on the computer. I told him we didn't need to go after all. I apologised for being pushy.

Hamish gave me a hug. "You wouldn't believe what I found," he said. There's a place north of the city that hires out camping equipment. It's $10 a night for a family-sized tent. Perfect for when we get the trailer fixed."

"Really?" I looked at the website. It was true. According to her description, a young woman had started a camping hire business as "something to do" while she was at home with a baby. Well that was one problem solved. We wouldn't have to spend $100 on a tent while the trailer was repaired. Giving up my plans was paying off already.

Thursday 26th July

I had lots to do today, including organising the second windscreen repair that I'd been putting off for two weeks now, and washing our stinky clothes. I read from Chapter 4 of James again to strengthen me:

"Now listen, you who say, "Today or tomorrow we will go to this or that city, spend a year there, carry on business and make money." Why you don't even know what will happen tomorrow. You are a mist that appears for a little while and then vanishes." (James 4:13-14)

I thought of the six-day schedule I'd been convinced we

should stick to. It was a relief to give up on my plans. I'd been wrong to hold on to them.

I found Hamish scrubbing the barbecue plate still covered in grease from the night before. A plane flew over us.

When the plane noise stopped, Hamish told me he'd had an idea. He placed the barbecue plate back in its place. "What if we went to Kakadu *after* we visit Jim and Debbie in Kalkaringi."

Kalkaringi was a two-day drive south of Darwin. I had a mental picture of a map with a route marked out—a series of arrows pointing all the way down to Kalkaringi, making a hairpin turn and pointing back up again, before turning around again. Like a paper clip. It would involve a lot of extra driving. Still, I did want to see those waterfalls and cave paintings.

"I've thought it through," Hamish said. "We can fit it in and still be back for the kid's school at the beginning of September."

A thrill went through me. I gave him a hug.

I definitely owed it to Hamish to get some things done. I filled three washing machines. Then I rang the insurance company. The cost of the windscreen would be covered, even though it was our second windscreen claim in six weeks. I booked in to have the glass replaced at midday on Saturday, giving us time to move spots in the caravan park that morning. A weight lifted off me.

Hamish helped me peg our clothes out in the courtyard behind the laundry shed. The Show had started. We could hear shouts and screams, and through the fence we could see the roller coaster cars dipping and diving as they hurtled around the track. A plane flew overhead, drowning out the screams.

Hamish shouted over the noise. "I had a message from Kathy Roberts. She saw my photos on Facebook. She's living in Darwin now. She wants to meet us at the Show tomorrow. Their kids are performing. Some Irish dancing thing."

Kathy had been part of the youth group Hamish ran twenty years ago. She was married to a guy in the army, and had her own large family now, even though she was fifteen years younger than Hamish.

"That's incredible," I told Hamish. "It's the first time you hear from her in twenty years, and we happen to be camped next to the Show where her kids are dancing tomorrow." Giving up on my own plans was definitely working.

"It's amazing alright. Especially the Irish dancing part." Hamish shook his head. "How can anyone do Irish dancing in this heat?"

The clothes dried in no time. After Hamish had helped me take them off the line, and pack them away, we decided to have another break from the barbecue. We drove to the Mindil markets, a night market of food and clothes and jewellery stalls, right on the beach. Jenna described it in her diary:

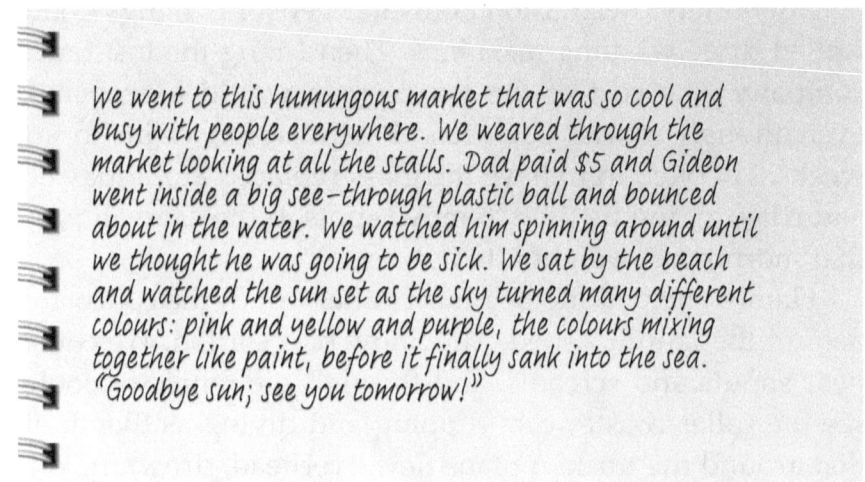

> We went to this humungous market that was so cool and busy with people everywhere. We weaved through the market looking at all the stalls. Dad paid $5 and Gideon went inside a big see-through plastic ball and bounced about in the water. We watched him spinning around until we thought he was going to be sick. We sat by the beach and watched the sun set as the sky turned many different colours: pink and yellow and purple, the colours mixing together like paint, before it finally sank into the sea. "Goodbye sun; see you tomorrow!"

It was beautiful watching the sun set. The kids were so excited about the market and watching Gideon spinning around in the see-through ball that they talked all the way home. Hamish asked them to be quiet. They got louder. Hamish tried to reverse into a tight spot next to the camper trailer. The car bounced into something and we were thrown forward. Hamish yelled at the children. They stopped talking. Then he got out to look for damage.

"We've broken the back windscreen," he told me.

"You're joking!" I said. "You *are* joking, aren't you?" I noticed Hamish's serious expression. My heart sank. "You're *not* joking."

Hamish had reversed into a power pole. Unlike the front windscreen, with its large star-shaped chip, the back window had cracked all over like a piece of honeycomb. Hamish taped a windscreen sun protector over the glass. I rang the insurance company right away. We were covered. It turned out there was no limit in our policy on how many windscreens we could break and have replaced, which was just as well. I arranged to have it fixed on Saturday afternoon at 12.30, straight after the front one.

It was another noisy night: the rush of roller coasters, the shouting and screaming of the show-goers and the German boys' repetitive music. Surprisingly, I wasn't bothered by the noise. I thought of the beautiful pink and purple sunset, and the people having fun at the Show, and how we were meeting an old friend there tomorrow. If I'd tried to organise a catch-up, I couldn't have arranged it more efficiently.

It made me think of James.

"Why you don't even know what will happen tomorrow. What is your life? You are a mist that appears for a little while and then vanishes." (James 4:14)

I liked thinking of myself as a mist. It was relaxing.

Chapter 14

Friday 27th July

It turned out the entrance to the Show was a long walk along the highway. There was a large queue of people waiting to pay the hefty admission fee. We arrived late to meet Kathy, who was sitting at a plastic table with her two youngest children, but we were just in time to see the other two performing.

The Irish dancing group wore black tights and green leotards, even though it was thirty-five degrees. Jenna and Faith watched open-mouthed as the girls jumped and kicked their legs in the air in unison without moving their arms. They were very impressive. I couldn't believe that anyone could wear tights and kick their legs that high in the sticky heat.

After the performance, the kids ate snacks Kathy had packed into Tupperware boxes.

"That was amazing girls," I told them.

The girls nodded. They were busy eating the carrot and cheese sticks Kathy had prepared.

"I remember you telling me you wanted five kids," I reminded Kathy.

"Well, she's not far off,' said Hamish. Her toddler shoved some cheese in her mouth.

Kathy was the daughter of the vicar at the first church Hamish and I attended. He and his wife had adopted Kathy and later Daniel. I recalled Kathy as a happy but thoughtful twelve-year-old, telling me that adoption had its benefits and its challenges. She seemed to be thriving as a mother. Her four-year-old climbed into her lap.

We reminisced about old times and caught up on everything that had happened since we'd last seen each other. Kathy's army husband Matt was away a lot on service. It was hard work having so many kids and being a solo parent for weeks at a time. They lived a simple life, she told us. I looked at the homemade muffins and fruit salad the kids were now hoeing into. It looked like she was doing a wonderful job.

The kids had finished their snacks and were restless. Kathy wanted to go home so her toddler could sleep. I gave her a hug. Hamish said we'd stay in touch. The girls said a shy goodbye and Jenna complimented the oldest two on their dancing.

We looked at cake contests and school art exhibits, and stalls advertising weird and wonderful products. Gideon even held a baby crocodile at a stand promoting four-wheel-drive accessories. But the kid's highlight was of course choosing show bags and going on the scariest rides they could handle. It cost more than a night in a motel, even with a packed lunch. But it felt like money well-spent.

Jenna wrote later:

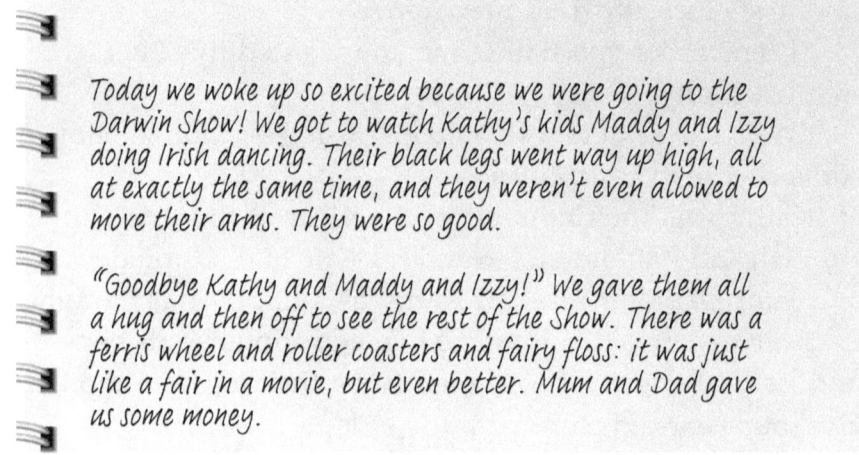

Today we woke up so excited because we were going to the Darwin Show! We got to watch Kathy's kids Maddy and Izzy doing Irish dancing. Their black legs went way up high, all at exactly the same time, and they weren't even allowed to move their arms. They were so good.

"Goodbye Kathy and Maddy and Izzy!" We gave them all a hug and then off to see the rest of the Show. There was a ferris wheel and roller coasters and fairy floss: it was just like a fair in a movie, but even better. Mum and Dad gave us some money.

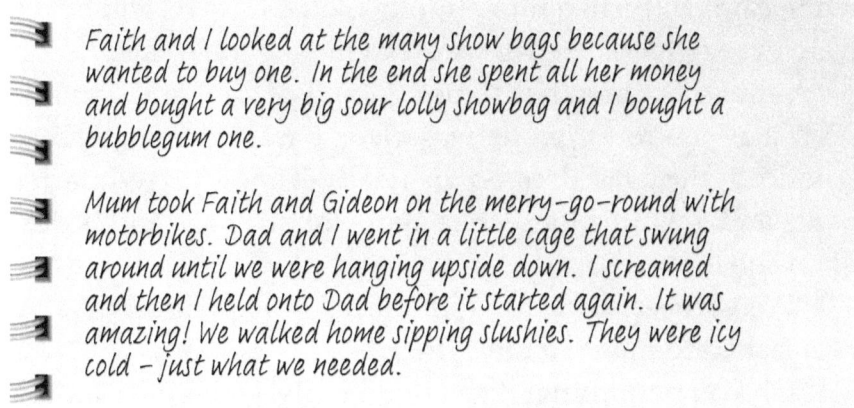

Faith and I looked at the many show bags because she wanted to buy one. In the end she spent all her money and bought a very big sour lolly showbag and I bought a bubblegum one.

Mum took Faith and Gideon on the merry-go-round with motorbikes. Dad and I went in a little cage that swung around until we were hanging upside down. I screamed and then I held onto Dad before it started again. It was amazing! We walked home sipping slushies. They were icy cold – just what we needed.

I was determined not to plan anything from now on. I would be like a mist. If God could put us next to the Darwin Show, at the same time a friend we hadn't seen for twenty years invited us to meet her there, who was I to try to improve on that?

Saturday 28th July

Hamish picked up the hire tent first thing this morning, so we could move into it after we'd made space for the caravan that had booked into our spot. He planned to pack up early, before going to get the windscreens repaired at 12 o'clock.

I talked to the woman at reception, in case she'd changed her mind about having to move us. She hadn't. She gave us the corner site which had just been vacated by the German boys, who were heading to Jabiru.

Hamish set up the hire tent on the new site, and we began moving our stuff onto the grass on the old site to make it easy to pack up the trailer.

It was half past ten when a Land Cruiser towing a shiny

white caravan turned into our old spot. Our beds and boxes were everywhere, like we were having a garage sale.

A slim woman in her sixties got out of the Land Cruiser.

"Gee, you're *early*." It was clear I was not impressed. I noticed she was dressed in neatly-ironed three-quarter pants and a white blouse. She stared at our bags and boxes. Then she looked at me.

"We've been here for four days," I explained. 'We've been asked to move to the corner."

"Oh you poor things," she said kindly. I felt guilty for being angry with her. "It's such a shame," the neatly-dressed woman continued. "We would have liked the spot on the corner. It's opposite our friends we're meeting here."

A tall man with grey hair had gotten out of the car and joined us. "Yes, that would have been much better," he agreed.

My shoulders sagged. Why couldn't the caravan park have been more flexible?

The new arrivals caught up with their friends while I helped Hamish carry the rest of our belongings to the new site. We'd done the hard bit already, it would be worse arranging to swap back. Hamish took the girls with him to get the windscreens repaired.

The tent Hamish hired had a small section at the back for the kids to sleep in, and an annexe at the front for our food boxes. The inside of the tent was cramped and hot. I bought Gideon an Icy Pole from the caravan park store and we sat in the shade on Gideon's sleeping bag.

James was right. I was like a mist. I had no control over anything. Not even where to camp in the caravan park. I took out my phone and opened a game Jenna had shown me called Fruit Blitz. The aim is to slice fruit before it explodes. It's pointless, but fun. Bananas, pineapples and mangoes whizzed across the screen. I sliced fruit with my finger until the juice ran out. The more fruit I sliced, the higher score I got. It was very satisfying. Between games, I gradually dragged beds and boxes inside the tent until it was set up.

After Hamish and the girls arrived back and everyone was settled, I picked up the game again. Each time I got a good score the screen erupted in little stars. It was mesmerising. I discovered a red spiky fruit that earned bonus points. I avoided the bombs. I tried harder and harder to slice fruit and avoid bombs. I kept slicing fruit until the early hours of the morning. The worry of having to get the trailer repaired and the irritation of having to move were forgotten.

Chapter 15

Sunday 29th July

I played Fruit Blitz all morning. It's fantastic. I remembered reading somewhere that games are good for mental agility. I passed 500 points. I was thrilled.

Hamish interrupted me to tell me he wanted to go to Leanyer Water Park. It was annoying as I just wanted to slice fruit. The water park had three massive slides. Jenna persuaded me to go on the yellow one, called "Go Bananas". I got water up my nose. I came home to a message inviting me to pay money to buy bonus fruit.

I couldn't improve on my 500. Realised I should have bought extra fruit. I'll keep trying.

Monday 30th July

I accepted an invitation to play Fruit Blitz online from someone called "Fruit Slayer." They're amazing. I couldn't beat them. We took the kids to a crocodile zoo in the centre of Darwin. The girls swam next to crocodiles they could see through glass. I came home to eleven requests to play Fruit Blitz. I matched with "Strawberry Shortcake".

Tuesday 31st July

I received a message from "Fruit Slayer" asking me to play in a tournament. I didn't win, but I'm definitely improving.

The car had to have its service. We caught the bus to town. We took the kids to see *Ice Age 4* at the cinemas. There was a teenage woolly mammoth in it called Peaches. I lost track of the story, wondering if I was missing something important on Fruit Blitz. We picked up the car and trailer. The electrics on the trailer were sorted. Hamish was happy.

I played Fruit Blitz until the early hours of the morning. I couldn't beat my previous score of 500. The games got harder and I got more and more messages asking me to spend money. I only stopped playing because my eyes were so sore I couldn't keep them open. I think I'm addicted.

Wednesday 1st August

I had to stop playing. I read somewhere that games like Fruit Blitz aren't good for mental sharpness. They're actually just a waste of time. My eyes were still sore this morning and my head hurt. I received an invitation to pay for Fruit Blitz VIP membership. I ignored it.

I read the end of James Chapter 4 again. After the verse about life being like a mist, there's a section on doing good.

> *"Instead, you ought to say, "If it is the Lord's will we will live and do this or that. As it is you boast in your arrogant schemes. All such boasting is evil. If anyone, then, knows the good they ought to do and doesn't do it, it is sin for them." (James 4:13-17)*

I noticed the word "boast." Perhaps that's where I'd been going wrong. I was convinced I had the best plan for our itinerary, and got angry with Hamish for not agreeing with me. But making no plans wasn't the answer. Since I'd decided not to make *any* plans, I'd gotten addicted to slicing fruit on a screen. What had I missed? Perhaps the best way to live was to set goals, but accept that God may have other ideas. Now I knew "the good I ought to do," I needed to do it.

It was a relief to make plans again, especially as we were heading to Kalkaringi. I needed to be useful to Jim and Debbie, or I wouldn't have an answer for James: *"Faith by itself, if it is not accompanied by action, is dead." (James 2:17).*

We thanked the caravan park staff for looking after us, returned our miracle hire tent, and drove back to Katherine where we stayed in a small and shabby motel room with peeling paint on the walls. (The luxury motel we'd booked during our previous visit to Katherine was booked out).

It seemed appropriate to be staying in humble surroundings. I didn't want to be distracted by luxuries on the eve of our missionary visit.

Thursday 2nd August

I wondered how Jim and Debbie were feeling about our visit. They were pastors in the Baptist church. Three years ago, they'd left their three adult children behind in Melbourne to start life in an indigenous community in the Northern Territory. They visited our church when they came back to Melbourne to see their kids. Jim told the congregation they hadn't gone to the outback to make a church like ours. They hadn't gone to bring God to the people either. God was already there. I couldn't wait to get a better understanding of what he meant.

Kalkaringi is 480 km south-west of Katherine. The big multi-laned highway out of Katherine dwindled to single lanes. Then the road narrowed to a one-way dusty track.

Hamish pulled over to give way to a road train stirring up dust as it headed toward us.

Late in the afternoon, we crossed a bridge over a small river and saw a sign for Kalkaringi. Further on an official looking blue and white sign read "Prescribed area. Absolutely no alcohol permitted." Hamish found some expensive port, a Christmas present from his parents, he'd been planning to have with cheese one night when the children were in bed. *Surely we could just keep it. Who would know?* Hamish upended the bottle and I watched as the expensive liquid spread over the rocks and seeped into the dust. My irritation changed to excitement. It seemed so radical to throw out something so expensive, a bit like burning money. I felt strangely alive.

We passed square houses made of breeze blocks painted in reds and browns to match the dirt. A group of children waved, then talked over each other with their enthusiasm to give us directions to Jim and Debbie's place at the end of the street.

Jim and Debbie were sitting on their verandah. Debbie was taller than I remembered, and had a smile that spread across her whole face. Jim was also smiling behind his beard, and they both hugged each of us warmly. Jim talked with great interest to the children, like they were the most important people he'd ever met, while Debbie showed us around the little weatherboard house.

After we had set up camp in their front yard, and enjoyed a welcome meal Debbie had made for us, Jim showed the kids his collection of children's videos. Jim told us he loved kids, and missed their children and grandchildren back in Melbourne. I was anxious to find ways we could help with their missionary work, but I couldn't think of anything I could do. I remembered an email from Debbie in which she'd mentioned the need for house repairs at Lajamanu, the other community they worked with.

"Hamish is really good at renovating. He can do anything," I offered helpfully.

Jim sat back in his chair and considered Hamish. "Our house at Lajamanu needs a *lot* of work. Are you any good at replacing weatherboards?"

Hamish nodded.

"That's a pity. We're not going to Lajamanu this week."

Oh no, I had been counting on Hamish being useful.

Jim stroked his beard thoughtfully. Eventually his eyes lit up. "Can you use a chainsaw?"

It was agreed that Hamish could have the job of sawing up some wood for the church camp taking place that weekend. *Thank goodness; we wouldn't be a complete burden.*

Jim explained in his slow quiet voice that they were here to support the indigenous community to run church their way, and had no interest in recreating a Western church in Kalkaringi. This approach meant respecting the indigenous language, and culture, and acknowledging their traditional system of elders. The indigenous elders were leaders in the church, and were the decision makers in all matters. Jim and Debbie provided training and encouragement to the elders. They often met outdoors. Jim had found the indigenous people were more receptive in the bush. Jim offered to ask the elders if we could attend the church camp, which was to be held not far from the town. We said we would be honoured to go if the elders agreed.

Later that night I thought about Jim and Debbie sitting on the verandah, and the warm welcome, and Jim telling us they were here to support the indigenous church, not run it for them. It no longer seemed so important to find ways to help out; perhaps the church didn't need us after all. But then I remembered James Chapter 2 on faith and deeds. I decided I should do my best to do some good deeds tomorrow. And I needed to do more than just offer Hamish's help. I needed to be useful myself. Perhaps I could help in the op shop where Debbie had suggested we visit her first thing in the morning.

Friday 3rd August

I couldn't believe it when I woke up and checked the time. It was nine o'clock already! The op shop was open between 9 and 11. I woke the girls, who wanted to swap some of their clothes. By the time they'd sorted through their donations, it was nearly 10 o'clock!

We crossed the road to the church building, which served as church, community centre, and twice a week as op shop. We found Debbie cheerfully sorting through a box of knitted beanies donated by a church in Melbourne. She had almost finished going through new donations but still had one small bag that I could sort through for her. I think she could easily have finished her work already but had set aside the bag especially. Debbie chatted to customers and helped the girls choose some new T-shirts to replace the ones they were tired of wearing. Debbie seemed so efficient, yet comfortable and at ease, and great to talk to as well. I was in awe of her and wondered how I could possibly be any real help.

Back at the house, Jim told us that the elders had agreed we could go to the church camp. We spent the afternoon packing up the trailer, then we followed Jim and Debbie in their four-wheel drive towing a trailer full of wood that the elders had collected (Hamish's chainsawing wasn't needed after all as it turned out) to a spot ten minutes out of town that Jim and one of the elders had selected earlier.

At the bush campsite, the ground was dry and dusty. There were only a few grasses, and shrubs along a creek on one side, and a line of small eucalyptus trees in the distance where the sun was starting to set. We chose a spot on the west side to set up the trailer tent. Jim went back to Kalkaringi to collect some of the church members. Debbie told us she was going to start a fire. We thought she meant a campfire for cooking. To our amazement, Debbie struck a match and set fire to a grassy area near our camp spot. The fire spread at a rapid rate. Jenna wrote:

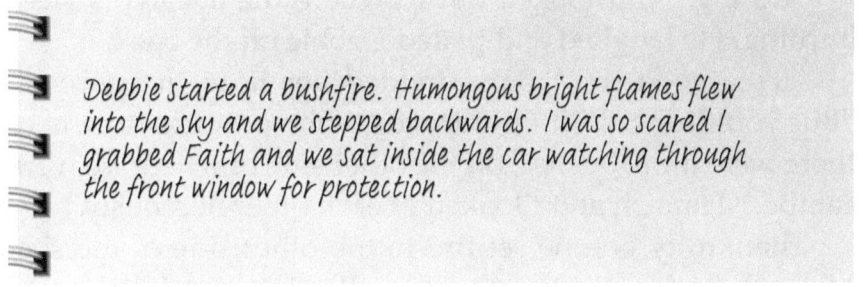

Debbie started a bushfire. Humongous bright flames flew into the sky and we stepped backwards. I was so scared I grabbed Faith and we sat inside the car watching through the front window for protection.

Hamish and I looked on in amazement as the fire spread from one patch of grass to the next. I kept watch on Gideon, who was trying to get as close to the flames as possible. At one point, the fire turned in our direction and some grass set alight a few metres from where Hamish was setting up the trailer.

"Do you think the fire's a bit close?" Hamish asked Debbie. He was trying to sound calm, but I could see that he wasn't. His left leg shook with anxiety.

"Don't worry," she told Hamish. "There's not much green undergrowth out here, so the fires don't get out of hand." She walked toward the patch of flames and stomped it out with a shovel. "The indigenous people always burn an area before camping. It makes access easier, and encourages new growth later. Because we're here first, I'm doing it for them."

The fire continued to spread and some small eucalypts in the distance set alight. Hamish and I kept watch by the tent. The eucalypts had burst into big flames that were shooting into the sky. It was spectacular. Gideon made "dingo" tracks in the dirt. The girls stayed in the car.

Jim returned from collecting some members of the church. We were introduced to Michael, in his thirties, and Barb and Linda, middle-aged elders of the church.

"What do you think of the fire?" asked Debbie.

"It's big!" Jim looked out to where the eucalypts were burning. He laughed and patted Debbie on the back.

"It's a good fire." Barb nodded her head in approval. "But you didn't do it on this side." She gestured to where there were more bushes, on the other side of where we were camped. Hamish and I looked at each other nervously.

Thankfully no-one set fire to the other side of the site. Michael, Barb and Linda began collecting wood for campfires.

By the time the rest of the church members arrived, there were only a few smouldering patches of the big fire left. The eucalypts were still standing but were much smaller now. Hamish let out a sigh of relief.

There were about fifteen of the congregation assembled now, including a couple, some young women, the middle-aged elders, and a family with small children. They seemed relaxed and at home. The women lit campfires for cooking and began making damper and heating tinned corned beef. Faith and Jenna warily emerged from the car. Linda showed them how to make damper. After dinner we sat in a circle while Jim, the teacher for the weekend, led a Bible study on the Holy Spirit. Debbie then shared about a time when she was not following what God wanted for her life and how sad she became. Now she felt a sense of peace from listening and being guided by the Holy Spirit. I decided if that was where Debbie's confidence came from, that's what I wanted.

Saturday 4th August

Jim led another study after breakfast. I was still looking for opportunities to be helpful. I noticed eighteen-month-old Isaiah wriggling on his mum's lap and volunteered Jenna as a babysitter while his mum stayed for the Bible study. Then I realised I'd done it again. I'd volunteered someone else for something, *and* she was only ten years old. I followed the kids into the camper trailer with Isaiah.

Isaiah had thick straight black hair and big brown eyes, and a habit of folding his hands behind his back while he walked with a kind of strut with his legs straight out in front of him. The kids sang him some nursery rhymes.

Then Jenna put a rug over our camp table and lined some of their teddies up behind it. She said, "Teddy can clap. Can you clap, Isaiah?" Faith made her teddy clap and Gideon demonstrated by clapping his own hands.

Isaiah started to cry. I picked him up to see if I could comfort him. He kept sobbing. Up close he had soft downy hair on the back of his neck and a beautiful smell.

Gideon made up a song to a kind of up and down, sing-songy tune, and sang: "The sun will come out. Everything will be okay. Your mother will never leave you. Your mother will always loo-ook after you."

Isaiah stopped crying. Then Gideon stopped singing and Isaiah started crying again. Isaiah's dad Levi came to collect him.

After lunch there was more Bible study, then we followed the others to a swimming hole. I noticed everyone seemed to look after Isaiah as he strutted happily along in between them all, without anyone in particular watching him. His parents and the others sat along the sandy bank fishing with hand reels. We'd brought a fishing rod we had never used, and I thought about asking the others for some bait, and whether any of them knew how to use a fishing rod, but they were all so quiet and absorbed in what they were doing, I didn't want to interrupt them. After a long time, Levi reeled in a turtle. It was too small to eat so he gave us all a good look at it, and then threw it back in the water.

Back at the campsite, Linda showed Jenna and Faith how to make damper, which was cooked over hot coals and was surprisingly light and delicious. Then after dinner, Michael and his wife Naomi led us in worship.

Jenna wrote:

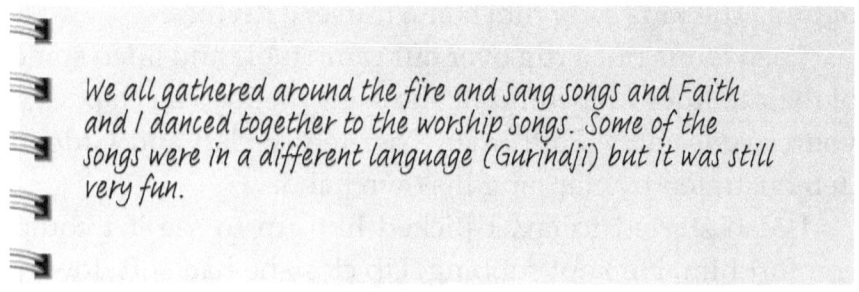

We all gathered around the fire and sang songs and Faith and I danced together to the worship songs. Some of the songs were in a different language (Gurindji) but it was still very fun.

After the singing, Jim suggested a time of praying for the Holy Spirit to direct us. Jim and the elders stood in a semi-circle and ministered to anyone who wanted it. One by one each member of the church came forward. As I watched them, my heart was pounding in my chest. I knew I had not been allowing God to direct my life, and I knew I should stand up and ask for prayer. I'd already accepted Jesus into my life and knew I had the Holy Spirit inside of me, but I wasn't sure I was allowing him to direct my life like Debbie had. But after the last person from the church was prayed for, the group of elders moved away and the opportunity had passed.

After the prayer time everyone broke up into little groups and sat around the fire. I talked to one of the church elders, Barb, who told me all about her experiences of the Holy Spirit. I felt the same pounding in my chest as before, and this time I asked Barb to pray for me. Her dark eyes widened. She looked toward Jim for help, but he was in conversation with Naomi, and she couldn't get his attention. Seeming a bit uncertain, Barb placed her hand on my shoulder, bowed her head and prayed. It was a beautiful prayer. She thanked God for his love for us, and asked the Holy Spirit to come and be in charge of my life.

Later putting the children to bed, I felt lighter. I let the girls pull their mattresses outside and curl up to sleep under the stars. They were still wearing the bathers they had swum in.

Sunday 5th August

I was sorry to see everyone packing up early this morning. I didn't want to leave. Thankfully we gathered around a campfire again to hear Jim's final message. He spoke about worshipping from John 4:23.

> *"Yet a time is coming and is now come when the true worshippers will worship the Father in the Spirit and in truth, for they are the kind of worshippers the Father seeks."* (John 4:23)

Jim explained that when we worship, we don't do it just with our heads, understanding the truth, but also with our hearts, allowing God to speak to our spirit. After the teaching, we shared communion of damper and black tea. There was more singing, and the girls, still in their swimsuits, danced again, something they would have been too inhibited to do at church at home. At the close of bush church, Jim asked the group where they would like to meet for church that night. The elders nominated Dagaragu, a town eight kilometres from Kalkaringi. Jim reminded everyone that tomorrow was Picnic Day, a Northern Territory public holiday for a race meeting in the south of the Territory. Hamish thanked the group for allowing us to come to the camp and share life with them for the last two days. The elders shook hands with each of us and Linda looked straight at me with her kind eyes and said that we were welcome any time.

We were the last to finish packing up. We took time saying goodbye to the campsite, with its blackened earth from Debbie's fire, the track leading through the grass down to the swimming hole, and the remains of the campfires where we had gathered and sung and listened and prayed. Back at Jim and Debbie's we spent the afternoon setting up the trailer again, then discussed whether to go to church at Dagaragu.

Night church in Dagaragu turned out to be similar to church camp. About forty people sat on plastic chairs around a campfire in front of the small church building and waited patiently while Michael and some others set up the audio equipment. Eventually a few worship songs were played, with lots of buzzing and crackling from the speakers which nobody seemed to mind, except Gideon, who dislikes loud noises. Gideon and I wandered around the small town lit by a few dim street lights, trying to avoid the donkey poo.

After the music and crackling stopped, I felt drawn back to hear the message. I picked up Gideon and ran back to the others. Michael shared that there was a spiritual revival in Kalkaringi and Dagaragu, with many people repenting and turning to God. There was praying and laying on of hands. It was a moving end to a wonderful weekend.

Chapter 16

Monday 6th August

I lay awake in the early hours listening to the dogs of Kalkaringi having a group barking session. Unable to sleep, I thought about the wonderful weekend at the church camp, and Jim preaching on worshipping in spirit and in truth. I wondered if I'd been trying to understand the Book of James with my head, and not trusting God from my heart. I prayed, asking God to show me. I didn't get an answer but felt overwhelmed by feelings of joy as I remembered Jim and Debbie's kindness, and the welcome from the church, and Barb's prayer for me. I let the feelings of joy wash over me.

We spent the morning of Picnic Day playing basketball with some kids at the courts at Kalkaringi school. Any time Gideon got his hands on the ball, he held onto it and ran off into the school grounds. The indigenous kids didn't complain. They watched Gideon run around for a while and when he took too long to return with the ball, they gradually drifted away.

We walked to the Arts centre near the entrance to Kalkaringi by the highway, and met some women using dot sticks to make traditional desert paintings on canvas. Dot painting seemed to be a slow and meticulous business, but the results were beautiful, and a complicated system of symbols represented people around campfires with digging sticks and traditional bowls called coolamons.

In the afternoon, Debbie drove us back to Dagaragu, so we could see it in daylight. She told us the history of the area, including how the Gurindji people had worked on cattle stations for next to no pay, and in terrible conditions. She showed us Wattie Creek, where the workers staged a strike, and the plaque that commemorates the day in 1975 when Gough Whitlam gave the workers' leader, Vincent Lingari, a handful of soil to symbolise giving back some of their land to the Gurindji people. It was sad to see that Dagaragu was almost deserted, in spite of land still being owned by the Gurindji; whereas Kalkaringi was growing, with its church, school, arts centre and strong community. I hoped that Michael was right when he told of the beginnings of a revival in Kalkaringi *and* Dagaragu.

The elders had organised a movie night to celebrate Picnic Day. Some teenage girls had dressed-up and wore bright blue eye shadow. It was obviously an important event in the social calendar. Inside the community centre, a dozen adults sat on a few church pews and the children lay on the floor. Jim played a DVD about a cycle race on the small flat-screen TV. After ten minutes, the children became restless, so Jim played a *Veggie Tales* movie, which held everyone's attention.

When *Veggie Tales* finished, Jim announced we would watch the feature for the evening: a film about Jacob from the Old Testament. Most of the children left, and the teenage girls moved inside. I thought having to look after Gideon was a great excuse to get out of movie night, with the small TV and unpredictable program, but after putting him to bed, I wanted to go back. I was drawn to the beautiful community. I left Gideon with Hamish and ran back to the church in the dark. It was warm and cosy. I found a seat next to Patricia, a woman I'd met at the op shop, who was unable to speak, and communicated with smiles and gestures. Everyone seemed fascinated by the movie, except a ten-year-old boy who rolled onto his stomach and banged his head on the floor when Jacob kissed Rachel. The rest of us stayed glued to the story of deceit and escape and eventual victory of Jacob. Patricia took my hand and held it in her lap.

Tuesday 7th August

The girls were nervous *and* excited this morning because Debbie had arranged for them to spend the day at the Kalkaringi Primary School. Faith was thrilled to play with some kids her own age. She wrote:

> On the sixty-fourth day of the holiday I went to the Aboriginal school. All the kids wanted to sit next to me. We had to do spelling and then we got to do dancing. We had hotdogs for lunch. In the afternoon we played basketball. My best friends were Ruby and Lily.

Jenna was very nervous about going to school, but I was pleased to read her interesting observations:

> This morning I had butterflies flying all around my tummy because I was going to the Aboriginal school. Mum said she would come with me. We went to the assembly and the Principal sang "heads, shoulders, knees and toes" with all the kids. It was really funny. I felt better after that. Faith went with the little kids and I went with the Peltophorums

> class. Peltophorums means a type of tree with yellow flowers. The Peltophorums are the oldest kids in the school, so they're in Grade 6. I thought that was pretty cool because I'm only in Grade 5, but I got to be a Peltophorum for the day.
>
> I really liked the teacher. She told us to write about the weekend. I wrote about the church camp, sleeping under the magnificent stars, jumping out of the tree, and singing at the campfire. The teacher got me to read first. Then the other kids read. They used really soft voices and I felt embarrassed that I'd been so loud. The kids spoke very quietly about camping and fishing and swimming with their families. Three of the boys had been to Melbourne for the weekend because it was a present from the school because they had good behaviour. They spoke a little bit louder than the other kids. They were talking about the cold weather in Melbourne, the orangutans at the zoo, the Eureka Skydeck and Luna Park.
>
> In the afternoon the teacher taught them maths. We had to make a graph of everyone's favourite meat. I said my favourite was chicken of course, which everyone else agreed with, followed by fish and sausages. After we finished the maths we could have free time to do whatever we wanted or play maths games on the computer. The teacher had a chat with me and told me that the other kids were at a lower level than me because English is their second language. If you think about that, they're really smart.

Once Jenna was comfortable at school, I decided to carry out my plan of finally being helpful to Debbie. Hamish was occupied making a special surprise with Gideon. I told him I was going to the op shop. I was determined not to be distracted by all the feelings of joy I was having, and do some good deeds. Hamish asked if I could first go to the Arts Centre to let them know he was having trouble making the electronic payment they were expecting for a painting we had chosen, and ask if we could pay cash. I wanted to purchase the painting, but I also wanted to get to the op shop in time to help Debbie before it closed. I ran all the way to the Arts Centre. When I got there, Robyn, the manager of the Arts Centre and a couple of the artists were standing outside the building watching me.

"I'm in a hurry," I said. I was breathing hard. "I have to help Debbie at the op shop." I bent over and rested my hands on my knees.

An older woman holding a dot stick looked at me with wide eyes. "I saw this woman running. I couldn't believe it. I thought why is this woman running?"

Robyn shook her head and laughed. "Nobody runs here."

I made an arrangement to pay cash, then went as fast as I could without running, to the petrol station / supermarket by the highway where there was an ATM. I paid for the painting, then waited for Robyn to carefully roll it and put it in a tube for me. I walked as fast as I could down the hill, dropped the painting off to Hamish, and crossed the road to the op shop.

Debbie was leaving the church.

"Wait! I've come to help!" I yelled.

Debbie closed the door with a thud. "I've finished. Don't worry; there wasn't much to do today."

I felt deflated. "Is there something else I can do to help?" *Please!*

Debbie suggested I help her with some housework, as she had to pack to get ready for their trip to Katherine for a conference the next day. While I manoeuvred their old vacuum cleaner around the tiny hallway, Jim kindly called out from his study that it was a luxury to have me clean for them. Jim was a people-person. He was being kind, trying to make me feel good about helping them.

After the housework was done, Debbie made us a cup of tea. We sat in their front room overlooking the verandah. Debbie told me she was studying a counselling course, to help her support people in the community in need. Encouraged, I told Debbie all my problems. Debbie kept nodding, and making "go on" noises, so I kept going, ending with the church camp, where I'd realised I wasn't trusting God's plan for my life. Debbie was an excellent counsellor. I told her everything. Ever since Barb had prayed for me at the church camp, I'd been feeling a lot of joy, but I didn't know what that *meant*.

Debbie leaned forward. I couldn't wait to hear what she had to say. Was I on the right track? Or was I still not trusting God?

Then a familiar voice called, "Debbie!"

Linda had come for a cup of tea. I never heard Debbie's advice. After we'd had tea and cake Debbie had made, Linda asked where Hamish was. I found him in the camper trailer reading the guidebook. The girls were trying to teach Gideon how to play jacks. One of Faith's new friends had given her some. They followed me back to the Smith's living room.

Linda gestured for us to sit down on the Smith's lounge chairs. Debbie had gone into the kitchen to get more cake. The children continued their game of jacks on the living room floor.

Linda leaned toward us. "I need to tell you something."

Hamish fidgeted in his chair. Linda kept looking straight at us. It was good having you and your family at the church camp. We liked having you visit our community."

Hamish let out a sigh. "Thank you. It's been wonderful. Thank you very much for welcoming us."

Linda continued. "We liked having you even though you didn't know how to look after the bush."

I wondered what was coming next. Linda looked at Hamish. "You were scared of the fire." He nodded. I remembered Hamish telling me he felt like a child at the bush camp, a total beginner in the company of people who understood the land.

Linda looked at me. "And you Jane. Your children did not know how to make bread. I had to teach them."

I nodded. It was true. "Thank you for the bread you dropped off on Monday by the way. It was delicious."

Linda nodded. "So the elders and I have made a decision." My heart skipped a beat. This was their land. Would they ask us to leave?

"Hamish," she gave him a serious look. "You are going to be my skin brother. This means you are part of my family."

I'd heard about the Aboriginal kinship system, known as the "skin" system. It determined who would look after someone's children if a parent died, and who could marry whom. It was a big deal.

Hamish's eyes had gone shiny. It always happens when he's happy.

"And you Jane. That means you are my sister-in-law." I nodded. It didn't sound as good as the full sibling, but I was pleased nonetheless. I took her hand and squeezed it. "Thank you Linda. That's an honour."

Linda looked up at the children, "And I am your Aunty. In Kalkaringi, we say "Naty.""

Jenna stood up and gave Linda a shy embrace. Then Faith gave her a tight hug. Linda laughed.

Debbie returned with a tray of cake and a teapot and put it down on the coffee table. Gideon threw one of his jacks high in the air and Hamish caught it just in time to stop it landing on the cake.

Wednesday 8th August

We were leaving Kalkaringi and going to Katherine ourselves, heading north again. I was sad to say goodbye. It helped when one of Faith's new best friends, Ruby, came to visit with photographs for the girls and a dinosaur book for Gideon as farewell gifts, with promises that she would keep in touch with Faith by email. Gideon presented Jim and Debbie with the surprise he and Hamish had been working on—a special snake made out of plastic bottles. Jim greeted the snake enthusiastically and made hissing sounds as he slid the snake across the floor.

After big hugs with Jim and Debbie, I apologised for not being any help, but no-one heard me because Gideon was copying Jim making hissing sounds with the snake.

We waved them off as they drove away in their old brown four-wheel drive headed for their mission leaders' conference. Then while Hamish and the kids were waiting for me to close the gate to the backyard behind me, Linda arrived, saying she had come to pray with us.

"In our church, we always pray for safe travels."

Hamish and the kids got out of the car where they were waiting for me, and we all huddled together on the dusty street. Linda explained that it is their church tradition to pray whenever anybody leaves Kalkaringi. She said a wonderful prayer for God's blessing on us.

We promised Linda to try to visit her again one day. At the supermarket filling up with fuel, we saw Levi (Isaiah's father), who told us in his lovely gentle voice how great it had been to have us in Kalkaringi. Driving up the Buntine Highway, tears welled up in my eyes when we passed the sign marking the border of the town. Six days before we had tipped out an expensive bottle of port. In place of the expensive gift, we'd gained new knowledge, new joy, and a sense of God's family. Being a Christian was full of surprises.

Chapter 17

Thursday 9th August

We were staying at the Katherine Gorge Caravan Park for a few days before heading to Kakadu. To celebrate, the girls set up a "restaurant" with a beach towel tablecloth weighted down with stones, and served "cakes" of cornflakes mixed with maple syrup.

We walked off our treats with a hike to the Katherine Gorge lookout. From our high vantage point we could see majestic red sandstone cliffs either side of a wide green river which flows all the way to Kakadu National Park. Katherine was more than a convenient stopping place after all. I could see why it was a popular place to visit.

Friday 10th August

The girls were excited about having a video call with their classmates today. I felt proud they would be able to share their amazing educational experiences, like the visit to the Bureau of Meteorology where they launched the weather balloon. I hoped their teachers would be impressed.

Faith's Skype session was scheduled first. Hamish set up our computer on the trestle table. Faith's teacher Jenny, a middle-aged woman with a flair for colourful clothing, was the first face we saw.

"Hello Faith," said Jenny. Her hair was tied in a purple scarf and she was wearing large blue hoop earrings. "Isn't technology wonderful?" She beamed at the camera. Then she sat down to reveal Faith's Grade 2 class—some were sitting at desks and some were on the floor. A few of them waved enthusiastically.

Faith was so overwhelmed to see her classmates she couldn't speak. Thankfully the other students asked her questions.

"Is it boring doing car trips?" asked a boy with long hair.

"No. We watch movies and go to a drive-through McDonalds." A few of the kids murmured their approval.

"Where are you now?" asked a girl with messy pigtails.

"We're in Katherine. We've been here three times and eaten pizza every time." It was true. But that was not the impression I wanted to give the teacher, that we ate takeaway food. The Skype session was not going how I imagined it.

"What else have you been doing?" asked Jenny. The class were starting to mutter among themselves.

"I liked going for walks in the Kimberleys. We went swimming," Faith said so softly no-one could have heard her. The noise in the classroom was getting louder. The kids on the floor rocked back and forth or lay on their stomachs.

Then the girl with pigtails had an idea. "Mrs Smith, can we sing Faith our song for the school production?"

Faith smiled with delight as her classmates sang *Joy to the World* with great gusto. The school production was always a big occasion.

Before Jenna's turn, I told her to make notes about the trip, and made sure she had the guidebook and photos to refer to. I didn't want a repeat of Faith's Skype session, which had not been educational.

All three Grade 5 classes and their young teachers were part of the Skype session. Jenna pointed out Katherine on a map from the guidebook. She showed them a photo of her class from the school in Kalkaringi. I was proud of her. But instead of asking questions, the class wanted to tell their news.

"You know how Mrs Jones is pregnant?" called out Chloe. She was one of Jenna's best friends.

Jenna nodded. She had been excited Mrs Jones was expecting a baby.

"Well Mrs Price and Mrs Delaney are pregnant too." Chloe grinned.

Mrs Jones held the computer out in front of her so Jenna could see her six-month belly bump. Then she went over to the other teachers, who turned sideways so Jenna could see they were also pregnant.

"Congratulations!" Jenna gushed. "That's wonderful." She pushed her notes on our trip aside. I was disappointed. She hadn't told them anything about the Bureau of Meteorology in Geraldton.

"Did you know that Chloe is leaving us?" said Amber. "She's going to live in Brisbane."

"Oh no! You can't leave me!" yelled Jenna. Chloe wiped away tears. A group of girls gathered around Chloe and gave her a hug. Jenna put her arms around the computer screen.

After the Skype session ended and Hamish had packed away the computer, Jenna was quiet. Seeing her friends had reminded her how much she missed them. I shouldn't have been focussed on creating a good impression for the teachers. Her connection with her friends was what mattered. What had I been thinking?

Faith was energised by seeing her class and didn't feel sad at all. She wrote:

> Yippee! Today we had Skype. I got to see my friends and they sang their production song. But of course if you're in my class you already know that.

Saturday 11th August

Jenna was still quiet this morning, probably thinking about her friends back home, and Chloe going to Brisbane. She stared out the window all the way from Katherine to Kakadu. I tried to cheer her up, telling her most people didn't get to visit Kakadu National Park, with its ancient cultural sites. She didn't answer.

We found a bush campsite near the township of Jabiru. Hamish has a knack for making people feel better. He got Jenna to help him make a fire.

She recorded it in her diary:

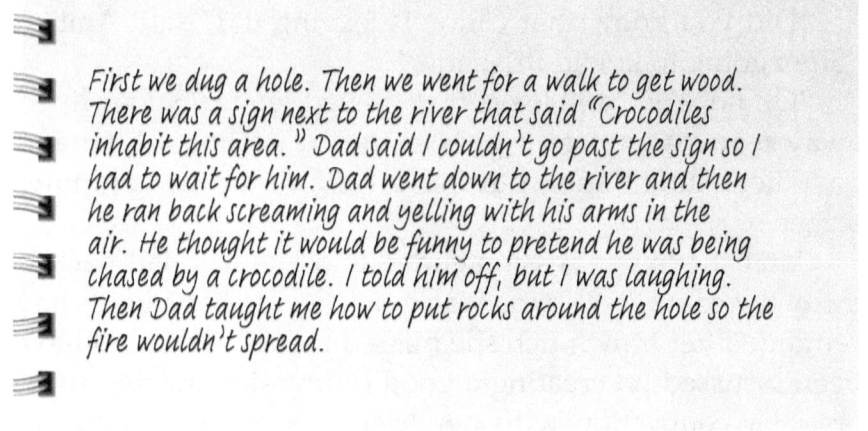

First we dug a hole. Then we went for a walk to get wood. There was a sign next to the river that said "Crocodiles inhabit this area." Dad said I couldn't go past the sign so I had to wait for him. Dad went down to the river and then he ran back screaming and yelling with his arms in the air. He thought it would be funny to pretend he was being chased by a crocodile. I told him off, but I was laughing. Then Dad taught me how to put rocks around the hole so the fire wouldn't spread.

Sunday 12th August

After learning to make a fire and spending some time with Hamish, Jenna was talking again, but she wasn't her usual bubbly self. I worried she was homesick. I decided to try to recreate the things we would do at home. She helped me make pancakes for breakfast, which was our Sunday ritual. Then I had another idea.

"How about we have a family church service?"

"Great idea. I can do the children's talk." Jenna helped with Sunday school at home.

"And I can talk about what I'm reading from the Bible." I was sure I could share something useful from James.

We set up the girl's bedroom side of the tent, pushing the beds aside and bringing in chairs. We sang some songs. Hamish sang loudly. Faith and Gideon held hands and danced. I raised my hands in the air, hoping to recreate worship back home. Jenna filmed it on my phone.

When Jenna handed back my phone I glanced at the video she'd taken. I looked ridiculous raising my hands inside a tent. I had a grey patch from not visiting a hairdresser since we'd left Melbourne. I felt miserable. I deleted it.

Then it was time for a Bible reading. I flicked through James. Chapter 1 was about learning from trials, not really relevant for a family message. Chapter 2 was about good deeds, but I realised I hadn't done any. I'd been counting on helping Jim and Debbie in Kalkaringi, but I overslept and then they didn't need my help. Then I got to Chapter 3, which is all about speech. This was where I'd had some success. It would be a good topic for a message. The family sat down and looked at me expectantly. I read from James.

"Not many of you should become teachers, my fellow believers, because you know that we who teach will be judged more strictly." I hoped I would measure up as a teacher. I was aware of the enormous responsibility.

"We all stumble in many ways." I continued. That was a relief. *"Anyone who is never at fault in what they say is perfect, able to keep their whole body in check."* Faith started to wriggle in her seat.

I skipped ahead to verse 4. This was the important part. *"Take ships as an example. Although they are so large and driven by strong winds, they are steered by a very small rudder wherever the pilot wants to go. Likewise, the tongue is a small part of the body, but it makes great boasts."* (James: 3:1-2; 4-5)

Now it was time for a message. What exactly had been helpful about the verse? I couldn't remember. But I'd been calm after reading it.

"Do you remember Karijini National Park? Remember how cold it was at night? And how hard the ground was? Dad had to use his drill to get the pegs in." Hamish nodded.

"That first morning I felt like yelling at the girls taking so long to wash up." Faith pushed herself as low as possible in her seat. "But I read this passage. I decided to tame my tongue. I pictured the family as a ship, and I was the rudder, steering you to hurry up."

Jenna was wriggling now. "That's not what it means."

She was interrupting! No-one interrupted the preacher at home.

"Our own bodies are the ship. You steer yourself, Mum, you don't steer your children." Jenna smiled sweetly at me. Was she right? I wasn't sure.

Now Hamish spoke. "That's true Jenna. But I think the passage is telling us more than that. Did anyone notice the part *"Anyone who is not at fault in what they say is perfect."* Why would James say that?"

Hamish was taking over, and he was complicating the message, when it was supposed to be a simple encouragement to stay calm. I felt myself getting angry.

Hamish continued. "Nobody is perfect." Faith nodded. Hamish leaned forward and looked around at the children. "When James says that anyone who is not at fault in what they say is perfect, he's reminding us we all need Jesus."

"All of us are sinners," added Faith. "That's why Jesus died for us."

I was surprised by a warm feeling that spread through

me. My indignation at Hamish taking over as leader melted away. I tried to find my anger again, but it had gone.

Gideon was banging two dinosaurs together. Jenna found a pink sock. She put it over her right hand and opened and closed the hand in imitation of talking.

"I'm a tongue," she said. Gideon stopped playing with the dinosaurs and stared at the pink sock. Faith giggled. "How can I be good?" asked Jenna.

"You ask Jesus to help you?" Gideon said shyly.

"That's right Gideon! I've got something special for you!" She sounded just like the children's worker at home. She fetched a pink love heart sticker from her pencil case and stuck it on Gideon's T-shirt. He looked down proudly at it.

As we drove to Ubirr in the afternoon I reflected that the family church service had been a success, even though the video (now transferred to permanently deleted status) had been horrible and the teaching had gotten off to a shaky start.

We visited the Ubirr caves - the reason I had been so keen to come to Kakadu. The ancient paintings stretched along sections of smooth wall underneath overhanging rock. Some showed fish and crocodiles painted in reds, browns and yellows, with lines showing the internal structures of bones and organs. My guidebook told me they were painted in the saltwater period and were known as X-ray paintings because of the ultra-realistic anatomy. Other paintings told stories and depicted kangaroos, emus, turtles and humans carrying spears. These were from a later period, when saltwater systems were replaced by freshwater pools, increasing food resources. It was thrilling to see a record of that history right in front of us.

Later the kids played on some nearby rocks overlooking the savannah. Hamish and I stretched out on the rock. I opened up James again. I was uncomfortable that Jenna understood it better than I did. I read through Chapter 3. The verses that stood out to me this time were further down in the chapter.

> *"Can both fresh water and salt water flow from the same spring? My brothers and sisters, can a fig tree bear olives, or a grapevine bear figs? Neither can a salt spring produce fresh water." (James 3:12-13)*

Hamish had put his hat over his face to protect him from the sun. I prodded him. "I think you're right about James trying to point out our need for Jesus."

Hamish took his hat off his face and turned to look at me. I read him the verses about the water and the figs.

"I get it Hamish! We need to have Jesus inside us to produce the fruit of Jesus. If we're going to control our tongue, we need Jesus."

"Hm-mmm." Hamish put his hat back over his face and rolled on to his other side. He wanted to nap.

The children were re-enacting *The Lion King* story. The pile of flat rocks overlooking the wetlands looked like Pride Rock. Jenna held Gideon up in the air like he was Simba. Faith was swaying one arm out in front of her like an elephant. My heart swelled as I watched her make trumpeting noises as she ran around the new king.

Chapter 18

Monday 13th August

Hamish had planned a trip to Jim Jim Falls, named for Andjimdjim, meaning water pandanus, the palm-like plants we'd seen everywhere in Kakadu. I felt nervous about the walk, which our guidebook described as challenging. Would there be large rocks we had to scramble over? Would I get left behind? I wondered if I should stay at camp and let Hamish take the children without me.

Then again, I didn't want to miss out on the falls. And it was a chance to redeem myself after my outburst when I got lost in the Kimberley. I braced myself for the journey ahead.

We drove over soft sand to the start of the walking track. The kids laughed as the car bumped over the sand. My stomach churned.

The walk began easily enough with a sandy path with no obstacles apart from a few tree roots. Hamish turned around every now and then to check I was still there. I was glad he'd learned his lesson and was looking out for me.

Then sand gave way to rocks. Painted arrows indicated the path over them. I followed carefully. I noticed the distance between me and the family got bigger. I could see the kids up ahead climbing elegantly over the rocks like spiders. I pushed myself to go faster.

I was out of breath and dizzy. I could see Gideon ahead of me stretching his tiny arms and legs, then getting pulled up by Hamish to get over the large ones. I tried to copy Gideon, stretching out my arms, but I couldn't extend my legs like he had. I grazed my elbow and banged my knee hard. *Ouch!*

I reached a vertical boulder. I couldn't see the family. A white arrow pointed toward the sky, and another one pointed to the ground, indicating the return journey. I found a toehold, and manoeuvred myself halfway up the rock. I perched there, spread out against the rock, wondering how to go any further. I felt humiliated.

Then I heard Hamish.

"Are you okay, Jane?"

"No! I need help! How did you get up there?"

Hamish reached down. I grabbed his forearm and he pulled me up and over the rock. I gave him a hug. My legs shook.

From the top we could see emerald-green water and a wide bank of yellow sand. The water sparkled in the sun. At the end of the gorge, we could see a large circular pool and Jim Jim Falls making a white line against the cliff face. It was breathtaking.

Hamish and I sat watching the falls, while the children played in the sand. A sign near the water's edge read, "It is currently safe to swim." I guessed there were no crocodiles in the pool at this time of year.

"Why don't you swim to the falls? I'll watch the kids," Hamish offered.

The circular pool was huge, and the cliffs were high. There was no sun on the water at that end of the gorge. It would be impossible to see what was below.

"Go on, you'll love it." He nudged me with his elbow.

Hamish was right. I nearly missed out seeing the beautiful gorge and the cliffs. I didn't want to miss out on a swim.

I walked past the children, who were gathering sand into mounds, and dipped one foot in the water. It was icy cold. Without thinking too much, I dived in. The shock of the cold water took my breath away. I stood on the sandy river bottom and gasped for air. Then I swam freestyle, arm over arm to warm up.

When I reached the circular pool, the water was black. I could no longer find the sandy bottom when my toes tried to find it. The cliffs were higher, and the pool wider than I'd realised. But I kept going. I wanted to reach the cliff face and see the falls up close.

When I was three-quarters of the way, I remembered a sign I'd seen at the start of the walk—"Swim at your own risk. Crocodiles can enter the water at any time." My heart rate quickened. I began swimming breaststroke, with my head out of the water. It was slower than freestyle, but I wanted to be able to see any crocodiles before they attacked me.

I made it to the cliff face next to the waterfall. I heard Hamish cheering from the riverbank. The rock was smooth and slippery. I grabbed onto a pandanus plant to steady myself. The falls hit the pool and sprayed me in the face.

On the way back, I alternated a few quick strokes of freestyle with breaststroke. I comforted myself that if there *were* crocodiles in the water, there wasn't much I could do about it now. The girls were standing in knee-deep water ready to meet me. Jenna looked at me in awe, her eyes shining. I hugged her and kissed the top of her head.

I was energised by my swim. On the walk back, I helped Gideon over the large rocks. I slid down the big boulder with him. I got scratches on the backs of my legs, but I wasn't worried.

Tuesday 14th August

Jenna wanted to see some more of Australia's "Big Things".

The kids had climbed the Big Rocking Horse and been photographed next to the Big Galah in the south, picnicked beside the Big Banana of Carnarvon and seen the Big Prawn of Exmouth in the west. Hamish had even gone all the way to Wyndham so Gideon could see the Big Crocodile. But Jenna thought we could do better. There was a Big *Boxing* Crocodile on the way to Litchfield National Park. And, with only a small detour, we could see the Big Stockwhip. Whips were apparently used to make a loud sound to help round up cattle. The Big Stockwhip was a large concrete structure that marked the entrance to a homestead and a factory that made whips.

Using the map book, I directed Hamish down a dirt track toward a town called Woolner, where I thought the Big Boxing Crocodile should be. Woolner came and went and all we could see was farms and paddocks, but no reptile statues. Hamish drove back to the highway and we stopped at a petrol station and asked the attendant, a middle-aged woman with bleached blond hair, about the Big Boxing Croc.

"Which one are you after?" She leaned toward us, resting her elbows on the counter.

"There's more than one *boxing* crocodile?" Hamish and I said at the same time.

"There's one near the Jumping Crocodile Cruise. But you probably want the *really* big one at Humpty Doo on the Arnhem Highway."

We all agreed we wanted to see the Really Big Boxing Croc, the kids for the obvious reason that it was bigger, and Hamish and I because we were heading that way anyway. She pointed to the location on our map. We thanked her and bought Gideon a squishy rubber crocodile he'd found by the counter.

We found him outside a petrol station on the Arnhem Highway. He *was* huge, at thirteen metres tall, with a big head and an open mouth full of teeth. The paint was coming off his red gloves. The kids thought he was the best big thing they'd seen. With the exception of the Big Rocking Horse, he was the biggest, and definitely the fiercest. They hopped around in front of him, pretending to box each other.

Once they'd had enough of stabbing their fists in the air, we made our way toward the Big Stockwhip, which was somewhere off the Stuart Highway. We had just turned onto the highway, when we heard a loud bang. We'd burst the driver's side rear tyre.

Hamish told the kids to stay in the car. I watched for oncoming traffic, while Hamish unhooked the spare tyre and fetched the jack from the well in the boot. He lay on the hot ground, precariously close to the highway. My job was to stand at the back of the trailer and yell every time I saw a car coming, so he could get off the road. When I saw a truck I shouted "road train" as loud as I could and Hamish scrambled out from under the car and ran to the back of the trailer to join me. We watched the heavy vehicle pass by. The car shook as the truck went past.

It was exciting being part of such a dangerous operation, like avoiding the crocodiles at Jim Jim Falls. Once again, I felt exhilarated. Was this what James meant by *"Consider it pure joy, my brothers and sisters, whenever you face trials of many kinds?"* (James 1:2) Had I finally learnt some courage?

Hamish seemed satisfied too when he'd finally replaced the tyre and we'd returned to the car, although he was bright red and sweat was running down his face. He took a long drink of water from his aluminium bottle.

"It's too late to go to the Big Stockwhip now," he told the children.

The kids groaned. "But you promised!" Faith was doing a series on Australia's Big Things in a scrapbook.

"We need to get to camp. We spent too long looking for the Boxing Crocodile, and changing the tire." Hamish took another long drink.

"Well can we go to the Big Strawberry then?" Faith stretched forward in her seat. Even though it was near home, we'd never been, although Faith often asked.

"Let's go during the Christmas holidays," I said. It would fill up the spot Faith had saved for the Big Stockwhip in her scrapbook. I handed Hamish some tissues so he could wipe the sweat off his face.

We still arrived late at the Litchfield National Park campground, which was already fully-booked. We found a private campground, which was more expensive, but also had more amenities, including flushing toilets and a cafe selling ice cream. The ice cream was perfect.

Wednesday 15th August

We chose one of the gorge walks described as "spectacular" in our guidebook for our day at Litchfield National Park. I braced myself for another walk, hoping I would be able to keep up with the family again.

I needn't have worried; everything about the walk to Florence Falls was easy. It was cooler than it had been in the Kimberleys and Kakadu. There were steps, instead of rocks, and now and then a section of boardwalk conveyed us over a peaceful stream. It was incredible, to be able to enjoy all this beauty with so little effort.

Because the walk was so accessible, there were many other tourists doing the same journey. We bumped into each other as we made the slight downhill trek on gravel. Then we saw the waterfall—a miniature Jim Jim Falls—with tall cliffs surrounding a perfectly round pool, fed by an impressive torrent of water.

Jenna was determined to swim across the pool and touch the waterfall like she'd seen me do at Jim Jim. While Hamish made a wall of pebbles with Faith and Gideon, I encouraged her to swim breaststroke, with her head out of the water, so she could avoid crashing into other swimmers. But she'd gone to a swim school that taught backstroke first. Because she was feeling nervous, she lay on her back and did the swimming stroke she was most confident with.

I steered her away from the rocks where teenage boys were jumping off into the water. As we got closer to the falls, the water became more turbulent. We knocked into other swimmers. I couldn't persuade Jenna to roll over. She couldn't get close to the cliffs, because the pressure of the water from the falls was so strong. I gave up. I called out to Hamish.

Hamish could see how nervous Jenna was about swimming in rough water. He helped her swim to the cliff edge where the water was calm and they made their way to the falls hugging the rock. I was impressed with Jenna's determination. Perhaps the whole family was learning to persevere. Jenna wrote later:

Mum and I tried to swim to the waterfall but we couldn't make it. Dad and I moved like crabs along the cliff. We had to stop and rest but we didn't give up. We set ourselves a goal to get to a particular rock, and when we made it, we set another goal. In the end we got right next to the waterfall. I was so happy. The noise of the water was really loud. I shouted to Dad, "we made it" and he put his thumbs up. Then we swam back to Mum.

Chapter 19

Thursday 16th August

The Northern Territory had been exhilarating. Now we were driving south. That meant going home.

"It feels like the end doesn't it, Hamish? Now we're heading back to Melbourne."

"We've still got Uluru, and Coober Pedy to go." Hamish stretched. "But I'm looking forward to getting home too. Working outside." Hamish had been building a deck for two years, but it still only ran alongside the kitchen. He hoped it would eventually wrap around the house. "It will be good to see Mum and Dad too."

"It will be great to see them," I agreed. But I was feeling unsettled. Going home meant trying to engage Gideon in wholesome activities instead of letting him watch TV shows about dinosaurs all day. And it meant getting a job. Gideon would be going to school next February. We'd agreed I'd go back to work to improve the finances.

"I'm worried, Hamish. What if I can't get a job? Or what if I'm no good at working? I've spent five years kicking balls around the backyard and reading books about velociraptors. I don't know how to do anything else anymore."

"You'll be fine. It'll come back to you." Hamish scanned the road ahead. There was a convoy of caravans in front of us. He wanted to overtake.

"You know I was meant to be a lawyer?" I'd fancied I'd be good at arguing.

"Well that was what your mum wanted."

"She wanted me to be a lawyer because she'd never gotten the chance. She was very smart, you know. She got lots of academic awards in high school, but had to drop out to help at home." Hamish nodded. He'd heard it all before. Her father, my grandfather, had drunk too much, was always losing work and moving the family to a new town, hoping things would be better. Eventually my grandmother couldn't cope. Mum gave up school to help look after her younger siblings.

"She was disappointed I didn't get into Law. She thought I'd been studying hard for years alone in my room. Sometimes I studied, but usually I just wasted time. Did you know I used to write poems or draw pictures?"

"That's not a waste of time." Hamish looked thoughtful. "Why didn't you spend time with your mum and your stepdad?"

"Sometimes I did. If he was in a good mood, John would let me help him cook dinner." I remembered getting told off, in a nice way, for pinching some of the grated cheese. "Most of the time, if I hung out with them, I felt like I was intruding on something and would go back to my room."

"I think Mum was impressed with you at least Hamish." I braced myself as he overtook the first caravan. The driver made space for Hamish to slot in behind another one. A sign above the back window read "Rae and Darren - Living the Dream." My thoughts drifted. I'd finished a second Arts degree, majoring in psychology this time, while Hamish supported me. Then I took a job as a research assistant in a government department, and supported Hamish while he studied social work. After graduating he worked as a case worker for a family services organisation, then quickly got promoted. He had an ability to make tough decisions and stick to them, which made him management material apparently. When I gave up work to look after Gideon, I got further behind Hamish. How would I ever catch up? Would I even be able to get another job now, after so much time?

Hamish overtook Rae and Darren. Now we had a clear view. The desert had given way to forest and palm trees. It made me think of childhood holidays to northern New South Wales, where the scenery was lush and tropical. Mum and John would alternate driving night and day until we got there. We would skip meals and buy chocolate bars from roadhouses along the way until we reached the tropics. I felt nostalgic for simple, spur-of-the-moment holidays.

Hamish turned into the Mattaranka Caravan Park. The campsites were on the side of a hill and overlooked tropical rainforest. Wild peacocks wandered amongst the tents, fanning their tails of blue, green and gold. The Eagles' *Take it Easy* was playing somewhere.

The children followed the peacocks, while Hamish and I selected a site.

"Shall we do a quick set-up Hamish? There's no need to put up the awning."

Hamish didn't answer. I left him unfolding the trailer tent, and walked in the direction of the music.

The voice of Glenn Frey floated on the wind, telling me to lighten up, and to take a stand.

Through some trees I saw young people drinking at wooden tables surrounded by palm trees. There was a stage with speakers.

It reminded me of those trips to New South Wales again. I loved eating out on holidays. It was thrilling to choose what you wanted to eat. Mum and John were always relaxed and happy. They drank gin and tonics in outdoor restaurants just like this one. I remembered a night Mum and John laughed every time I told them how beautiful the night sky was.

Hamish was threading the poles through the top of the tent when I got back.

"There's a really nice restaurant with music. Let's eat there."

Hamish sighed. He was already annoyed. I'd told him I didn't want to make a big meal. I'd asked him to cook sausages to have in bread. Another change of plan was obviously irritating.

I decided to take a stand. "Go on Hamish. You know it makes sense."

Hamish drummed his fingers against the tent pole he was holding. "Fine, we can go. But let's set up first."

I helped Hamish with the poles, then arranged the camp chairs. When I thought we'd finally finished, Hamish unpacked some new LED lights he'd found in Darwin and attached one to every pole. I felt a flash of irritation. I wanted to listen to the Eagles.

Eventually, Hamish had set up. Eating out wasn't as happy a time as I'd expected. The children were not as excited about ordering at a restaurant as I thought they'd be. The highlight was meeting a family from Red Hill. The children danced together next to the stage while a band played seventies' music, and the adults shared travel stories. I hoped it wasn't too obvious to Andrew and Janet that Hamish and I were barely speaking to each other. I think we got away with it.

Friday 17th August

I woke up feeling miserable. I was embarrassed about not speaking to Hamish in front of the couple from Red Hill. It *was* obvious. And there was a new thought: Hamish didn't care about whether I had fun. That was why he didn't want to eat out, and then barely spoke to me at the restaurant. If

Hamish didn't want me to have fun, maybe my fear I'd had after getting left behind in Manning Gorge was true after all. Perhaps Hamish *didn't* want to be with me anymore!!

Tears rolled across my cheeks and over my nose and wet the pillow. Memories of childhood came flooding back. I had a mental image of my mum barely able to get out of my bed after John left. I'd take her toast and a cup of tea and put it on the table next to her. After two weeks, things went back to normal, minus John. She got up and started cleaning the house and talking to the cats.

I overheard Hamish help the kids find clothes and breakfast. Then I heard the couple from Red Hill. Their voices were so normal and happy, as they told Hamish they were heading to Darwin. I lay as still as possible behind the canvas wall, so they wouldn't know I was there. It was very awkward to be crying while Hamish had visitors.

I cried out silently to God, asking him to send Andrew and Janet away. A new thought came into my mind, as if the Holy Spirit had other concerns: "Get up!" I pushed the thought away, wanting to stay in the safety of my bed, but it came back: "Get up!" (There was also an undertone of "You're fine, you don't need to hide, just *get up*!!")

By the time I was dressed, Janet and Andrew had gone. I was sad I hadn't swapped phone numbers with Janet. I asked Jenna to help me with the laundry. In the bright sunshine, I noticed the state of our clothes. I showed Jenna how to spray the marks with stain remover, telling her to use more until the clothes were drenched and smelling of chemicals. Surprisingly, they were still covered in red and brown marks when we came back to the clothesline after a visit to the thermal springs a couple of hours later.

Later I broke the silence with Hamish and told him I wanted to spend another night in Mataranka. I was feeling more cheerful since getting out of bed, but I wanted to delay going home. We still had stains on our clothes, and I couldn't face all the collapsing the hundred and one camping items Hamish had set up for a two-night stay, and packing them in boxes and finding places for them in the car. Hamish wanted to stick with the original plan and head south the next day. But he compromised. He offered to give me a morning off. If Jenna helped, it would only take them *two hours* to pack the car, and the rest of us could go for a walk in the park.

Saturday 18th August

I wondered if I really needed a day off packing up. It wasn't really that bad a job, and it would be nice to help Hamish, wouldn't it? Then I remembered that, since he had agreed to give me a morning off already, it would irritate Hamish more than anything if I changed the plan.

While Gideon and Faith built "dams" in a trickle of water we found on our walk in the park, I opened James on my phone Bible app. I remembered Chapter 2 was about doing good deeds, and that faith without deeds was useless. I wanted some inspiration to stop feeling sorry for myself and start doing some of the hard work I was clearly avoiding.

Someone had linked my phone Bible with an app called *Understand your Bible*. The link was written in pink and appeared on the bottom of the screen. I suspected Jenna had added the app after it became obvious that I didn't understand James Chapter 3 at the family church service in Kakadu.

I read from Chapter 2:

> *"You foolish person, do you want evidence that faith without deeds is useless? Was not our father Abraham considered righteous for what he did when he offered his son Isaac on the altar? You see that his faith and his actions were working together, and his faith was made complete by what he did. And the scripture was fulfilled that says 'Abraham believed God, and it was credited to him as righteousness,' and he was called God's friend. You see that a person is considered righteous by what they do and not by faith alone." (James 2:20-24)*

I clicked on the link below. The "Understand your Bible" notes were written in a cute font that looked like handwriting.

> James is not suggesting we must add works to our faith to ensure God's love for us. His point is that a real faith, that believes God, will be accompanied by acts of obedience. Abraham believed God, therefore he obeyed him, putting Isaac on the altar. A real faith, a faith that believes God, will be accompanied by a changed life. To quote Martin Luther, "faith alone saves, but faith that saves is not alone."

It was like the rest of James: *Do not ask God for wisdom and then doubt him (James 1:6-8). Do not read the word and ignore what it says (James 1:22-25). Do not call yourself "religious" and act like someone who isn't (James 1:26).* And now this. *If your faith is real, your life will show it (James 2:24).*

Something loosened inside me. I'd been looking at things the wrong way. I wanted to work hard and excel at something to please God, like I should have pleased Mum and made her happy. In fact God wanted my obedience, like

Abraham leaving Isaac on the altar. I wasn't quite sure what obedience would look like, but it wasn't about trying to be useful, or successful.

I told Hamish on the way to Tennant Creek, while the kids watched movies and Hamish and I shared a bag of licorice I'd found in the park shop. After I'd calmed down on the walk, we were speaking again.

"I've been learning how our deeds are an expression of our faith, but they're not what makes God love us. I've heard it lots of times in church, but it hadn't sunk in. I'm still trying to be useful to God."

Hamish swallowed a piece of licorice. "I remember when I really got close to God as a teenager when I was in youth group. I was happy. I volunteered in hospitals visiting the patients. I didn't do it because I had to. I was full of joy. I *wanted* to do it. I felt close to God when I was helping."

I'd heard all about Hamish's youth group days. He went to meet girls. But he ended up meeting God, and volunteering.

Hamish turned toward me. "I feel the same way about you. I don't love you because you *do* things for me. I just love spending time with you."

I felt a bit uncomfortable. I would rather rely on my usefulness, uncertain as that was, than Hamish's goodness in loving me, just for me.

I ignored Hamish's gaze. "You didn't want to spend time with me at the restaurant." I looked out the passenger window, as far away from Hamish as possible. I didn't want to get hurt. "My family were always relaxed when we ate out. I wanted to relive a happy memory."

"I didn't know that." I glanced back at Hamish. He seemed thoughtful. "How about we go out in Alice Springs? I've been doing some research. There's a restaurant that serves Australian bush food—crocodile and stuff."

It wasn't very spontaneous. We wouldn't be in Alice Springs until later in the week. What was the atmosphere like? Would the wind be blowing the right way that night? I'd rather respond to the feeling of the moment. It *was* sweet though, the idea of Hamish *enjoying* my company. Planning a special meal for us all. I stared out at the flat barren landscape. I found the biggest piece of licorice in the bag and handed it to him.

Chapter 20

Sunday 19th August

The Tennant Creek Museum wasn't far from our camping ground at "The Pebbles". We could spend a day peacefully absorbing information, without any decisions to argue over. And it would be another educational experience for the children, that they could tell their teachers about when they got back to Melbourne. It was easy to persuade Hamish to go, once I discovered that you could visit the museum for as long as you wanted, at the price of only $15 for a family ticket.

As we walked up the steps of the Tennant Creek Museum of Natural Mineralogy and Social History, Gideon ran toward some brightly-coloured plastic windmills spinning in the wind, grabbed one and watched the petals turn. A Scottish lady with grey hair and a thick accent (Volunteer Joan, according to her name badge), yelled "Stawp! They are very fragile!"

I thought the wooden stem Gideon was holding looked very sturdy, but obediently told Gideon to return it to its basket with the other windmills. Then while I was paying the $15 entry fee, Volunteer Joan looked over my shoulder and shouted "Stawp! Don't pull them apart!"

I turned around warily, expecting Gideon to be tampering with something delicate, like those Japanese paper cuttings you can buy at the National Gallery, but he was examining a stand covered in fridge magnets, with his hands by his side.

Gideon ran over to a ramp that led away from the shop

and down toward the museum itself. There was no merchandise there for him to play with. I could relax. While Jenna was showing me a badge in the shape of a gold nugget, I heard a scream of "Stawp! Don't do that! That railing is intended for downward pressure, not outward pressure!"

I looked up to see Gideon swinging on the ramp railing, unknowingly creating outward pressure. I decided we needed to leave the shop and visit the museum as quickly as possible.

Volunteer Joan accompanied us to the first room, which held the rock crushing and gold sorting exhibit. I could see her features soften and she seemed to breathe evenly as she explained what each piece of machinery was for. Then she opened the minerals room. I noticed with relief that every crystal and accompanying sign was enclosed in a glass case a long way off the floor, making breakages unlikely. Volunteer Joan announced we could tour the rest of the museum by ourselves, as the exhibits were self-explanatory, and she was not comfortable to leave the shop unattended for very long.

Left alone, Hamish read some of the information to Gideon, while the girls and I discussed which of the crystals we thought was the prettiest. Faith and I liked a giant purple crystal; and Jenna chose a milky white one in a hexagonal shape.

Jenna and I read every sign in the social history building. Tennant Creek was the last town in Australia to have a gold rush, and lived through prosperity even in the Depression. The first gold nugget was found by a local Aboriginal man, who showed it to a white man who formed a gold mining syndicate without him. In spite of the wealth from gold, the miners lived in basic conditions, adapting to life in the outback with all sorts of innovations such as keeping their beer cold in a wet sock.

Gideon had a good run around outside, and we fed him lunch, before exiting nervously through the museum shop. I wanted to avoid any further conflict with Volunteer Joan, so I acted as if all the shouting at Gideon had never happened. I told her that we were camping at the Pebbles.

"Are you going to the Devil's Marbles?" she asked.

"Yes, we're going there tomorrow, on our way down to Uluru". I was pleased we were getting on.

Volunteer Joan's eyes narrowed. "Go there at midday", she instructed. "The sun shines directly on the Devil's Marbles and they glow bright red. Otherwise they're nothing much to look at".

"Thank you," I said, a bit uncertainly. I would have liked her to be a bit more enthusiastic about our travel plans.

As if to make the point she was not at all enthusiastic about our travel plans, Joan declared, "Uluru is pretty boring most times of the day too, just an uninteresting grey rock".

Hamish arrived to pay for some Tennant Creek badges, saving me from trying to work out what to say next. While making his purchase, he told Joan how impressed he was with the minerals museum. This started a warm and happy conversation. Volunteer Joan was relaxed, and made eye contact, so long as she was talking about gold or minerals.

Hamish doesn't care whether people like him or not. He's told me before that he doesn't need to make friends with everybody. And yet clearly she enjoyed her conversation with Hamish. I was amazed at the unfairness of it.

Hamish took a nap back at the campsite, while the kids and I went for a walk in the flat barren landscape nearby. Gideon collected rocks, which he was sure were crystals, while the girls collected wildflowers. Hamish was still asleep when we got back. Gideon arranged his "crystals" while the girls "planted" the wildflowers to make a garden for when Hamish woke up.

Monday 20th August

We arrived at the rocks known as the Devil's Marbles (or Karlu Karlu, meaning round boulders), at midday. The enormous spheres glowed red in the sun, just as Volunteer Joan had said they would. A sign explained that they were "degraded nubbins" created when granite expanded causing the sandstone above it to crack into blocks, which formed into balls when the edges were worn away by wind and water. I imagined this was a fact Joan would find interesting. We took photos mimicking the ones in our guidebook, with the kids standing between two big round boulders, with arms outstretched to show the enormous size of them.

Hamish was excited to arrive in Alice Springs, the only place in Australia he'd heard of as a boy. We both expected a laid-back country town in the middle of the desert. Instead, the road into "Alice" curved around a hill and was bordered by green grass and spinifex. A large sign, with white letters etched into red rock, welcomed us, and after that, the bustling town sprawled out in every direction.

We found a caravan park on a main road opposite the Alice Springs Cultural Centre, and were allocated a spot next to the amenities. The young man in the office apologised for our location, but I thought it would be convenient, especially if we woke up to the kids needing the toilet. I was pleased Alice Springs turned out to be a bona fide town. It would be a good place for a rest, and to take Hamish up on that meal out he had been talking about.

Chapter 21

Tuesday 21st August

All the travelling, and setting up and packing up, or watching Hamish set up and pack up, had caught up with me. I didn't have the energy to shower, even though the amenities were next to the tent. I took Gideon to a park across the road next to the Cultural Centre. I thought it would occupy him and be easy. My brain was not working properly, so I forgot the road we had to cross was two-way. I was surprised out of my stupor by the sound of a truck coming from the left. At the park, I opened up the Fruit Blitz app on my phone and sliced fruit to get over the shock. I told Jenna later how tired I was. She said, "Me too!" She told me she was sick of travelling. She just wanted to read her novel about a dragon. She hadn't written in her diary for a week. Hamish is still writing his. He never gives up once he starts something.

Wednesday 22nd August

My foggy-brain feeling was worse this morning. I thought I should shower, but it seemed like a lot of effort. I wore bathers and sat on the floor and let the water rain down on me. I wondered why I wasted energy standing in the shower normally. I couldn't face making lunch. It was too hard to remember who liked what in their sandwiches. I felt frustrated. I knew Hamish didn't *need* me to do things for him, but he'd already taken over the shopping and dinner-making, and a million other things. I felt I couldn't put sandwich making on him as well. I sent out a tired desperate prayer to God. It soon occurred to me Jenna could make sandwiches. She did an excellent job, while I had a nap. She still wasn't writing in her diary. I didn't care.

Thursday 23rd August

My brain was still foggy and when I moved it felt like I was walking through water. I agreed to go to West MacDonnell Ranges National Park to see Ormiston Gorge (we did literally walk through water for a bit), the ochre pits, and Stanley Chasm, because I was too tired to tell Hamish I was too tired. I didn't take a lot of notice of the national park. I worried what I was missing. Thankfully Hamish and Faith were still keeping diaries. Faith wrote:

> On the eighty-first day we went to Ormiston Gorge. Jenna found dragon eggs and showed Gideon. Dad told me it's a bush melon, but don't tell Gideon or Jenna. Jenna said Gideon should only take one egg home or the mother dragon will get angry. At the ochre pits I saw bright red and yellow rock. Jenna said the indigenous people used it to make paint. At Stanley Chasm the walls were really tall and I found a pink sparkly rock. Dad says the rock could have gold inside.

Friday 24th August

My thoughts were a little clearer today, but my body still felt like I was walking through water. I remembered we had to shop for Father's Day. It meant expending energy, but it would save any stress or embarrassment of having mucked up, in ten days time. I took the girls with me and walked in a daze unable to find the shopping centre. Faith used her excellent sense of direction to find an Australia Post shop and bought Hamish an umbrella with a light on the end of it she'd seen in a catalogue. I realised Faith was turning into a mini, female version of Hamish. Jenna bought Hamish a box of chilli sauces allegedly from around the world. I found a frog you could blow up like a balloon. I knew Gideon would love giving it to Hamish. We all enjoyed the pre-Father's Day night out that Hamish had planned. It wasn't spontaneous, but I had to admit the kids enjoyed it. Hamish wrote:

Got ready in our posh clothes (the ones not stained red yet) for our night out at Red Ochre restaurant. We decided as we had after studying the menu online for a few days now to have an outback meat experience so ordered two plates of the "Taste of the Outback" which consisted of kangaroo steak, camel sausages, crumbed crocodile and pan-fried barramundi with a side of chips. Gideon who was eating for free (large amounts) had the pasta bolognese. Did have to ask our waitress if the crocodile was freshwater or saltwater, thinking I might react to the saltwater variety, given my allergy to fish. She never came back with the answer to my question. Still very excited to get our tasting plates and risked eating a small amount of crocodile which didn't taste fishy, or of anything at all. The girls tried everything and enjoyed it. Very proud of them being so adventurous.

Saturday 25th August

My brain felt clear again. I could think, and set goals, and work toward them. I decided to return to reading James. I didn't have a solid grasp of Chapter 2 yet. It was all about faith and action. Action was definitely where I was struggling.

> *"My brothers and sisters, believers in our Lord Jesus Christ must not show favouritism. Suppose a man comes into your meeting wearing a gold ring and fine clothes, and a poor man in filthy old clothes also comes in. If you show special attention to the man wearing fine clothes and say. "Here's a good seat for you," but say to the poor man, "You stand there" or "Sit on the floor by my feet," have you not discriminated among yourselves and become judges with evil thoughts?" (James 2:1-4).*

I don't tend to judge people by the state of their clothes, which would be rather hypocritical. Did I judge people for other reasons? My mum believed our family was superior to other families, who ate too much fried food, or didn't get regular dental check-ups. We were definitely better than families who left their pegs on the clothesline to rust. The solution was to put them in a peg basket. I'd suspected we weren't *actually* superior to anyone else. But I might have absorbed some of Mum and not realised it.

We packed up easily today. A family with teenage children was also leaving. I noted their clean clothing, but didn't feel inferior. They were probably just at the start of their travels. Hamish noted with satisfaction that we were packing up faster than them. I realised Hamish, in spite of his self-confidence, can be very competitive. We said goodbye to the teenagers, who were still struggling to pack everything away, and headed for King's Canyon (Wattarka).

We stopped at the Henbury Meteorite Reserve, which is full of craters formed when a fragmented meteorite hit the Earth's surface. Our guidebook said the site has been extensively studied for information about meteorites, and visited by US astronauts to learn what the surface of the moon would be like.

As we wandered around the barren rocky landscape, I wondered what the chances were of this spot getting hit by a meteor again? Faith picked up a piece of rock and handed it to Hamish. He told her it was definitely a piece of meteor, known as a meteorite, as it felt heavier than the other rocks. Hamish handed me the "meteorite" to look after. Gideon then entrusted me with a dozen pieces of what he believed to be from a meteor, grey rocks of various shapes and sizes. I let a few pieces slide out of my hand when no-one was looking. I was sure there was no way of knowing what was actually from a meteor. The more pressing issue was whether we were in danger of being hit by one.

I decided it was highly unlikely the same spot would get hit twice. My shoulders relaxed. Faith had given up looking for meteorites and asked for her original piece back. Unfortunately, I no longer had it. She glared at me then blinked back tears. I searched for rocks of a similar size and shape, but she was not satisfied until Hamish said he'd found what was definitely another meteorite. It was an impressive-looking rock: dark grey and jagged, with a pattern of little holes on the surface. Faith smiled and hugged Hamish.

We arrived at our next destination, Kings Canyon Resort Caravan Park, in mid-afternoon, and found a spot beside a grassy reserve and some barbecues. To my amazement, Hamish decided not to put up the awning. I tried to appear calm and not show too much excitement as he explained the reasons for his decision: there was a nice table next to the barbecue we could sit at, without setting up our own eating area; and we were only staying two nights and would be out most of the next day. He also had a sore elbow from banging in so many tent pegs.

I couldn't believe my luck. In order not to risk doing something that might cause Hamish to change his mind, I wandered around diligently after Gideon while he made friends with a number of small boys. The boys chased each other around the toilet block, laughing and shouting. I put one of the camping chairs on the grass and watched them. I was so happy Gideon had made some friends and I didn't have to help Hamish set up the awning, that I couldn't stop smiling.

Sunday 26th August

Gideon wanted to play with his new friends, but most of them were heading off, leaving only four-year-old Charlie. The two boys took it in turns riding Charlie's blue bike up and down the length of the caravan park.

We left Charlie's parents, Annette and Chris from Richmond, watching Gideon and Charlie and went to the park office to find information on walking tracks.

A lady with white hair noticed us studying the brochures. "You should do the walk around the rim. It's spectacular. But ignore where the brochure tells you it takes three hours. It took us six, didn't it Ivan?" The old man beside her nodded.

"But it was worth it." Ivan added. "You really should do it. But leave plenty of time."

Hamish was sure we could go faster than Ivan and Joyce, and do the rim walk in the advertised three hours. But I was worried. What if we got caught out in the dark, like we had in Exmouth? I persuaded Hamish we should collect Gideon and the girls, and leave straight away.

There were 500 steps to the top (the kids counted). It was easy walking; nothing like clambering over boulders in the Kimberley. Hamish still had a twinge in his hip from chasing Gideon, but it wasn't slowing him down yet.

We reached the top puffing but not exhausted. From the top we could see rich red ochre cliffs against a brilliant blue sky. It was exhilarating.

Even when it became obvious we would complete the walk easily, Hamish encouraged the kids and I to go as fast as possible. I wasn't sure why. Brilliant greens dotted the gully below and the white of the ghost gums looked stark against the red earth. Although it was spectacular, Hamish discouraged photos, or detours such as the track to the Garden of Eden, a lush oasis we could see in the gully below. All that seemed to matter to Hamish was making good time.

Hamish recorded in his holiday diary that we completed the walk in two hours and twenty minutes. Afterward I wondered: why did we rush? What did we miss? Was Hamish trying to prove how much faster we were than Joyce and Ivan? They were at least seventy. What was the point of that?

Gideon played with Charlie, and the girls swam at the resort pool. Charlie's dad Chris paid us a visit at the picnic table next to the barbecue. He was wearing a button-up shirt and perfectly round sunglasses like I'd seen celebrities wearing on TV. Was there bad news? Had Gideon bit Charlie? Or used bad language?

"The boys are really getting on, aren't they?"

I breathed a sigh of relief. "Thanks for watching them earlier."

"Would Gideon like to have dinner with us? We're having kangaroo sausages."

"He'd love that. That's so *kind* of you." I was using a slightly British accent I saved for people who were well-dressed. Hamish shot me a strange look.

Not only had Gideon made a friend, he'd been invited for dinner. Not since the three of them were asked to watch telly in Karijini, had any of the kids been invited anywhere. And *kangaroo* sausages. I was impressed.

Chapter 22

Monday 27th August

It was time to do what all tourists come to central Australia for—visit Uluru, the great big rock in the geographical centre of Australia. It was a shame to leave Charlie behind, as he and Gideon were getting on so well. I made sure to say a proper goodbye to Chris and Annette, while Hamish and the kids waited in the car. They were hanging laundry on the line next to the amenities. I noticed Annette's hair was cut in a choppy style, with chunks of brown hair breaking up the blond. It must have been fashionable in Richmond.

"Thanks so much for having Gideon over," I told her. I was using my British accent again.

"No problem. Enjoy the rest of your holiday." Annette brushed a chunk of two-tone hair off her forehead.

"Maybe we could see you in Coober Pedy. We're staying at the caravan park on the 31st of August."

Chris was hanging some colourful board shorts on the line. "I'm really not sure what our plans are."

My heart sank. They didn't want to be friends. They probably knew plenty of people in Richmond. Charlie would probably have no trouble making other friends on their holiday. I felt my cheeks get hot. I thanked them again and made a quick exit, so they wouldn't see me blushing.

Hamish concentrated on driving as efficiently as possible to Uluru, while I kept an eye on the map. About 130 km from where Uluru should have been, Hamish called out "There it is!!"

Hamish leaned toward the passenger side, trying to get

as good a look as possible. The children gasped, then sat in hushed silence. I felt goosebumps forming. It was special to be experiencing this moment together.

Then it occurred to me. Was it really possible to see Uluru from 130 km away? It must have been bigger than I realised.

As we continued along the highway, I got a different view. The rock was long and flat. From photos I knew Uluru was curved on top, like a croissant.

"Are you sure that's Uluru, Hamish? I studied the map. One hundred and thirty kilometres east of Uluru was another rock. "I think it's Mount Conner."

Jenna groaned. "You mean it's not Uluru? How far is it to Uluru, Mum?"

"Are we nearly there?" groaned Faith. She kicked the back of the passenger seat.

It was a long ninety minutes before we arrived at Uluru resort. We were given a space too small for the camper trailer. After two visits back to the reception desk, we were eventually allowed to use two spaces that didn't have a barrier between them. The feeling of walking through water I'd had in Alice Springs was coming back. But we wanted to visit Kata Tjuta (the Olgas) before the main event, Uluru, the next day.

Kata Tjuta is actually a series of domes, made of sedimentary rock and covered in sandstone, with a layer of minerals including iron oxide which give it the bright red colour. Our guidebook recommended a walk through Walpa Gorge, between two of the larger domes. The gorge was unexpectedly green and lush. I was slowed down by the sight of amazing flowers—pink daisies on long stalks without leaves, the pink beautiful against the red cliff backdrop.

The walk ended in a viewing platform before the two

domes merged together at the end of the gorge. The two cliffs rose steeply upward, leaving a V-shaped sliver of blue sky. I rested against the wooden railing. Gideon ran up and down the viewing platform, while Hamish and the girls pointed out the ridges in the cliffs. Gideon ran against my side and felt my phone in my pocket. He'd recently discovered it had a camera, which he thought was great fun. I let him take it. It would keep him occupied so I could catch my breath.

Gideon took videos of the steel mesh walkway of the platform. A couple were taking photographs of the cliffs with traditional cameras that weren't phones.

The woman was wearing a puffer jacket and jeans which seemed unnecessary in the heat. She looked toward Gideon and then at me. "Vot is he doing?"

"He just discovered the camera on my phone," I explained. "He likes to take videos."

"He vill drop your phone," the man observed. He put his camera down. "If he dropz your phone it vill go through the slatz." He pointed to the steel mesh.

"Somesing to sink about!" shouted the woman in the puffer.

I realised they had a point. "Danke." It was the only German word I knew. I asked Gideon to give me back his phone. He ran away from me. The fascination of taking videos was too strong. I began chasing him around the platform, while the German couple watched me. I eventually caught up with him and wrestled the phone off him. My rest was ruined.

We returned to Uluru "resort" in time to watch the sunset at the Uluru viewing platform. So we would finally see Uluru. The *real* one this time, not Mount Conner, or "Fooluru" as it's sometimes called, apparently. I wondered what the *real* Uluru would be like? If I'd had goosebumps from seeing Fool's Uluru, imagine my reaction to the *real* thing?

It turned out to be much more subdued than my response to Fooluru. Perhaps there was a limit to how many times a day the body would produce the surge of adrenaline that formed goosebumps. My surge had been used already, when Hamish spotted Mount Conner. The girls were more interested in swinging upside down, a compulsory activity whenever they saw a railing, than they were in looking at the real Uluru.

Hamish and I studied the rock, while the girls hung upside down and Gideon played in the dirt. It *was* curved at the top, unlike Mount Conner, I pointed out to Hamish. It was almost symmetrical. There were swirls and crevices, but it was a unified monolith, unlike the separate domes of Kata Tjuta. It was a ten kilometre walk around the base apparently.

"It *is* impressive isn't it Hamish?"

"I'm glad I get to see this with you - Fooluru *and* Uluru."

"Me too. Let's take it slowly tomorrow Hamish, and make sure we take the detours this time." I didn't want a repeat of racing around King's Canyon.

Tuesday 28th August

I was excited about walking around Uluru. It was a significant part of the First Nation's history. I wondered what traces of ancient indigenous culture would be left. I waited impatiently for the rest of the family to wake up so we could get going.

We were delayed by Hamish wanting to visit the Uluru viewing platform again. It looked much the same as it had the night before. When we finally arrived at the Uluru walking track, a half-hour drive from the resort, we were held up again when Hamish found one of the park rangers and waited for him to finish telling a young couple about the best sites to take photographs.

"Which way is the walk around the base?"

Really Hamish. *Which way*? As long as we kept the rock in sight we would eventually get back to the carpark. We should go whatever way we *felt* like.

The ranger stroked his chin. I could see he was trying to avoid stating the obvious.

"Perhaps go this way." He pointed in a clockwise direction. "Many of the tour groups go that way. If you're walking in the opposite direction, it might feel crowded. And make sure you take the detours signposted along the way." I hoped Hamish would listen. I didn't want to miss something as important as the Garden of Eden again.

Finally we started the journey. It was an easy walk, on a wide gravel path. The rock rose sharply out of the flat earth, looking even more impressive than it did from the resort viewing platform.

Signs told us there were four main sections of the base walk. The first section contained caves where the Mala people, ancestors of the present-day Anangu, taught adolescent boys to track and hunt by painting on rock. So this was the evidence of ancient culture - not the neat anatomical paintings of Kakadu, but a series of squiggles where the cave walls had been painted over and over again, like a teacher's blackboard, initiating boys into the responsibilities of manhood.

In the second section, the rockface was flat, except for small holes and crevices, which held stories important to the Anganu. Signs told us that photographs are prohibited, as the Anganu believe the stories should only be viewed in their actual location. So that was why we never saw photographs of this view - the sites were sacred to the locals.

We took a detour to Mutitjulu Waterhole. Hamish had listened to my request to slow down. It turned out to be a shady lush oasis, full of long grass and gum trees. I closed my eyes and listened to the trickling water and the croak of frogs.

On the final section of track, Gideon sat on the gravel track and refused to walk any further. Hamish and the girls were far ahead. I picked him up and carried him the last few kilometres, enjoying the birdsong and the way Gideon's hair felt against my neck. There were sections where the sides of Uluru slanted down to meet the path, and elevated caves and crevices dotted the rock. It was bliss.

By the time we arrived back at the carpark, Gideon's weight hung heavily around my neck, my shoulders hurt and I was sweating in the middle-of-the-day sun.

I set Gideon down on the track, relieved to be free of his weight. "That was amazing."

Hamish had his hands on his hips. "Why didn't you walk Gideon?"

"I'm hungry," he tugged on Hamish's arm. "Where's the scroggen?" We hadn't packed the mixture of chocolate and nuts this time.

I stretched my arms in the air, trying to relieve the pain in my shoulders. "What did you think girls?"

"It was beautiful," said Jenna. She wrapped her arms around my waist.

"I liked the waterhole," said Faith. She joined Jenna, hugging us both around the middle.

"That was special, experiencing that altogether." I gave them a squeeze.

Wednesday 29th August

There weren't many towns between Uluru and Coober Pedy, on our way south. We opted to stay at Marla, a tiny town on the Stuart Highway, with a roadhouse and a general store, and set up camp next to a patch of red dirt. It was a quiet spot, next to nothing, aside from a solitary caravan belonging to a couple from Ballarat. The kids helped Hamish gather wood for a fire.

Thursday 30th August

I was awakened to a loud clacking sound. It sounded like thunder, or gunfire. Had a war broken out? Were we being raptured?

"What's that?" I reached for Hamish's left hand under the covers. He was shaking.

Hamish took a while to answer. He must have been going through the options. "A train?"

Oh of course. So *not* a war, or the end of the world. I felt relieved. I didn't want this current life to be over - there was still so much I didn't understand.

"Do you think it was the Ghan?" There was a passenger train that travelled the three thousand kilometres between Darwin and Adelaide.

"That'd be it. How did we miss the track?" Hamish looked at his watch. "It's 3 a.m. Can you believe the children slept through that?"

In the morning light, after a few hours more restless sleep, we found the track a hundred metres from the trailer. The copper-coloured steel shone brightly in the sun. "How did we miss that?" Hamish wondered again. We decided not to move the trailer. If we were woken up again at least we would know it was the Ghan, taking sleeping tourists through the desert.

Before the kids woke up we discussed how to spend the day. I wanted to give the children one more educational experience before we got home.

"There's an Opal Field in the West," I told Hamish. According to the guidebook, you could look for opals on a heap of dirt. The kids might enjoy that. "Or in the other direction there's an indigenous community, with an art's centre that's open to the public."

Hamish stretched. "It will be good to see another indigenous town."

I agreed. It would be interesting to see how the community compared with Kalkaringi.

When the kids awoke after an apparently blissful peaceful sleep, we ate toast cooked over the gas flame, then headed to the indigenous town, known as the Anangu Pitjantjatjara Yankunytjatjara lands.

A wide dirt track led away from the highway. To our left, was an Australian Rules Football field of red dirt. The goal posts were streaked with red dust. At one end was a Ford Falcon from the 1980s, rust halfway up the doors. I thought it would make a great photo. But Hamish didn't want to stop. He said I was treating the indigenous community like a tourist attraction, wanting to take photos. I sighed. I would never be as good as Hamish.

The streets were quiet. There were no children running to greet us like there had been in Kalkaringi. Then again it was mid morning. Perhaps they were at home or in school. We found the arts centre, a low building with dot art paintings behind the windows. Three men were painting at tables. They seemed surprised to see us. One stood up abruptly.

"Clarice is not here," he said.

"We'll just have a look, if that's okay." One of the men nodded. Hamish took the kids over to the displays near the window. There were racks of bags and cushion covers with indigenous designs.

Two of the men left what they were doing and walked to the back of the arts centre, talking loudly. Every now and then I could hear one of them say "Clarice." The other artist, an old man with grey hair and a lined face, stayed where he was.

"Can I have a look at what you're doing?" There was a series of lino prints of an aeroplane drying next to him on the table.

"Oh they're wonderful."

The old man stood up and beckoned for me to follow him to a large drawer. It was full of lino prints of more aeroplanes and cars. I wondered if they were for sale. It would be nice to support the arts centre.

The front door swung open.

"Well, hello, hello, " said a female voice with a middle-class accent.

"Clarice!" shouted the younger men. "We didn't know where you were!"

Relieved, they returned to their table, relaxed now that the manager was here and could attend to us.

"Are these prints for sale?" I held up one of the aeroplanes. Clarice looked at me in surprise. She had blond hair cut in a choppy bob. She walked over to the counter next to the rack of handbags, I never got an answer.

I returned the print to the old man, who smiled and returned it to the drawer. I joined Hamish who was looking at cushion covers. "Do you like any of these?" he asked.

They were geometric designs in bold colours. I couldn't imagine them in our house.

Clarice swept toward us. "They're wonderful, wonderful. They're made in India but ten percent of the price goes to the indigenous artist who designed them. It's a fabulous, fabulous way of supporting the community," she said. Clarice wore a bold blue print dress with strappy blue sandals and large silver hoop earrings that could have come from a boutique in South Yarra. Her way of repeating random words was annoying.

I wasn't going to be fooled by Clarice. I remembered James chapter Two: *If you show special attention to the man wearing fine clothes …. have you not discriminated among yourselves and become judges with evil thoughts? (James 2: 2-4).*

I turned my back to her and focussed on Hamish.

"I like these ones." I pointed to some covers with a bold pattern of dark green and red triangles. I thought they might fit somewhere in our house.

Hamish shook his head. "What about these." They were edged in bright orange, with smaller brown and lime green squares within.

I took a step back. "Where would we put them?" I asked Hamish. "They'll clash. Think of the living room." I could barely remember it, but it came back to me dimly. "The rug is red and dark green."

"It's not a good idea to match colours. It looks like you're trying too hard. It's better to mix and match," Felicity said. She looked at me. I looked away. Then she held up the red and green cushion covers and the multi-coloured ones to demonstrate. I squinted. I tried to imagine the cushion covers and the rug together. I couldn't. Above all it was surreal to be discussing living room decor in the middle of the desert.

"Okay, we'll take the orange ones," I gave in.

"Wonderful, wonderful."

Clarice chatted happily to Hamish while she wrapped the cushion covers and took the payment.

I thanked the old man for showing me his artwork before we left. He smiled again. He didn't seem bothered he hadn't made a sale. He was enjoying what he was doing.

"What were you thinking?" I asked Hamish when we left and walked around the town so the kids could run off some energy. "Those cushion covers won't look good anywhere."

"Why did you buy them then?"

"Well you liked them. We'll make it work." I hoped so, but I doubted it. "What did you think of that woman?"

"She was lovely. Very helpful."

"I thought she was strange! The way she kept repeating words. And did you notice her outfit? Why dress like that, with those expensive looking shoes, in the middle of the desert?"

"I don't judge people on what they wear," said Hamish.

Hmmm. Hamish was right. It was wrong to judge people for being middle class. When James said not to discriminate against the poor, he didn't say anything about discriminating against the rich. I felt ashamed.

When we returned to the car we found a dog had torn apart the vinyl trash bag that hangs off the spare tyre. Hamish and I scooped the rubbish off the footpath and put it in a plastic bag. I went to look for a bin, but Hamish said we should take the rubbish with us.

We only had a week left before we got back to Melbourne. Would I ever learn the lessons in James? I called out to God in a silent prayer. I asked him to change me, no matter how much it would hurt. I needed him to do something big.

Chapter 23

Friday 31ˢᵗ August

It was my last week to study the final chapter of the Book of James. I read:

> *"Be patient, then, brothers and sisters, until the Lord's coming ... You have heard of Job's perseverance and have seen what the Lord finally brought about. The Lord is full of compassion and mercy." (James 5:11)*

So, the last chapter of James focused on perseverance. I remembered how helpful the opening verses had been, especially verse 2: *"Consider it pure joy whenever you face trials of many kinds"*. James started and finished with perseverance. It was the theme of the whole book.

Arriving in Coober Pedy, it was obvious the townsfolk had learnt to persevere. It was a flat treeless desert, with doorways built into the side of stony mounds, leading to underground houses known as "dugouts" built as an escape from the searing summertime heat. I read in my guidebook the town was the home of international grade opal mining, but the population had recently declined. Only small holdings were allowed to prevent large-scale mining of the region, and while some prospectors found lots of the sparkling gems, others found nothing and went into tourism or left.

We had promised Faith we would stay in an underground house, but it was expensive, so we were spending the first two nights in a caravan park, before moving underground on Sunday, which was Father's Day. This meant having to set up camp *twice in the same town*. That was annoying, but at least we would see what an underground house was like.

Saturday 1st September

We visited the Old Timer's museum, where the children searched for opals; and then had cake in a cafe in the main street, where Hamish was a blessing to the owner. He wrote in his diary:

Old Timer's Mine has a self-guided walk through the mine under the shop. We donned the regulation helmet (we all needed extra large). The children had so much fun running through the maze of tunnels looking for the next number on the map and then reading the facts on display there. The second part of the tour was through an historic old underground house that was, well, remarkable. It was fascinating to see the children's bedrooms, kitchen etc. that was part of everyday life underground. Did wonder if there were cases of rickets and depression from lack of light but there was no information about that. After an extensive look through the gift shop for the children and a lesson from the owner about opals (in particular the triplets and doubles), we went outside to a largish pit full of rocks and stones where the children could forage for opals (known as noodling). This entertained us for over an hour, with shrieks of excitement as we found the smallest slither of opal in a bit of rock.

On the way back to the campground we stopped in at a little bakery for afternoon tea, run by an old German couple. As the shop was just closing up they offered us the cakes for half price, but the wife's calculations by hand were so amiss she asked us the full price. I was about to challenge her adding up but felt quite strongly that God wanted me to be generous.

The rest of the day was uneventful as Jane fixed up the washing she had started earlier and the girls made up an Angry Birds game. They threw rocks at a tree and tried to hit the targets which were screwed up pieces of paper tucked in between the branches. They argued non-stop about the rules. I think they need to go back to school.

Sunday 2nd September

After a Father's Day breakfast (I made it easy by reheating ready-made hotcakes), we visited the Anglican church, the underground Catacomb Church, for their 9.30 service. The church is cut into the side of the hill in a cross shape with the altar at the head, and the rest of the cross formed by two wings and the entrance.

The vicar, who introduced himself as Gerald, played the guitar while we sang some hymns. I recognised one of them from the Anglican church we attended years ago. After the singing, Gerald put down his guitar and made some announcements, including a request for volunteers to lead Sunday school the following week. Then he invited Elizabeth, a large middle-aged lady with long wavy hair, to give the reading.

Elizabeth adjusted the microphone behind the lectern and cleared her throat. "Today's reading is from James Chapter 4: verses 13-16." I couldn't believe it! Of all the books of the Bible, she was reading from James.

"Now listen, you who say, "Today or tomorrow we will go to this or that city, spend a year there, carry on business and make money." Why, you do not even know what will happen tomorrow."

Elizabeth readjusted the microphone and spoke directly into it. Her voice came through loudly and clearly.

"What is your life? You are a mist that appears for a little while and then vanishes."

I squirmed in my seat. I remembered thinking of myself as a mist in Darwin. It had been relaxing at first, but then I didn't bother to do anything and wasted two days playing a silly game on my phone. I tried to remember what came next.

"Instead, you ought to say, "If it is the Lord's will, we will live and do this or that.""

That's right. I remembered thinking that verse was like a line from the Lord's prayer. *"As it is, you boast in your arrogant schemes. All such boasting is evil." (James 4:13-16).*

Elizabeth snapped her Bible shut and returned to her seat.

Gerald had a thin whiny voice, not at all like Elizabeth's rich and melodious tone. It took a while for me to tune out the quality of his voice and listen to his message.

Gerald paced in front of us, not concerned about using the microphone at all, although he was the one who needed it. He began by discussing plans. He pointed out planning wasn't bad per se. He quoted a verse from Proverbs about it being foolish not to plan. The bit God was interested in, Gerald explained, was the attitude of our hearts when we made plans. It was wrong to assume we knew with any certainty what was going to happen.

I agreed with Gerald. I had no idea about the future. Would I go back to paid work? Would Gideon be okay? All of it was unknown.

"There's never been a culture, like the present Western culture, that is less resilient to hardship, than we are. The Book of James is more relevant to you and I, than it was when it was written."

I sat up straight. What did he mean? Gerald's voice might have been small and whiny, but he had some big ideas.

"People from Western cultures think that if they work hard enough, if they do their research, if they do their due diligence, they can control the future. Psychologists call it the "Life Control Illusion." But it's false. We have no idea what will happen to us."

I couldn't see where this was going. I agreed I didn't know the future, but if I worked hard, I'd at least have a chance of success.

"Why is the Life Control Illusion a problem?" Gerald looked from side to side at the congregation. No-one made a sound.

"Because it leads to over-confidence." I remembered being full of confidence when I had an idea: writing a book, the six-day plan to go to Kakadu, leading a family church service. Each of these ideas had met with failure. I shifted again in my seat.

"But it also leads to under-confidence. We think we *know* how our life ought to turn out, and when it doesn't, we worry. We think it's up to us to create success, so if we're not successful, it must be our fault. We can't handle the pressure."

I thought of myself unable to get out of bed in Mataranka, thinking I'd failed as a wife, and even a daughter.

"If we trust in our own plans, we've taken the role of God, and we're not qualified. Whenever we have a job we're not qualified for, we feel uncomfortable." Gerald smiled. An older man in the front row chuckled.

"So what's the answer?"

I leaned forward to make sure I heard it.

"It's in verse 15: *"Instead, you ought to say, "if it is the Lord's will, we will live and do this or that.""* (James 4:15)

I thought that would be a good place for Gerald to stop. My head was bursting with new ideas. But he continued.

"When James says you are like a mist, do you know what he means? He's comparing you to the mist when it's cold and you open your mouth and let out a breath. It's there for a split second and then it's gone. That's how fleeting your life is." I remembered the cold mornings in Adelaide and Norseman, drinking tea with Hamish and noticing the puff of mist when either of us opened our mouths to take a sip. Were our lives really that insignificant?

"Everything you do will be forgotten. Nothing you do will make any lasting difference." That was a horrible idea. Gerald had gone too far. I looked at the children next to me. Jenna's mouth had dropped open slightly. Faith and Gideon were busy colouring in the pictures of Noah's Ark Elizabeth had handed them when we walked in. Thank goodness the younger two were not hearing this.

"Unless …," Gerald continued. Thank goodness there was an "unless". "Unless there's a God in eternity, nothing you do has lasting value." I felt hopeful again.

"Do you know what the answer is to being like a mist, like a breath that comes out of your mouth and disappears in an instant? It's another breath." What did he mean? I looked at the children again. Jenna had started helping Gideon with his colouring in. I would have to listen hard so I could tell her later.

"It's the breath that comes from God. When Jesus appeared to the disciples after his resurrection, he *breathed* on them, and they were filled with the Holy Spirit." I felt goosebumps forming. Gerald's message was really good. Was he wasted in Coober Pedy? I looked around me. There was only a small congregation of locals and a few passing tourists, most of whom probably came to see the church building. A couple of older people had fallen asleep. Did they not realise how amazing the message was?

Gerald continued. "Because we have the Holy Spirit, our

inner nature is changed by God, and it's our inner nature that lasts forever. Turn in your Bibles to 2 Corinthians Chapter 4 verses 16 and 17." I fumbled in my handbag for my phone, and opened the verse.

> *"Though outwardly we are wasting away, yet inwardly we are being renewed day by day. For our light and momentary troubles are achieving for us an eternal glory that far outweighs them all." (2 Corinthians 4:16-17)*

I looked at Hamish. He'd opened the pew Bible at the verse and was nodding.

"Go in peace to love and serve the Lord! Amen!" Gerald tried to raise his voice, but his voice cracked and it sounded like he was choking. A few people echoed the "Amen."

When we left the underground church and went outside, the mid-morning sun was scorching and shone on the stony mounds which contained the underground houses, making every surface sparkle. I knew I was going to be thinking a lot about Gerald's sermon, but for now I had to focus on the day in front of us. I blinked, trying to adjust to the bright light.

Firstly, we had to move into the underground house. Our new accommodation was cut into the side of the hill at the top end of the town. We went through a door in the rock, as if entering another world. It was pitch black inside until Hamish found the light switch. The house was surprisingly big, with a lounge room, kitchen, and two bedrooms with ensuites. Some of the walls had been plastered over, and painted in a milky white, like the base colour of opals. In the bedroom the walls were exposed rock. Faith was satisfied. It really was the underground situation she'd been hoping for.

Now we'd moved, I had important business to think about. I had the responsibility of Father's Day. Hamish always made a big deal of birthdays and celebrations. I once told Hamish he went overboard. It was stressful how much effort he put into the kids' birthdays, Mother's Day and other special days. But he said he refused to apologise for doing something well. He was proud of it.

I owed it to him to do Father's Day well, but I couldn't decide how to celebrate. As we had recently been out for dinner, something we rarely did, I thought we shouldn't spend money on restaurants. I wondered about home-made pizzas for dinner, but then dismissed it. It would be too much trouble. I considered takeaway pizzas, but Hamish might not think that was special. Perhaps we could eat out at a pizza restaurant? It wouldn't cost much, and Hamish might consider it a *little* bit special to have pizza somewhere in the main street of Coober Pedy.

But it didn't feel good enough. I felt uncomfortable. Then it hit me! I was trying to find a low-cost way to celebrate Father's Day, while at the same time impressing Hamish doing it. It reminded me of a book I'd read by the Christian humourist Adrian Plass. It was called, *Looking Good Being Bad*. I could do better! We already had the umbrella, the blow-up frog, and the chilli sauce. This could be the best Father's Day ever. And no, we would *not* have pizza. The cost of celebrating Hamish was irrelevant. I would find the best restaurant in town.

I made an excuse to Hamish and set off with Jenna up the main street of Coober Pedy in search of its best restaurant. We went in and out of buildings that looked like they might serve food. Inside one establishment that had been half built into rock, a young man informed us that there used to be a restaurant there, but it closed recently. The town was not doing well and businesses were failing, he told us. Another place built above ground had a small window through which we could see some tables and a few diners. I got excited and went inside. The waitress told me they would be opening for dinner soon, but at the moment they only served lunch. She hoped we would come for lunch tomorrow.

We came to a big resort that advertised it had a restaurant. The resort had the ambience of an inner-city office complex. We went up a lift and down several corridors to find the restaurant. The air conditioning was blowing hard. A menu displayed at the front advertised a $65 per person set menu of risotto, steak and crème brûlée, with matching wines. I was torn. Perhaps this *was* the best restaurant in Coober Pedy. It was certainly expensive. But it wasn't really suitable for taking children. And maybe spending a whole lot of money wouldn't ensure Hamish had a wonderful Father's Day.

After a long search our only other options were the pizza restaurant and a Greek restaurant at the other end of town. The Greek restaurant won easily. I knew Hamish liked Mediterranean food. It reminded him of when his family lived in Cyprus. I booked a table for 6 pm.

The children gave Hamish his gifts over our first course of dips and olives. Hamish took his time over each present, exclaiming about them. He could see the benefits of the umbrella with the light, he got excited about the chilli sauce, and he blew up the frog and let it go to make a farting noise. It ended up landing face down in the hummus dip. Everyone laughed. It *was* turning out to be the best Father's Day ever.

After our first course, we had souvlaki and feta, and a bean salad that Hamish recognised from his childhood.

He told Christos, our waiter, a large man with a full head of dark curly hair, that the food was as good as he used to eat in Cyprus.

Christos smiled at Hamish. "Ah, that is because I'm Cypriot. My family came out here twenty years ago, when the mining was good. Now the mining is bad, so we opened this restaurant." Christos topped up our glasses with more Greek wine. "This is Greek-Cypriot food, but we don't tell anyone, because no-one in Coober Pedy has heard of Cyprus." He smiled.

Hamish and Christos talked about Cyprus. Then Christos brought out another bottle of Retsina, on the house this time, he said, and then gave us a large platter of baklava and Turkish delight to finish off our meal.

Hamish said he'd had enough wine. I didn't want to offend Christos. It had been so kind of him to give us free food and wine, especially when he'd been through the hardship of a failed mining business. I accepted Christos' gift and did my best to drink the bottle on my own. It had a strange flavour, like turpentine. When the bottle was almost empty, Hamish suggested I stop. Then Christos brought out some ouzo to finish the meal with. They were large glasses. I wanted to get rid of the taste of turpentine. I downed my ouzo in one gulp. It was much nicer than the wine. It tasted like licorice.

Walking home, I noticed I was swaying slightly. Then, even more alarmingly, I could see two of everything: two neon signs of the Coober Pedy pizza restaurant, two of the Big Miner statues outside the miner's museum, two windows in front of the opal shop. Hamish steadied me by putting his arm around my waist, gave Jenna the house key and told the children to go ahead of us and let themselves inside. They started running down the hill, excited to be given so much freedom.

"Are you seeing double, Hamish?" I asked him, when the children were out of sight. I could see two crosses of the Catholic church, next to the Catacomb Church where we'd been that morning.

Hamish sighed. "When we get home, you're going straight to bed. I don't want the kids to see you in this state."

I easily complied. Hamish led me to the bed in the Master bedroom with the exposed rock walls. I knew he'd sort out the children. He's good like that. I fell asleep instantly.

When I woke, my head felt like it was in a vice being pressed in on both sides. I wondered why it was so black. It wasn't like normal darkness. Usually in the middle of the night it's possible to make out the shapes of things, even if there's no detail. But I could see nothing. Had the wine and ouzo permanently affected my vision?

I held my arm up. I couldn't see anything. A wave of nausea washed over me. Everything was spinning. I thought I might throw up. I couldn't remember which side of the bed the ensuite was.

I could hear Hamish snoring softly beside me. I didn't want to wake him. I was embarrassed I'd made myself so ill.

I stared into the darkness. I couldn't remember ever feeling so bad. My head throbbed. The nausea brought me nearly to the point of heaving. But even worse than that, there was a feeling of self-loathing for having made myself so ill. The hatred I felt for myself made the physical symptoms unbearable. This was worse than the sadness and self-pity I'd felt in Mataranka.

"Help!" I cried to God silently. I remembered just that morning I'd been impressed by the Catacomb Church's vicar, Gerald, sharing God's word. What had that been about?

It was something to do with humans being like a mist. Three words came into my mind. "I am nothing." They came to me over and over again. "I am nothing." Was that why I couldn't see my arm? Had I ceased to exist? No, I could still feel it.

I held my right arm in the air again and waved it around. I still couldn't see anything. Then I remembered we were underground, with no windows to let in light from the moon or the street. So I still existed, it was just impossible to see. I wondered if Hamish had remembered to set up nightlights for the kids.

The thought "I am nothing," came back. After a while I stopped fighting it. I started to relax. The nausea was bearable while I allowed the thought to persist. It was a bit like the time I thought of myself as a mist in Darwin, which had been relaxing. But it was deeper than that. It was as if God himself was joining with something deep inside me while I focused on those words. The self-hatred was replaced with a feeling of peace.

It reminded me of an experience I'd had years ago. Some close friends of ours, Hugh and Wendy, decided not to come to our wedding. They thought we shouldn't have lived together before we got married. In their eyes we were setting a poor example by living together, especially as Hamish was a youth group leader in the church. Hamish and I disagreed - we thought it would be too hard to live apart, and Hugh and Wendy were being narrow-minded.

One Sunday we drove to the mountains near Melbourne on a sunny day. I told Hamish how much I missed our friends. "Maybe they were right," I said spontaneously. "Maybe we shouldn't have lived together." I didn't really believe it, but I was trying desperately to resolve the situation. As soon as I'd said it, I was flooded by a conviction that our friends *were* right, and a feeling of joy that was so intense I couldn't speak. When I'd eventually recovered I told Hamish. He agreed that, since I'd had such a powerful experience when I said those words, we should apologise to our friends for disagreeing with them. Hugh cried huge sobs when we told him.

Like in the car all those years ago talking about Hugh and Wendy, it was as if God's spirit had taken over me, giving me no choice but to meditate on the words "I am nothing." I was filled with a surprising sense of joy and freedom. I spent a long time letting those words wash over me. I didn't want to miss out.

Chapter 24

Monday 3rd September

My headache had gone, after a good breakfast and some fresh air, and I was still feeling the sense of peace from the night before. I told Hamish about it on the drive to Port Augusta, how it had come to me again and again, the words "I am nothing."

The children were watching *Home Alone* in the back seat.

"What do you think it means?" Hamish asked.

"I think it has something to do with James, and that amazing message we heard yesterday."

"That Gerald was good, wasn't he?"

I nodded. "I think it relates to the verse about being like a mist; how nothing we do will have lasting value, unless there's a God in eternity. If we focus on ourselves, instead of God, it causes all sorts of problems. If I realise I am nothing, I have no value, except the value God gives me." Wow, it made sense. Maybe this was it. Maybe God had given me the big revelation I'd prayed for.

"And the value God gives us is infinite value, " Hamish interjected.

"Yes, you're right, Hamish. And if I have no value apart from God, it solves a lot of problems." I was warming up to the topic more and more. "If I try and I don't succeed, it means nothing."

"And if you do succeed, it means nothing either."

"Yes, you're right." I couldn't remember a time when Hamish and I had been so much in sync. "Well maybe a small sense of satisfaction, but in terms of my eternal value, it means nothing. Therefore, it's okay to take a risk. For example, I could apply for a job when we get back home. If I'm unsuccessful, it means nothing. If I succeed, it means nothing. Nothing really important anyway. I'm not scared of applying for a job anymore."

"But that feeling won't last. You say that now, but you'll get scared again."

Hmmm. Hamish was right. I latched on to a good idea, then forgot it after a few days, maybe a few weeks if I really put my mind to it. But this felt different.

"I will forget. But then I'll remember. Sometimes. And it's not just about being unafraid to do big things, like applying for a job. Just think of all the problems that will go away if I remember I'm nothing. I don't have to get offended. I am nothing. So there's no-one to be offended. I don't have to get embarrassed, or hurt, or feel sorry for myself." I remembered Faith running into the petrol station in Perth, telling me to spend money so I could save money on petrol. If I hadn't been embarrassed, I could have thought more clearly. I never would have picked up sixteen chocolate frogs and then yelled at Hamish for making a fool of me. Then I remembered feeling sorry for myself in Mataranka. If there'd been no-one to pity, I could have got on with enjoying myself, spending time with the family.

"The thing I'm puzzled about is this. There seems to be all these things we have to avoid as Christians, like pride and self-pity."

"And anger," Hamish added. I heard the kids pull their headphones off in the back seat. *Home Alone* had finished and the hero, Kevin, was reunited with his family.

"Yes, anger." That was definitely relevant. "Is that what being a Christian is about, getting rid of stuff? It seems very negative. Do we just have to turn away from sin? Can't we be a bit more *proactive*."

"When we get rid of sin, we can be our real selves, who Jesus meant us to be," Hamish said.

"You're right, Hamish." I twisted around to see what the kids were doing.

"Haven't you heard of the gifts of the Spirit, Mum? It's love, joy, peace, forgiveness, kindness, goodness, faithfulness, gentleness and self-control. That's what happens when you get rid of sin." I hadn't realised Jenna was listening.

"But the greatest one is love," added Faith. Ah, she was listening too. Good.

"Love, love, love," sang Gideon, in imitation of the Beatles. Jenna and Faith laughed.

Hamish narrowly missed an emu which darted across the road. We camped in a small camping area on the side of the road. It was an amazingly harmonious evening. Everyone did their chores without arguing.

Tuesday 4th September

We spent our very last night of the holiday at a motel in Mildura. It was small, clean and comfortable, but we weren't focussed on our accommodation. All we were thinking about now was getting home. Jenna and Faith wanted to see their friends. Gideon wanted to be able to play with *all* his dinosaurs. I wanted to live in a house where I didn't have to cram everything into tiny spaces. Hamish had finally had enough of driving. We couldn't wait to get home.

Wednesday 5th September

Australia is big. After three months of travelling and thousands of kilometres, fears, fun and adventure, our trip was coming to an end.

Hamish was looking steadfastly at the road in front of him. It was his third day driving in a row.

"Do you remember our goals for the trip, Hamish? You said you wanted to experience something new as a family."

"I think we achieved that, don't you? We had so many amazing experiences—snorkelling in Ningaloo, hiking in the Kimberley, you getting lost. I think Kalkaringi was a real highlight. The faith of the indigenous church was inspiring, and the community was amazing. They really know how to look after each other."

Hamish took his eyes off the road and glanced in my direction. "What about you? Do *you* think we achieved our goals?"

"Well, I said I wanted the same things as you, but really I wanted a break. I wanted life to be easy. I wanted you to help occupy Gideon seven days a week instead of just the weekends.

Hamish looked surprised. "So how did that work out?"

"It wasn't easy at all. The camping part was so hard, setting up and packing up. And Gideon was hard work, even with the two of us. Remember when we lost him in Monkey Mia?"

Hamish shuddered. "Remember how he started a fire in the Kimberley? He got so filthy. And you dobbed on the policemen, for leaving hot ash."

It was my turn to shudder, with embarrassment. But I didn't dwell on it. "I'm glad it wasn't easy. The challenging parts are the ones we'll remember the most."

"So what do you think about that verse now? *"Consider it pure joy, my brothers and sisters, whenever you face trials of many kinds?" (James 1:2)"*

"I think you were wrong."

"Really?"

"You said you thought the verse meant that if we struggle, it forces us to change. If everything's easy, we never have to change, so we don't grow, we don't mature."

Hamish looked at me, his eyebrows raised. "I think that's exactly what it means."

"I don't think so anymore. To understand that verse you have to look at the whole of James. Remember the message about Chapter 4, about how we're so insignificant without God, we're like a mist?" Hamish nodded. "We need to have trials so it forces us to turn to God. We have to realise, when we're in trouble, we can't help ourselves. By trials we learn we are nothing without God, so we turn to him."

Hamish shook his head quickly. "Well, that's the same thing."

"No, it's not. It's about maturing by turning to God specifically. You were talking about maturity in general."

Hamish wiped his forehead with the back of his hand. "Actually, I think every interpretation I suggested was true. It just depends what you're focusing on."

"Alright, all your suggestions were good," I conceded.

We sat in silence for a while. Then I had an idea.

"Can I read you the last bit of James? I'm at the end."

I took Hamish's silence as agreement. It was a new thing I was trying instead of getting offended he wasn't more attentive. I opened Chapter 5 on my Bible app.

"As you know, we count as blessed those who have persevered. You have heard of Job's perseverance and have seen what the Lord finally brought about. The Lord is full of compassion and mercy." (James 5:11)

"Ah, the story of Job." So, Hamish *was* listening. "He stayed faithful even though he lost everything. He didn't have faith *because* God blessed him. God wants a relationship with us like that. He wants us to love him whether he blesses us or not."

"Hmm. We don't get salvation because of what we do for God. In the same way, God doesn't want us to love him just because of what he does for us."

"Exactly. It's not a transaction. It's like marriage. We don't love each other just because of what we do for each other."

"My brothers and sisters," I continued. *"If you wander from the truth and someone should bring that person back, remember this: Whoever turns a sinner from the error of their way will save them from death and cover over a multitude of sins."* (James 5:19-20)

"If you wander from the truth, I promise to try to bring you back Hamish."

"Thanks." Hamish smiled. "I think God invented marriage so that we could grow. It works like this: two people annoy each other, then have to turn to God, then figure out where they went wrong, then try to do better."

"Yes, you're right." I thought back over all the arguments and problems we'd had over the trip. I thanked God for forgiveness.

"Can we play some music," Jenna called out. After so much time in the car, she was sick of movies, and her scrapbook.

"Why don't we sing a song?" suggested Hamish.

"How about *Amazing Grace*?" asked Jenna.

"Really Jenna?" Hamish was clearly surprised. "What about Taylor Swift? *You Belong With Me*? You love that one."

"I used to like that one, Dad. It's old now. *Amazing Grace* never gets old."

Jenna and I started singing. The others joined in. We got very loud, especially when we got to the verse about worship.

"When we've been here, ten thousand years, bright shining as the sun. We've no less days to sing God's praise, than when we first begun." We sang until our voices were hoarse. Then we drove in silence until we got home. When we pulled into our driveway, I looked behind me. The kids were sound asleep.

Epilogue

It was wonderful to be home. It seemed our house had grown while we were away, so it was as if we owned a mansion. I wondered if I could use more of the house, now I was so grateful for all the different spaces. For a while, I sat on the couch against the back wall in the family room (the room with the red and green rug that the new orange cushions clash with, as I knew they would) and I sat up at the desk in the study to use the computer, the way the study was always intended to be used. After a while I found I went back to my old favourites, sitting up in bed to read, and at the kitchen table to answer emails.

I went back to using the house pretty much the same way I always had, but I had changed. I noticed I figured things out for myself, like how to clean the barbecue on the deck, instead of waiting for Hamish to get home and do it. I seemed to whinge less about trivial problems because they didn't seem so hard anymore.

Gideon started school in February. His lovely teacher made him a book tub with a picture of a dinosaur on it. Jenna got a speaking part in the school play. Faith was excited to join the Girl Guides. She's brilliant at organising activities and helping with meals when they go on camps. She hardly ever complains.

I got a job in administration with a research organisation. It's not very challenging, but it helps pay the bills. Hamish got promoted *again*. Now he's something called a *Program Manager*. I didn't feel jealous. I was pleased for him.

I decided to write a book. It won't be a list of practical instructions for families who want to go on a camping trip.

I'm going to take Hamish's idea and make a book out of these reflections. It doesn't matter if I succeed or fail. Except for God, my achievements are insignificant anyway. Well, some days I tell myself that. Other days I'm terrified. What if no-one reads it? Or what if people read it, and they hate it? Hamish tells me it will be fine either way. Some days I believe him.

Discussion questions

1. (Chapters 1-2) Jane can relate to the idea of God showing his love for people through a sacrifice, because her Dad explained his love for her that way. How can our experiences of family impact our relationship with God?

2. (Chapters 3-4) James has been described as a practical book, about how Christians should live. What practical advice in the first chapter of James (or a later section) challenges you most?

3. (Chapters 5-6) Jane tries to make a deal with God, asking him to show her more tropical fish. How does that work out? Why?

4. (Chapters 7-8) James describes the importance of consistency between faith and action. Is this a challenge in our modern Western culture?

5. (Chapters 9-10) What contributes to gaining wisdom with age? Do people always become wiser as they get older?

6. (Chapters 11-12) How does forgiveness contribute to the reconciliation that occurs at the end of Chapter 11. Why is forgiveness so important in relationships?

7. (Chapters 13-14) James warns against boasting about plans. What should our attitude be when we set goals and make plans?

8. (Chapters 15-16) Jane worries the family will be a burden to the community of Kalkaringi. Are they? Who, if anyone, benefits from the visit to Kalaringi?

9. (Chapters 17-18) The children understand James' teaching about speech (James 3: 3-12) much better than Jane expects them to. What can children teach us about Jesus?

10. (Chapters 19-20) Jane struggles to believe Hamish loves her because of her experience of family breakdown and instability. What is the answer to Jane's insecurity?

11. (Chapters 21-22) Jane realizes she is impressed with the family she meets at King's Canyon. What are some of the ways you show favouritism? How can we make sure we treat all people as children of God?

12. (Chapters 23-24) The vicar Gerald has a whiny voice but some big ideas. Jane worries his message will be missed. Do we sometimes overlook a message because it's not delivered in the way we expect it to be?

Note from the Author

Let's talk about creative bible studies. By creative I don't mean creative interpretations of the bible, like taking challenging verses from the Sermon on the Mount such as Jesus' exhortation to love our enemies, and saying Jesus didn't really mean we had to love our enemies. (I believe he did mean exactly that). And I don't mean bible studies that include pages for you to colour in (although that could be cool). By creative, I mean bible studies that are embedded in a creative story, like a memoir, or a novel, in which the protagonist of the story grapples with a book or passage from the bible, and the bible impacts on their life story.

Travels of a Wimpy Mum: Finding courage through the Book of James, is a memoir of my family's trip around Australia, and how I used my readings from the Book of James to help me handle challenges along the way. The idea evolved from emails I sent to friends and family to let them know what was happening on our trip. In my emails I included what I was reading from the bible. It was a way of being real about my thoughts and experiences, and I believed it would let my non-Christian family and friends know I was serious about my faith. It was a little awkward at times, but being real about our faith can be like that.

When I had the idea of turning these emails (and my children and husband's diary entries) into a book, my bible readings that I had included to "be real" turned out to be the very thing that gave the book the substance and structure that was needed to write a memoir. The bible passages turned it from a series of funny travel stories into a story with a point and a purpose: the point became Jane's growing understanding of the message of James and how it impacted her personal and spiritual growth. Through reflecting on James (both on holiday and writing this book) I have memorised verses from James (to store them up as a resource for future calamities) and have come to a deeper understanding about a real faith being reflected in our actions, and about our worth coming from God.

I realised God had led me into creating something new: a creative bible study in which the reader might become better acquainted with the bible and develop a richer understanding of the meaning and application of bible verses by becoming engaged in a creative story in which the main character grapples with verses themselves. It won't be for everyone, of course, but I think many people will find this way of studying the bible engaging and enjoyable.

I am working on another creative bible study. *Travels of a Wimpy Mum: finding joy in 1 Corinthians*, is the memoir of our family's trip to visit my husband's family in Europe in 2015. While marvelling at the history and beauty of ancient buildings and cities, Jane will grapple with challenges from 1 Corinthians. What did Paul mean when he said he had become like all people to win them over for Christ? How far should Jane go, in being like the laid-back Geordies in the north of England, or the Parisians with their insistence on speaking French perfectly, or not at all? A work of historical fiction (untitled as yet) is also in the planning stages. This will be a challenge, and a change from family travel memoirs, but I am keen to explore the history of the pre-reformation, in the times of Wycliffe, using a main character, like Alice Dexter from Leicester, England, who learns to read and write using the newly available bibles in the English language, and becomes a spirit-filled Christian in the process.

I am thrilled to have the opportunity to learn more about

God's word by writing these books. As I write them, I will become more acquainted with bible verses, I may even remember a few, and I will grapple with how they apply in my life, and the lives of my main characters. My prayer is that seekers might be encouraged to explore the life God has for them through reading these books, and that fellow Christians, like me, might become closer to Him, through being more familiar with the bible and grappling with its application in their own lives.

Acknowledgements

Travels of a Wimpy Mum is loosely based on my family's trip around the western half of Australia in 2012. I am grateful to my husband Hamish and our children Jenna, Faith and Gideon for letting me share their stories and their diary extracts. Their writings have been edited to reduce ambiguity and repetition, but I have retained their individual writing styles and unique ways of observing the world. As well as allowing me to share their stories and writings, Hamish and Jenna listened to me reading the drafts of the book on Saturday mornings, and provided helpful suggestions and motivated me to keep going.

The wonderfully original, insightful and funny Adrian Plass read an early draft and provided encouragement and advice. His interest helped me believe that I could write a book. Cecily Paterson, author of *Love, Tears and Autism*, and creator of The Red Lounge for Writers on-line writing courses, taught me the elements of good writing. Her high standards had me wanting to quit at times, but ultimately her coaching transformed my book.

My thorough and common-sense editor Nola Passmore helped fix and smooth out the final draft and was a pleasure to work with. Laura Tharion skilfully boiled the book down to its key elements and wrote my blurb.

I am grateful to my publisher Susy Lee of 598 Press, who believed in my book and generously shared her time, expertise and enthusiasm to bring it to readers.

Many friends read drafts and helped me stay on the journey. I am indebted to Lynnette Pizaro, Jan Lancaster, Chris Rowney, Janine Drakeford, Lwendyl Anderson, Naomi

Brown, Roger Rich and Tilly Roe for reading early drafts. Ethan Toll and Grace Robinson provided early design ideas that informed the final look of the book. My girl pals Lucy Roe and Vicky Robinson helped me through times of doubt and fear of failure. I am grateful for their prayers and steadfast support.

While researching the Book of James, I read many illuminating bible studies and listened to many insightful podcasts. Especially helpful were the sermons of the late Dr Tim Keller, recordings of which can be found on the *Gospel in Life* website. The sermon preached by the whiny-voiced Gerald in chapter 23 was based on Dr Keller's sermon "A Community of Justice Part 2," which was part of a series of messages he preached on the Book of James in 2010. (On our trip we did visit the Catacomb church on Father's Day in 2012 and were made very welcome by the congregation, heard a wonderful message delivered by a vicar with a pleasant speaking voice and ate a delicious morning tea put on for visitors which impressed us greatly).

Finally, thanks to God for my growing relationship with him and enabling me to experience and share some of what I have been learning in writing this book. I pray that it will inspire readers of all backgrounds, whether they be seekers, new Christians or those mature in their faith, to take heart as they seek a closer walk with him.

About the Author

Vanessa Foran is a psychologist living in Melbourne, Australia with her social worker husband and three children. She enjoys travel (preferably when it's easy and comfortable), learning new things, making quilts and slow-stitching. She became a Christian as a young adult when she was also exploring psychology, and ever since then has been interested in the relationship between faith and mental health.

To stay in touch, please send an email to vanessajforan@gmail.com and write "send me your newsletter" in the subject line. You can find background information about *Travels of a Wimpy Mum*, and updates about her new books on the Vanessa Foran author page on Facebook.
https://www.facebook.com/profile.php?id=61556180737697.

Also from 598 Press you might like:

Raising KIDS Who CARE:
Practical conversations for exploring stuff that matters
by Susy Lee

This book will change the world, one family at a time. If our child-raising is dominated by our surrounding culture of consumerism and wealth, by individualism and tech gadgets, then our societal future is in trouble. If parents are intentional though, having conversations with their kids about these influences and better ways to journey through life, then we could have a culture marked by compassion and contentment, driven by values and purpose.

This book resources parents with research and vision for better ways to ensure happy kids – through gratitude and caring and contribution. Then the book takes whole families along 40 structured conversations – all to be led by the kids!

More info at https://www.raisingkidswhocare.info/

www.ingramcontent.com/pod-product-compliance
Lightning Source LLC
Chambersburg PA
CBHW022041290426
44109CB00014B/931